I have been a disciple-making pastor for over four decades. Twenty years ago I discovered Dr. Anderson's teachings and they revolutionized my approach to ministry. Life is a spiritual battle, not a Sunday school picnic—and Neil's message is a practical way to win this battle. Neil helped me realize repentance, faith, forgiveness and knowing our identity in Christ are essential for making disciples in the local church. Read, study, and learn from this book.

David Jenkins, pastor, Evangelical Free Church

I have been involved in local church leadership for over 30 years. In that time I have always endeavored to ensure that Christians are discipled rather than treated as merely "sermon fodder." Over the years I have tried a number of different approaches to discipleship. Some have been more successful than others. However, I have found the Freedom in Christ approach to be the most consistently effective aid to practical Christian discipleship. I have been using Freedom in Christ material for over 15 years now, and it is still proving to be fruitful.

John Groves, pastor, Hope Church, Winchester, England

We have found the Freedom in Christ resources to be invaluable for our church community. We introduced FIC two years ago to our pastors and leaders. Since then we've had well over 400 people go through FIC, with amazing testimonies of healing and freedom impacting people's lives. Freedom in Christ will continue to be a major part of Bayside Church's Pathway of Discipleship. We highly recommend this book and the Freedom in Christ course.

Rob and Christie Buckingham, senior ministers,
Bayside Church, Melbourne, Australia

God has gifted Dr. Anderson with the ability to systematize truth in a way that touches the intellect and transforms the heart. I have introduced his teachings in France, Switzerland, and Belgium. The response has been overwhelming, and lives have been revolutionized.

Dr. Walter Stuart, missionary to France
and adjunct professor at Tyndale Theological Seminary, Holland,
and Geneva Bible Institute, Switzerland

We have found the truth that Dr. Anderson teaches and the way in which he presents the message are absolutely vital to effective and sustained discipleship. The message and method of Freedom In Christ Ministries are crucial in helping both new Christians and those who have known Christ longer to walk in freedom in Christ and to make reproducing disciples. That is why we recommend this book to help carry out our Lord's mandate to make disciples of all peoples.

Dr. Rick and Laurel Langston,
International School of Theology, Singapore

I first met Dr. Anderson more than 20 years ago when he did a Freedom in Christ conference in the church I was pastoring. Lives were changed when people heard the good news of who they are in Christ, and had the opportunity to repent and find their freedom in Christ. Building on his internationally acclaimed Christ-centered teaching, Neil is now bringing to the global church a proven strategy for making fruitful disciples. His teaching on discipleship will change your life, ground you in your position in Christ, and move you forward in the power of Christ. I can't recommend it highly enough.

Dr. Byron Spradlin, president,
Artists in Christian Testimony International

The message of Freedom in Christ Ministries has touched thousands of lives in South Africa and it has liberated me as a pastor. Just knowing that I am not responsible FOR others, but responsible TO others, in terms of ministry, and knowing that I am accepted, secure, and significant in Christ has taken off the pressure of trying to have a "successful" ministry. All that God desires is that I be a godly minister of the gospel.

Rev. Jonothan Christie, Methodist minister, South Africa

The evil one has mined the path of "making disciples of all nations" with lies and deception. Almost as one crying in the wilderness, Dr. Neil Anderson teaches us again that freedom is available to anyone who would read and believe God's Word, place our trust in the "Wonderful Counselor," and believe what He has to say to the church!

Dr. David Kyle Foster, president, Mastering Life Ministries

I have found Dr. Anderson's materials to be an invaluable tool in helping the men we are discipling. *Victory Over the Darkness, The Bondage Breaker,* and *Discipleship Counseling* are used on a daily basis. The Steps to Freedom in Christ are critical in helping the men become free from their past trauma, unresolved conflicts, and their own misunderstanding of who they are in Christ. Every thought, every idea, is supported by Scripture, and presented in an easy-to-understand format. Because of God's Word and the resources He has provided through Freedom in Christ Ministries, I personally am a free man in Christ!

Derek Faulkner, executive director,
Renewed Life Ministries Outreach (RLMO)

My identity was wrapped up in being a mother and the wife of a pastor. With the children leaving home, I was looking for a greater sense of purpose and thought I would find it by leading the Freedom in Christ course. But to my surprise I learned from the course that my identity is found in Christ and not in what I do. A mild depression left and two people said I appeared happier. So many lives were influenced and many testified of feeling light, happy, and warm all over.

Lisa Fenton, Hastings, New Zealand

The Freedom in Christ course connects the truth of God's Word to our everyday reality, allowing for a precious time of discussion on relevant issues. Individuals are given the opportunity to examine themselves, and are shown from God's Word how they can overcome the challenges of life.

Majlind Gegprifti, Kisha Rilindja (The Reborn Church),
Tirana, Albania

For many years, Dr. Neil Anderson's books *Victory Over the Darkness* and *The Bondage Breaker* have been a great blessing to the church in India across denominations, and many in our own churches have been influenced. With the Indian church's practice of legalism on one end of the spectrum and the emerging hypergrace teachings on the other end, balanced biblical teaching of grace and truth is much needed, and Freedom In Christ Ministries' latest discipleship resources meet this critical need.

Jeyakaran Emmanuel, pastor and church planter,
Powerhouse Churches, India

I was in the ministry for more than 15 years and a defeated Christian when I was introduced to Dr. Anderson's teaching. When I read *Victory Over the Darkness* and *The Bondage Breaker*, I understood my problems and took time to go through The Steps to Freedom in Christ. It was a new day in my life and ministry. I always carry at least one of Neil's books wherever I go, and I use the principles from the books in my teachings. Every pastor and Christian worker who longs for a fruitful ministry should read these books because they will change their ministries with lasting fruit. I am committed to introduce Neil's writings to as many people as possible.

George Philip, country director,
Trans World Radio, India

I had already read *Victory Over the Darkness* and *The Bondage Breaker* before I attended Dr. Anderson's Discipleship Counseling conference in Chennai, India. I was personally and richly blessed by the balanced blend of psychological and spiritual truth, along with a healthy acknowledgment of spiritual forces. I was able to relate the teaching to the needs of my people and their various struggles.

Rev. Johh Simeon, senior pastor,
Emmanuel Methodist Church, Chennai, India

My late husband and I were victims of spiritual abuse when we attended Dr. Anderson's conference Resolving Personal and Spiritual Conflicts. We were both set free from our bitterness when we forgave our pastor, and I had 75 others I needed to forgive, encompassing decades of abuse, victimization, and even rape. My life changed that day, and we started a Freedom in Christ ministry in a new church. That experience has opened doors for me to teach these same principles of forgiveness and identity in Christ to thousands of leaders across the United States and around the world.

Sheryl Giesbrecht, DDiv, author of
Get Back Up: Trusting God When Life Knocks You Down;
radio host and director of public relations,
International Christian Ministries

Few ministers have this kind of in-depth knowledge, wisdom, and insight for life application of the Scriptures. There are many good theologians. There are many good psychologists. There are very few disciple makers who are able to combine the principles of sound theology and sound psychology as Dr. Anderson does to help fellow Christians grow in Christ.

Dr. Phyllis Davis and Rev. Carrol Davis,
The Journey Pathways to Healing

Dr. Neil T. Anderson is one of the most important teachers of the gospel in the postmodern era, a friendly and warm human being, and a wise pastoral counselor. His ministry has brought a powerful renewal to our churches, focusing on our identity in Christ, spiritual freedom, and holistic healing for the purpose of building up new believers, and the consolidation and restoration of more mature believers. Our church regularly and methodically uses Freedom in Christ materials.

Dario Silva-Silva, founder and pastor,
Casa Sobre La Roca Churches, Colombia, South America

This material has been an amazing tool for the church in Venezuela. It has relieved my counseling load in a much-needed way. We have seen people released from their past due to recognizing their position in Christ. They have stopped blaming others, have allowed the Lord to do His work of healing from the inside, and changed their outward behavior.

Adam Nathanson, pastor

After nearly ten years of using Freedom in Christ materials, I learned that this ministry is not simply about setting people free from bondages to sin; it is a discipleship ministry that frees people to become Christlike. Freed people make wonderful disciples of Jesus. Our church became more than a hospital for the wounded. We became a school for developing disciples. Over 1,500 people who have gone through The Steps to Freedom in Christ now worship with all their hearts, pray with power, and disciple others.

Dr. Irv Woolf, director, National Coalition for Purity

I was blessed by this servant of God who wisely presented principles for ministry in our Christian community of different denominations. His anointed teaching on who we are in Christ, winning the battle for our minds, becoming the person God intended us to be, and knowing how to stand firm against spiritual forces opened our eyes to a complete and integrated message that is so necessary in the spiritual life of every believer. Our congregation continues to see great results using his Steps to Freedom in Christ.

Alberto Benigno, pastor, past president of
Council of Baptist Pastors of Cordoba, Argentina

We are thankful to God for Freedom in Christ Ministries and the blessing it has been to our church. We have employed these materials since we started the church, with excellent results in transformed lives. It is being used constantly in our School of Life in the different levels of classes, resulting in beautiful testimonies. Both *Victory Over the Darkness* and *The Bondage Breaker* are indispensable for discipleship.

Graciela Sanchez, senior pastor,
New Generation Church, Lanus, Buenos Aires, Argentina

Freedom in Christ ministries has had a profound impact on our personal lives and our ministry. Being part of an evangelistic ministry for 34 years and as a church growth pastor, we have led many people to Christ. We have also had the privilege of leading about 500 people through The Steps to Freedom in Christ. Freedom in Christ Ministries' repentance and discipleship strategy is the key to making fruitful disciples. It has given us the tools to help develop Christians to become the people God desires them to be and be true followers of Christ.

Earl and Trish Pickard, senior staff, CRU Ministries

THE
BONDAGE
BREAKER®

NEIL T. ANDERSON

HARVEST HOUSE PUBLISHERS
EUGENE, OREGON

Cover by Bryce Williamson

THE BONDAGE BREAKER is a registered trademark of The Hawkins Children's LLC. Harvest House Publishers, Inc., is the exclusive licensee of the federally registered trademark THE BONDAGE BREAKER.

The names of certain persons mentioned in this book have been changed in order to protect the privacy of the individuals involved.

The Bondage Breaker®
Copyright © 2000/2019 Neil T. Anderson
Published by Harvest House Publishers
Eugene, Oregon 97408
www.harvesthousepublishers.com

ISBN 978-0-7369-7591-9 (pbk.)
ISBN 978-0-7369-7592-6 (eBook)

Library of Congress Cataloging-in-Publication Data is on file at the Library of Congress, Washington, DC.

Printed in the United States of America

24 25 26 27 / BP-SK / 16 15 14 13

CONTENTS

ACKNOWLEDGMENTS AND DEDICATION

I want to acknowledge all the good people who have shared their lives with me. Every freedom appointment was a learning experience. There were many emotional moments working through the pain and torment they suffered. How wonderful to see God demonstrate His sufficient grace in their lives! There is no greater joy than to see God set a captive free and heal the wounds of the brokenhearted.

Harvest House Publishers has been a true partner in ministry. Eileen Mason was the editor who took the initiative to contact me about writing the first edition of this book, and she chose the title *The Bondage Breaker*. Bob Hawkins Jr. has followed in his father's footsteps of being a Christian publisher committed to God's Word. They are more than a company to do business with. They are a partner in ministry to serve the Lord with.

No person helped refine my message more than Dr. Robert Saucy. He was my friend and colleague at Talbot School of Theology, and served on the board of Freedom in Christ Ministries for the first ten years. I am fully aware of my need to be accountable to others, and not just for moral reasons, but for the credibility of the message and integrity of the ministry. Bob was my rudder, and sometimes my anchor when tempted to proceed without due reflection. I count it one of my greatest privileges to have coauthored a book on sanctification with him.

Writing a book on spiritual warfare was breaking new ground at Talbot School of Theology, and I needed someone to stand with me who had impeccable credentials. Dr. Saucy was the most respected man on campus, and I cherished the many hours that we spent discussing the message and methods in this book. He is now fully in the presence of God, whom he served for so many years. I dedicate this latest edition of *The Bondage Breaker* to the memory of the most gracious and humble servant of God that I have ever known.

A NOTE FROM NEIL

When I was a pastor, I taught God's Word to the best of my ability, but I didn't see much substantive change in the lives of the faithful people who attended the church regularly. Many had problems I didn't have adequate answers for. I was sharing information, but not seeing the transformation that I believed was possible. In 1982, I left the pastorate to teach at Talbot School of Theology.

At the seminary, I offered a Masters of Theology elective on spiritual warfare. In truth, I was searching for answers myself. I was looking for a wholistic, Christ-centered, biblically based answer that was true for all people irrespective of culture and time. This left-brained ex-aerospace engineer went through a lot of paradigm shifts during those ten years at Talbot. The class I started nearly doubled in size every year, and I began to see the lives of my students change as they discovered who they were in Christ and learned how to resolve their personal and spiritual conflicts. At the same time, God was directing a lot of hurting people to me with all kinds of problems, and I slowly learned how Christ really is the answer and how the truth really does set us free.

I loved teaching at Talbot, but I knew that God was directing me to take this message to the world. So in 1989, I founded Freedom in Christ Ministries, which now has offices, staff, and representatives all over the world. In all my years of ministry I have never gone where I haven't been invited. Half the churches that have invited me were evangelical, and the other half have been Pentecostal or Charismatic. I have never attempted to raise money for the ministry, and we don't charge a fee for helping people. Our staff raise their own support. We don't advertise, and don't spend any money marketing our product. I share my story in *Rough Road to Freedom* (Monarch).

A lot has happened since the first edition of this book. I have learned so much from interacting with various denominational leaders around the world. I see myself as a pastor-teacher, and I have written books on reconciliation, prayer, marriage, parenting, anger, fear, anxiety, depression, chemical addiction, and sexual addiction. I don't believe I have any special anointing or giftedness. I believe God has given me the gift of exhortation, but that's it. I believe it is the work of a pastor-teacher to equip the saints to do the work of ministry. All our staff are liberated children of God, and none are better than any others. Any mature Christian can do what we do to help others if they are equipped, and that is why our ministry exists. Our purpose is to glorify God by equipping the church worldwide, enabling churches to establish their people, marriages, and ministries alive and free in Christ through genuine repentance and faith in God. Our US office offers online training (www.ficm.org). Our international director, Steve Goss, is based in Reading, England (www.ficminternational.org).

I have since retired, and for the last six years I have cared for Joanne, my wife of 52 years, who was promoted to glory on October 2, 2018. I have experienced the peace of God during this time in a rather remarkable way, which I wrote about in *The Power of Presence* (Monarch).

The core message of *The Bondage Breaker* hasn't changed, and I'm thankful that Harvest House asked me to do this new edition. I am a better writer now, and I have more insight about this fallen world and its inhabitants than I did 30 years ago. I pray that you will read this book carefully, and take the opportunity to go through The Steps to Freedom in Christ. You have nothing to lose, and much to gain. It was for freedom that Christ set us free.

Neil T. Anderson

FREE AT LAST!

Years ago I was speaking in a Southern California church on the subject of the New Age movement. My text was 1 Timothy 4:1: "The Spirit clearly says that in later times some will abandon the faith and follow deceiving spirits and things taught by demons" (NIV). After my message, I was surrounded at the front of the sanctuary by a mob of people.

Sitting halfway back in the auditorium was a 22-year-old woman who had been weeping uncontrollably since the service ended. Several people had tried to comfort her, but she wouldn't allow anyone to get near her. Finally, a church staff member cut through the crowd around me and said, "I'm sorry, folks, but we need Dr. Anderson back here right away."

As I approached the young woman, I could hear her sobbing, "He understands! He understands!" We were able to get her out of the sanctuary and into a private office. After she calmed down, I scheduled an appointment to meet with her the next week.

When Nancy arrived for her appointment, her face was covered with open wounds. "I've been scratching myself like this ever since last week, and I can't control it," she admitted sheepishly.

Nancy described her horrible childhood, which included an abusive father and a grandmother who identified herself as a black witch.

"When I was three years old, I received my guardians—spirit guides," she continued. "They were my companions, telling me how to live and what to say. I never questioned whether having spirit guides was anything but normal until my mother took me to Sunday school. Then I began to suspect that my spirit guides might not be good for me. When I asked my parents about it, my father beat me. I never asked again!"

In order to cope with the increasing torment that her spirit guides brought to her life, Nancy resorted to rigid personal discipline. In her high school years, she decided to believe in God. But instead of leaving, her "guardians" continued to harass her.

After high school, Nancy turned to the epitome of discipline: the Marines. Determined to become the toughest of the lady leathernecks, she won awards for her discipline. But her spiritual torment kept pushing her mind and emotions to the edge. She refused to tell anyone about her mental battles for fear that she would be labeled insane. Finally, the pressure overcame her, and she snapped. Nancy quietly accepted a medical discharge and retreated to a lonely existence of inner turmoil and pain. This was Nancy's condition when she came to church that day and heard me talk about deceiving spirits.

"Finally, someone understands me!" Nancy concluded tearfully.

"Would you like to get rid of your spirit guides?" I asked.

There was a long pause. "Will they really leave, or will I go home and be thrashed by them again?"

"You will be free," I assured her.

Two hours later Nancy *was* free—and was hugging us with an openness she had never known before. "Now I can have people over to my house!" she exclaimed joyfully.

THE REALITY OF THE DARK SIDE

There was a time when I thought Nancy's experience was an unusual exception to the norm. Although the degree of her problem was somewhat exceptional, I have come to realize that the apostle Paul had in mind every believer when he wrote, "Our struggle is not against flesh and blood, but against the rulers, against the powers, against the world forces of this darkness, against the spiritual forces of wickedness in the heavenly places" (Ephesians 6:12). After more than 45 years of ministry as a pastor, seminary professor, and conference speaker, I have ministered to thousands of Christians all over the world who are being deceived and living defeated lives. This is a real tragedy, because their heavenly Father desires for them to live a free and productive life in Christ.

My own journey into this realm of ministry did not come by choice. I was a left-brained aerospace engineer before God called me into ministry. Even as a Christian layman I wasn't curious about demonic activity or the occult. The lure of esoteric knowledge and occultic power never appealed to me. I never played with a Ouija board, Tarot cards, a Magic 8-Ball, or had my palms read or fortune told, and I don't know what my astrological sign is to this day.

On the other hand, I have never doubted what the Bible says about the spiritual world, even when it seemed to conflict with my Western worldview. Initially I understood pastoral ministry as the application of sanctified common sense. I would try to speak the truth in love and encourage Christians to live accordingly by faith. It didn't take me long to realize that giving good advice wasn't enough for those in bondage and struggling with anger, fear, anxiety, and depression. These dear people had no mental peace, and I slowly began to understand the battle that was going on in their minds. I kept going back again and again to Scripture, looking for the truth that would set them free. In the process, I discovered who I was in Christ, how to resolve personal and spiritual conflicts, and then I started to see God set His children free and heal their wounds.

GOD WANTS YOU FREE
AND GROWING IN CHRIST

The apostle Paul wrote that "we are to grow up in all aspects into Him, who is the head, even Christ...to a mature man, to the measure of the stature which belongs to the fullness of Christ" (Ephesians 4:15,13). If God has given us everything we need to mature in Christ (2 Peter 1:3), then why aren't more Christians growing in Christ? Some are no more like Him now than they were 20 years ago. Paul said, "The goal of our instruction is love from a pure heart and a good conscience and a sincere faith" (1 Timothy 1:5). We should be able to say, every year, "I am more loving, patient, and kind and experiencing more joy, peace, and self-control than I was last year." If we can't say that, then we are not growing.

Part of the reason for this carnality is given in 1 Corinthians 3:2-3: "I gave you milk to drink, not solid food; for you were not yet able to receive it. Indeed, even now you are not yet able, for you are still fleshly. For since there is jealousy and strife among you, are you not fleshly, and are you not walking like mere men?" According to Paul, some Christians are not even able to receive good biblical instruction because of unresolved personal and spiritual conflicts in their lives. What is needed is some way to resolve these personal and spiritual conflicts through genuine repentance and faith in God. That is the purpose of this book.

My first book, *Victory Over the Darkness* (Bethany House Publishers), focuses on the believer's life in Christ and walk by faith. The book deals with the foundational issues of our identity in Christ and outlines practical steps on how to live by faith, walk according to the Spirit, renew our mind, manage our emotions, and resolve the emotional traumas of our past through faith and forgiveness.

Before we received Christ, we were slaves to sin. Now because of Christ's work on the cross, sin's power over us has been broken. Satan has no right of ownership or authority over us. He is a defeated foe, but he is committed to keeping us from realizing that. The father of lies can block your effectiveness as a Christian if he can deceive you into believing that you are nothing but a product of your past—subject to sin, prone to failure, and controlled by your habits.

Paul said, "It was for freedom that Christ set us free; therefore keep standing firm and do not be subject again to a yoke of slavery"

(Galatians 5:1). You are free in Christ, but you will be defeated if the devil can deceive you into believing you are nothing more than a sin-sick product of your past. Nor can Satan do anything about your position in Christ, but if he can deceive you into believing that what Scripture says isn't true, you will live as though it isn't. People are in bondage to the lies they believe. That is why Jesus said, "You will know the truth, and the truth will make you free" (John 8:32).

I don't believe in instant maturity. It will take us the rest of our lives to renew our minds and become like Christ. But it doesn't take long to help people resolve their personal and spiritual conflicts and find their freedom in Christ. Being alive and free in Christ is part of positional sanctification, which is the basis for progressive sanctification. In other words, we are not trying to *become* children of God, we *are* children of God who are becoming like Christ. Once people are established alive and free in Christ through genuine repentance and faith in God, watch them grow! They have a new thirst for the Word of God, and they know who they are in Christ because "the Spirit Himself testifies with our spirit that we are children of God" (Romans 8:16).

In this book, I have attempted to clarify the nature of spiritual conflicts and outline how they can be resolved in Christ. Part One explains your position, protection, and authority in Christ. Part Two warns of your vulnerability to temptation, accusation, and deception. Part Three shares how we can help others experience their freedom in Christ.

Since the publication of the first edition, there have been several exploratory studies that have shown promising results regarding the effectiveness of The Steps to Freedom in Christ. Judith King, a Christian therapist, did several pilot studies in 1996. All three of these studies were performed on participants who attended a Living Free in Christ conference and were led through The Steps to Freedom in Christ during the conference.

The first study involved 30 participants who took a 10-item questionnaire before completing the Steps. The questionnaire was re-administered 3 months after their participation. The purpose was to assess them for levels of depression, anxiety, inner conflict, tormenting thoughts, and addictive behaviors. The second study involved 55 participants who took a 12-item questionnaire before completing the Steps, and it was then readministered 3 months later. The third pilot study involved 21 participants who also took a 12-item questionnaire before receiving the Steps, and then again 3 months afterwards. The following table illustrates the percentage of improvement for each category.

	DEPRESSION	ANXIETY	INNER CONFLICT	TORMENTING THOUGHTS	ADDICTIVE BEHAVIOR
Pilot Study 1	64%	58%	63%	82%	52%
Pilot Study 2	47%	44%	51%	58%	43%
Pilot Study 3	52%	47%	48%	57%	39%

The Living Free in Christ conference is now available as a curriculum entitled *Freedom in Christ: A 10-Week Life-Changing Discipleship Course* (Bethany House Publishers, 2017). It has a leader's guide with all the messages written out, which leaders can teach themselves, a participant's guide for each person that includes the Steps to Freedom, and a DVD with messages presented by the staff of Freedom in Christ Ministries, should a leader prefer the course to be taught that way.

Research was also conducted by the board of the Ministry of Healing, which is based in Tyler, Texas. The study completed there was done in cooperation with a doctoral student at Regent University under the supervision of Dr. Fernando Garzon (Doctor of Psychology). Most people attending a Living Free in Christ conference can work through the repentance process on their own using The Steps to Freedom in Christ. In our experience, about 15 percent can't do so because of difficulties they have experienced. A personal session was offered to them with a trained encourager. They were given a pretest before a Step session and a posttest three months later, with the following results given in percentage of improvement:

	OKLAHOMA CITY, OK	TYLER, TX
Depression	44%	52%
Anxiety	45%	44%
Fear	48%	49%
Anger	36%	55%
Tormenting Thoughts	51%	27%
Negative Habits	48%	43%
Sense of Self-Worth	52%	40%

The contrast between bondage and freedom in a believer's life is powerfully illustrated in the following letter from a professional man. Unlike Nancy, by all appearances, this man was a normal, churchgoing Christian who appeared to be living a very successful life in both his family and career. But he wasn't experiencing his freedom in Christ.

Dear Neil,

I contacted you because I had been experiencing a host of seemingly inexplicable "psychologically related" attacks. My emotional troubles were probably rooted in my childhood experiences with horror movies, Ouija boards, and so on. I clearly remember fearing a visit from devilish forces after I saw the movie titled *The Blood of Dracula*.

My father had a pretty hot temper and was given to emotional outbursts. My survival response was to sulk and blame myself for upsetting him. Bottling my emotions inside became a way of life. As I grew into adulthood, I continued to blame myself for any and all personal shortcomings and misfortunes.

Then I accepted Christ as my personal Lord and Savior. I grew spiritually over the next several years, but I never enjoyed complete peace. There was always a lingering doubt about my relationship with God, whom I saw as distant and stern. I had difficulty praying, reading the

Bible, and paying attention to the pastor's sermons. I seriously questioned the purpose of life. I experienced horrible nightmares that woke me up screaming.

It was during my time of prayer with you that I finally found freedom in Christ. I realized that God is not a harsh, aloof disciplinarian, but a loving Father who takes joy in my accomplishments. I experienced a great release when I prayed through the final Step.

Now when I read God's Word, I understand it like never before. I have developed a more positive attitude, and my relationship with my Lord has completely changed. Since our meeting, I haven't had one nightmare.

Neil, I'm afraid there are many Christians like me out there leading lives of "quiet desperation" due to the attack of demonic forces. If I can fall prey to these forces and seem all right, so can others.

Are you one of those Christians who lives in bondage to fear, depression, habits you can't break, thoughts or inner voices you can't elude, or sinful behavior you can't escape? God has made every provision for you to be alive and free in Christ. In the pages that follow, I want to introduce you to the One who has already overcome the darkness and secured your freedom: Jesus Christ, the Bondage Breaker!

PART ONE

TAKE COURAGE!

Furthermore, we are instructed by our sacred books how from certain angels, who fell of their own free will, there sprang a more wicked demon brood, condemned by God... Their great business is the ruin of mankind. Accordingly, they inflict upon our bodies diseases and other grievous calamities. And by violent assaults, they hurry the soul into sudden and extraordinary excesses...By an influence equally obscure, demons...breathe into the soul, and rouse up its corruptions with furious passions and vile excesses.

TERTULLIAN (AD 160–220)

CHAPTER ONE

YOU DON'T HAVE TO
LIVE IN THE SHADOWS

Paul also says, "The unspiritual man does not know the things which
come from the Spirit of God." Contentious and proud wisdom is
rightly described as earthy, unspiritual and devilish because as
long as the soul seeks earthly glory it is deprived of spiritual grace
and remains cut off from God. For now it thinks only what comes
naturally to it since it originally fell. It is persuaded by the delusion
of an evil spirit to do things which are wicked and harmful.

BEDE (AD 673–735)

I was asked by a local Christian counselor if I could provide a spiritual assessment of one of his clients. He had given her several psychological tests, but never got to the root of her problem. After four years of professional counseling with no results, he finally considered the possibility that his client could be in some kind of spiritual bondage. Because there was a pentagram cut into her skin, it didn't take me long to give an assessment. I explained the spiritual battle going on for her mind, and she said, "Finally, someone understands." Although she had been struggling for years, she never sought out counseling until she tried unsuccessfully to commit suicide with an overdose of pills ten minutes after writing the following prayer:

Dear God,

Where are You? How can You watch and not help me? I hurt so bad, and You don't even care. If You cared, You'd make it stop or let me die. I love You, but You seem so far away. I can't hear You or feel You or see You, but I'm supposed to believe You're here. Lord, I feel them and hear them. They are here. I know You're real, God, but they are more real to me right now. Please make someone believe me, Lord. Why won't You make it stop? Please, Lord, please! If You love me, You'll let me die.

A Lost Sheep

The kingdom of darkness was far more real to her than the presence of God. Over the past 40 years, I have encountered hundreds of Christians like the woman who wrote this heartrending note. Most of them didn't attempt suicide, but many of them talked about dark impressions to do so. Nearly all of them admitted to the presence of "them"—inner urges or voices which badgered them, tempted and taunted them, accused them, or threatened them. We often tell people who come to our ministry for help that they will struggle with thoughts such as, *Don't go; they can't help you*—or they will think disruptive thoughts in first-person singular, like *I don't want to go*, or *I've tried this before, and it didn't work*. One person wrote: "Every time I try to talk to you, or even think about talking to you, I completely shut down. Voices inside literally yell at me: 'No!' I've even considered killing myself to end this terrible battle going on inside. I need help!"

Others may not be hearing voices, but their minds are so distracted that their daily walk with Christ is unfulfilling and unproductive. When they try to pray, they are tempted and bombarded by all sorts of things around them. When they attempt to read the Bible, they can't concentrate, and when they finish a chapter, they can't remember any of what they read. The same thing happens when they try rereading the chapter. Instead of being victorious, productive, joy-filled Christians, they trudge through life under a cloud, trying to hang on until the rapture. It could be a lack of mental discipline or stubborn flesh patterns, but if they go through The Steps to Freedom in Christ and the interference stops, then it can't be either one. I have seen thousands of people freed from this kind of mental torment, and most experience for the first time "the peace of God, which surpasses all comprehension" because now their hearts and their minds are being guarded in Christ Jesus (Philippians 4:7).

COMMON MISCONCEPTIONS ABOUT SPIRITUAL BONDAGE

Where do these voices come from, and what is the cause of all the mental confusion that plagues so many lives? One of the main reasons I fumbled and failed in my early days of ministering to people in bondage was because I didn't know the answers to these questions. Transitioning from my Western worldview to a biblical worldview has required several paradigm shifts. I labored under a number of misconceptions about the spiritual world that had to be dispelled. Perhaps you are struggling with some of these same faulty ideas that keep Christians in darkness.

1. *Demons were active when Christ was on earth, but their activity has subsided.* The Bible teaches just the opposite. False prophets, false messiahs, and spiritual deception will become more prevalent before the second coming of the Lord. Believers have wrestled "against the rulers, against the powers, against the world forces of this darkness, against the spiritual forces of wickedness in the heavenly places" (Ephesians 6:12) throughout the church age. Ephesians 6 then goes on to itemize the pieces of spiritual armor that we are to put on in order to defend ourselves against "the flaming arrows of the evil one" (verses 13-17). In 2 Corinthians 10:3-5, Paul declared that believers are engaged in a spiritual battle against forces that are raised up against the knowledge of God. If dark spiritual powers are no longer attacking believers, why would Paul alert us to them and encourage us to arm ourselves against them? The armor of God is for the believer, not the unbeliever.

Late-night television is dominated by psychic hotlines. Cable channels on history and science offer a variety of paranormal programs and push the concept of ancient aliens and UFOs, but offer no historic Christian commentary. Numerous cults and occultic practices seduce a gullible public, and the New Age movement is thoroughly entrenched in our college campuses. There is nothing new about New Age, of course. People are practicing the same old spiritism mentioned in the Old Testament. All they have done is change terms from *medium* to *channeler*, and from *demon* to *spirit guide*.

The kingdom of darkness was established at the fall of humanity and is still ruling this world. The battle from Genesis to Revelation is between good and evil, between the Christ and the Antichrist, between the Spirit of Truth and the father of lies, between the prophets of God and the false prophets, between the wheat (sons of the kingdom) and the tares (sons of the evil one—see Matthew 13:38). Wrestling against dark spiritual forces is not a first-century phenomena. The kingdom of darkness is still present, and the devil still "prowls around like a roaring lion, seeking someone to devour" (1 Peter 5:8). In light of this, Peter instructed us to "be of sober spirit, be on the alert...resist him, firm in your faith, knowing that the same experiences of suffering are being accomplished by your brethren who are in the world" (1 Peter 5:8-9). If your biblical worldview does not include the kingdom of darkness, then either God or you will have to take a bum rap for all the corruption Satan is foisting on you and the rest of the world.

2. *What the early church called demonic activity we now understand to be mental illness.* Such statements undermine the credibility of Scripture. The first demonically plagued Christian I counseled was diagnosed by medical doctors as a paranoid schizophrenic. After several attempts at medication and many hospitalizations, the medical establishment finally gave up on her. The diagnosis was based on her symptoms. She was nearly paralyzed by fear and was plagued by condemning thoughts, as is almost anybody who is under spiritual attack.

Any diagnosis based on observed or client-revealed symptoms offers by itself no explanation for the cause. Terms such as *schizophrenia, paranoia*, and *psychosis* are labels based on the classification of symptoms. But what or who is causing the symptoms? Is the cause spiritual, psychological, hormonal, or a neurological chemical imbalance? Certainly all these options must be considered. Consider this email I received:

> For years, ever since I was a teenager (I am 36 now), I had these voices in my head. There were four in particular, and sometimes what seemed loud choruses of them. When the subject of schizophrenia would come up, I would think to myself, *I know I am not schizophrenic, but what is this in my head?* I was tortured, mocked and jeered. Every single thought I had was second-guessed; consequently, I had zero self-esteem. I often wished the voices would be quiet, and I always wondered if other people had this as well, and if it was common.
>
> When I learned from you about taking every thought captive to the obedience of Christ, and read about people's experiences with these voices, I came to recognize them for what they are, and I was able to make them leave. That was an amazing and beautiful thing. To be fully quiet in my mind, after years of torment. I do not need to explain further all the wonderful things that come with this freedom of the mind; it is a blessing you seem to know well.

We should not be surprised when secular psychologists and psychiatrists espousing a natural worldview attempt to offer natural explanations for mental problems. Their worldview does not include God or the god of this world. Even many Christians who reject the scientific community's explanation for the origin of the species naïvely accept the secular psychologist's and psychiatrist's explanation of mental illness. Research based on the scientific method of investigation of mental health problems is not necessarily wrong; it's just incomplete. It ignores the influence of the spiritual world because neither God nor the devil submit to our methods of verification. To be effective, we have to acknowledge the neurological and biological basis for mental illness *and* a spiritual battle for the mind. I have attempted to do this in my books *Overcoming Depression* (Bethany House Publishers), and *Managing Anger* and *Letting Go of Fear* (Harvest House Publishers). I am certainly not against psychology, which by definition is a study of the soul. But I am not in agreement with secular psychology, just like I am not in agreement with liberal theology. What is needed is a truly biblical psychology.

3. *Some problems are only psychological, and some are only spiritual.* I believe such thinking creates a false dichotomy that implies a distinct division between the human soul and spirit. There is no inner conflict that is not psychological because there is never a time when your mind, emotions, and will are not part of the equation. Similarly, there is a spiritual component to every problem. There is no time when God is not present. "He…upholds all things by the word of His power" (Hebrews 1:3). The unseen spiritual world is just as real as the natural world that we observe through our physical senses, "for the things which are seen are temporal, but the things which are not seen are eternal" (2 Corinthians 4:18). Nor does the Bible designate any time or place when and where it is safe to take off the armor of God. As long as we are living on planet Earth, the possibility of being tempted, accused, and deceived is continuous. If we can accept that reasoning, we will stop polarizing toward medical answers only, or psychological answers only, or spiritual answers only.

Dr. Paul Hiebert, who taught at Trinity Evangelical Divinity School, contends that as long as believers accept "a two-tier worldview with God confined to the supernatural and the natural world operating for all practical purposes according to autonomous scientific laws, Christianity will continue to be a secularizing force in the world."[1]

4. *Christians cannot be affected by demons.* There are some who believe that Christians cannot be afflicted by Satan. Even the suggestion that demonic influence can be part of the problem prompts the hasty disclaimer, "Impossible! That person is a Christian!" Such thinking removes the church from the position of having an adequate answer

and helping those who are under attack, and it leaves people without hope. Yet we must remember that we are the only ones who can help them.

Nothing has done greater damage to arriving at a proper diagnosis and treatment than this unbiblical assertion. If Satan can't touch the church, why are we instructed to put on the armor of God, resist the devil, stand firm, and be alert? If we aren't susceptible to being wounded or trapped by Satan, why does Paul describe our relationship to the powers of darkness as a wrestling match? Those who deny the enemy's potential for destruction are the most vulnerable to it and are actually aiding his clandestine role. (Our vulnerability to demonic intrusion and influence is the subject of Part Two of this book.)

5. *Demonic influence is evident only in extreme or violent behavior and gross sin.* I labored under that kind of thinking for years when I was a pastor and therefore missed the subtle deceptions that rendered many Christians fruitless. Although there are some cases today that are similar to the wild demoniac called "Legion" in Luke 8, most deceived Christians lead relatively normal lives while experiencing personal and interpersonal problems. Because they view satanic involvement as being limited to the cases of mass murderers or violent sex criminals, these seemingly ordinary problem-plagued individuals wonder what's wrong with them and why they can't just "do better."

Satan's first and foremost strategy is deception. Paul warned, "Satan disguises himself as an angel of light. Therefore it is not surprising if his servants also disguise themselves as servants of righteousness" (2 Corinthians 11:14-15). It is not the few raving demoniacs who are causing the church to be ineffective. It is Satan's subtle deception and intrusion into the lives of seemingly normal believers. One Christian psychotherapist who attended my conference said, "I had never seen any evidence of demonism in my fifteen years of counseling until I came to your conference. When I returned to my practice, I discovered that my clients were being mentally deceived—and so was I."

Why didn't he see this before? If all that counselors are doing is listening to their clients, offering an explanation for their difficulties, and suggesting ways to change, they will probably never see the opposition. Only when you work toward resolution through prayer do you see what's really happening. The same holds for pastors. If all they are doing is preaching and teaching, they probably won't see evidence of demonism either. Most pastors don't have a clue as to what is going on in the minds of their congregants, and most congregants are not likely to tell them. During my first ten years of ministry, I didn't understand the battle for their minds either. One man did come up to me and say, "Pastor, I have this voice in my head." But I had no idea what he was talking about, and even if I had, I wouldn't have known what to do about it. I watched his marriage and family fall apart, and they left the church.

6. *Freedom from spiritual bondage is the result of a power encounter with demonic forces.* Freedom from spiritual bondage and conflicts is not a power encounter; it's a truth encounter. Satan is a deceiver, and he will work undercover at all costs. His demons are like cockroaches that scurry for the shadows when the light comes on. Satan's power is in the lie, and when his lie is exposed by the truth, his plans are foiled.

When I was a boy, we lived on a farm. My dad, my brother, and I would visit our neighbor's farm to share produce and help with chores. This neighbor had a yappy little dog that scared the socks off me. When it came barking around the corner, my dad and brother stood their ground, but I ran. Guess who the dog chased! I escaped to the top of our pickup truck while the little dog yapped at me from the ground.

That little dog had no power over me except for what I gave it. Furthermore, it had no inherent power to get me onto the pickup; it was my *belief* that put me there. Because I chose to believe a lie, I essentially allowed that dog to use my mind, emotions, will, and muscles, all of which were motivated by fear. Finally, I gathered up my courage, jumped off the pickup, and kicked a small rock at the mutt. Lo and behold, it ran!

Satan is like that yappy little dog, deceiving people into fearing him more than God. His power is in the lie. He is the father of lies (John 8:44) who deceives the whole world (Revelation 12:9), and consequently, the whole world is under the influence of the evil one (1 John 5:19). He can do nothing about your position in Christ, but if he can deceive you into believing his lies about you and God, you will spend a lot of time on top of the pickup truck! You don't have to outshout him or outmuscle him to be free of his influence. You just have to *out-truth* him. *Believe, declare, and act upon the truth of God's Word,* and you will thwart Satan's strategy.

This concept has had a dramatic effect on my ability to help struggling Christians. Prior to this, when I exposed a demonic influence, it would turn into what looked like a power encounter. With such a process, I saw counselees become catatonic, run out of the room, or become disoriented. One person jumped across my lap to grab a pencil and rake it across her wrist. I thought, *Dear God, there must be a better way.* My first approach was to get the demon to expose itself; then I would command it to leave. This exchange often resulted in a great deal of trauma for the counselee. Although some progress was made, the episode would usually have to be repeated.

I have learned since from the Scriptures that *truth* is the liberating agent, and that has proven to be the case in every successful counseling session. Jesus is the Truth, and He is the One who sets the captive free. Power for the believer comes in knowing and choosing the truth. We are to pursue *truth* because we already have all the power we need in Christ (see Ephesians 1:18-19). Furthermore, people in bondage are not liberated by what I do as a pastor, but by what they choose to believe, confess, renounce, and forgive. Notice the prominence of truth in the following passages:

- You will know the truth, and the truth will make you free (John 8:32).

- I am the way, and the truth, and the life (John 14:6).

- When He, the Spirit of truth, comes, He will guide you into all the truth (John 16:13).

- I do not ask You to take them out of the world, but to keep them from the evil one…Sanctify them in the truth; Your word is truth (John 17:15,17).

- Stand firm therefore, having girded your loins with truth (Ephesians 6:14).

- Finally, brethren, whatever is true…dwell on these things (Philippians 4:8).

God sent a powerful message to the early church in Acts 5 when Peter confronted Ananias and Sapphira: "Why has Satan filled your heart to lie to the Holy Spirit?" (verse 3). They were struck dead! Why the severity of discipline? God wanted the church to know that Satan, the deceiver, can ruin us if he can get us to believe and live a lie. If Satan could secretly infiltrate a church, a committee, or a person and deceive them into believing a lie, he could exert some measure of control over their lives! You may be tempted to dismiss Ananias and Sapphira as unbelievers, but that is not the case. F.F. Bruce, a New Testament scholar, wrote that Ananias was a believer[2] and Ernest Haenchen wrote that he [Ananias] was a Jewish Christian and commented, "Satan has filled his heart. Ananias has lied to the Holy Spirit, inasmuch as the Spirit is present in Peter (and in the community). Hence in the last resort it is not simply two men who confront one another, but in them the Holy Spirit and Satan, whose instruments they are."[3]

Some people say, "But I am a good Christian. How can I be deceived?" You are probably not as good as Eve was before the fall. She was sinless when she was deceived and believed a lie. Good people can be deceived, and if they are deceived, they don't know it. The battle began in the Garden of Eden and continues throughout the Bible. The contest depicted in the book of Revelation is not about dysfunctional families, sexual addiction, drug abuse, crime, or any other corruption. In fact, the word "sin" doesn't even appear in the book of Revelation. In the end, the battle between Christ and the Antichrist (Satan) is finally resolved. In between these two periods of history is "the church of the living God, the pillar and support of the truth" (1 Timothy 3:15).

SETTING CAPTIVES FREE

To my knowledge, there are no specific instructions in the epistles to cast demons out of someone else. That has led some to conclude that such a ministry is unwarranted. That is unfortunate, because the need is just as great, but the means by which we establish believers alive and free in Christ has changed under the new covenant.

Prior to the cross, divinely empowered agents—such as Jesus and His appointed apostles—were necessary to take authority over demonic powers in the world. Notice what Jesus did when He commissioned the 12 disciples to go on a training mission: "He called the twelve together, and gave them power and authority over all the demons and to heal diseases" (Luke 9:1). At that time Satan was not disarmed, and believers were not seated with Christ in the heavenlies.

A radical transformation took place at the cross and in the resurrection that changed the nature of spiritual conflicts forever. First, Jesus's death and resurrection triumphed over and disarmed the rulers and authorities of the kingdom of darkness (Colossians 2:15). Jesus proclaimed, "All authority has been given to Me in heaven and on earth" (Matthew 28:18). Because of the cross, Satan is a defeated foe, and he has no authority over those who are alive together with Christ and seated with Him in the heavenly places (Ephesians 2:5-6). Affirming the truth of Christ's victory and Satan's defeat is the primary step toward successfully standing against the enemy's attempts to intimidate you.

Second, because you are alive in Christ and seated with Him in the heavenlies, you no longer need an outside agent to exercise authority for you. You now reside "in Christ," who has all authority. In order to resist the devil, you first need to understand and appropriate your identity, position, and authority in Christ. Freedom in Christ is your inheritance as a Christian. That's why Paul wrote,

> I pray that the eyes of your heart may be enlightened, so that you will know what is the hope of His calling, what

are the riches of the glory of His inheritance in the saints, and what is the surpassing greatness of His power toward us who believe. These are in accordance with the working of the strength of His might which He brought about in Christ, when He raised Him from the dead, and seated Him at His right hand in the heavenly places, far above all rule and authority and power and dominion, and every name that is named, not only in this age but also in the one to come (Ephesians 1:18-21).

There is no need for the Christian to defeat the devil. Christ has already accomplished that. We just need to believe it. When we read through the epistles, it is obvious that Jesus has already delivered us from Satan and sin. That was the good news Paul conveyed in his prayer. God has done all He needs to do for us to live a victorious life in Christ. Now we have to assume our responsibility.

It is your individual responsibility as a believer to repent and believe the truth that will set you free. Nobody else can do that for you. I can't put on the armor of God for you, believe for you, repent for you, forgive others for you, and take every thought captive to the obedience of Christ for you, but I can help you. Finding your own freedom in Christ and helping others do the same is the focus of Part Three of this book.

The woman who called herself "A Lost Sheep" finally gained some measure of freedom. Four years after she wrote her desperate prayer, she was sitting in church on Sunday when she sensed God leading her to write His response. This is what she wrote:

My Dear Lost Sheep,

You ask Me where I am. My child, I am with you and I always will be. You are weak, but in Me you are strong. I love you so much that I can't let you die. I am so close that I feel everything you feel.

I know what you are going through, for I am going through it with you. But I have set you free and you must stand firm. You do not need to die physically for My enemies to be

gone, but be crucified with Me and I will live in you, and
you shall live with Me. I will direct you in paths of righteousness. My child, I love you and I will never forsake you,
for you are truly Mine.

Love, God

CHAPTER TWO

FINDING YOUR WAY IN THE WORLD

The stronger you are in your faith, the greater will be your confidence that you can overcome the wiles of the devil. You will also be aided in this endeavor by the knowledge that what you are going through is something common to the fellowship of all Christians throughout the world. Ever since the beginning of time it has been the lot of the righteous to suffer, and what a shame it would be if you were to be the only ones unable to endure.

BEDE (AD 673–735)

Several years ago, CRU[4] invited me to speak on a number of university campuses in the United States and Canada. Flyers were distributed and invited students to attend a meeting to hear about demonic influences in the world today. The purpose was evangelistic, and at the end of each meeting, an invitation was given to receive Christ or request an appointment. To my surprise, several hundred students filled each auditorium, and many did come to Christ. These were not fad-seeking teenagers or argumentative hecklers (although a group of Satanists did gather outside one meeting to chant!). Nor did they come to hear Neil Anderson, because they had no idea who I was.

They wanted to hear about demons! How many would have come if the flyer had invited them to hear about Jesus?

Around the same time, two of my seminary students, for the sake of research, attended a New Age conference being held two blocks from Biola University, where Talbot School of Theology is based. When they arrived at the door and discovered the cost to be 65 dollars each, they started to walk away. However, two strangers approached them, saying, "We were told to give you these tickets." The surprised students took the tickets and walked in.

They reported that one of the speakers led conference participants in a meditation exercise. He challenged everyone to imagine a spirit guide coming alongside. The speaker concluded the exercise by saying, "Now invite your spirit guide to come in." The devil was giving altar calls two blocks from Talbot School of Theology!

A lot has changed since I wrote the above in the first edition of this book. Now, 20 years later, a conservative voice can scarcely be heard in public education. Postmodernism has undermined objective truth, and civil discourse about subjects that really matter is nearly impossible in a public forum. Authoritative structures are crumbling, and educational administrators are capitulating to the demands of a spoiled generation. The trend is to be spiritual but not religious, yet no attempt is made to define what it means to be spiritual. Postmodernists argue that what is spiritual for me may not be for you, and what is true for you may not be true for me!

THE TWO-TIER WORLDVIEW

The Western world I grew up in saw reality in two tiers (see Figure 2a). The upper tier is the transcendent world where God, ghosts, and ghouls reside, a world that is understood through religion and mysticism. The lower tier is the empirical world, which is understood through observation and empirical research. In this two-tier scenario, the spiritual world has no or little practical bearing on the natural world; it is practically excluded from our understanding of reality. Humanistic rationalists reject the upper tier altogether.

In stark contrast to Western rationalism and naturalism, the rest of the world has a different view of reality. Missiologists report that spiritism is the most dominant religious orientation in the world. In many third-world countries, religious practices or superstitions have more practical relevance in daily life than science does. People in animistic cultures appease their deities with peace offerings, and consult their shamans to ward off evil spirits or to gain their favor. The fact that Jesus came to "destroy the works of the devil" (1 John 3:8) is that part of the gospel they are waiting to hear.

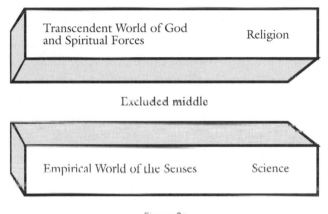

Figure 2a

It is tempting for those who are educated in the West to dismiss other worldviews as inferior on the basis of our advanced technology and economic success. But why, then, do we have the highest crime rate and divorce rate of any industrial nation and the greatest distribution of pornographic filth? Neither our materialistic worldview nor spiritism reflect a biblical worldview.

Between the two tiers is what Dr. Paul Hiebert calls the "excluded middle," the real world of spiritual forces active on earth. The challenge is to understand, from God's perspective, how the spiritual world impinges upon the natural world. A mute man who was demon-oppressed was brought to Jesus, and "after the demon was cast out, the mute man spoke" (Matthew 9:33). I can't explain how a demon can keep a man from talking, but I have seen it in my office, and seen God set a person free to speak. When Paul talked about the spiritual battle in the heavenlies, he was not referring to some distant place like Mars or Pluto. He was referring to the spiritual realm, the kingdom of darkness that is all around us and governed by "the prince of the power of the air" (Ephesians 2:2), "the ruler of this world" (John 14:30 NKJV).

PSYCHOSOMATIC ILLNESSES

Medical doctors know that many of their patients are sick for psychosomatic reasons. The most conservative estimate I've heard or read is 50 percent. How people would explain the cause for such illnesses varies greatly, depending on their worldview. To illustrate, a colleague asked us to pray for his daughter, who was experiencing symptoms of multiple sclerosis (MS). I felt sorry for the family when I heard about her condition and the prospect of living with this debilitating illness, but I couldn't get her off my mind. I believe God arranged an opportunity for us to meet. As she walked by my office, I invited her in and asked, "When did you first become aware of the symptoms?"

"I started feeling the first tingling sensations about six months ago."

"Was there anything traumatic or unusual going on in your life at the time?" I asked.

"I was feeling a little sorry for myself because I haven't yet attained the monumental achievements that my parents and brother have. I was reading the passage in 2 Corinthians 12 where Paul wrote about his thorn in the flesh. He said that God's power was perfected in his weakness, and I wanted God's power in my life. So I asked God to give me a thorn in the flesh."

"You asked God for a thorn in the flesh?"

"Yes."

"Do you know what Paul's thorn in the flesh was?"

"Some sort of physical problem, wasn't it?"

"We're not told how it was manifested, but 2 Corinthians 12:7 clearly states that it was a 'messenger of Satan,' literally an angel of Satan—a demon! Paul never asked for it. In fact, he 'implored the Lord three times that it might leave' him [verse 8]. I strongly recommend that you renounce your request for a thorn in the flesh and pray that any influence by Satan be removed from your life."

She did so and immediately felt better. She said even the room seemed lighter to her. The symptoms disappeared, and she resumed her normal activities. Several months later, the symptoms began to reappear. Then I led her through The Steps to Freedom in Christ, which was far more thorough than what we had time for originally. Today she is free, with no symptoms of MS.

A seminary professor attended my conference with his wife, who had been struggling for years with the symptoms of MS. She came with a walker and occasionally used a wheelchair. My wife, Joanne, led her through the Steps. The professor's wife walked out free of any aids, and the symptoms never came back. Twenty years later she was still doing fine.

I have personally met with three people who had been diagnosed with MS, and were set free in Christ after going through the Steps. From my understanding, there are two types of MS. One is a progressive degenerative disease, which I believe is primarily a physical problem. The other has MS symptoms that seem to come and go, and that was the case for the three mentioned above. I also led a godly man with the other MS through the Steps, and nothing changed. I told him that I couldn't find any spiritual basis for his illness, and he agreed. He just wanted to make sure, and I was privileged to help him come to the right diagnosis.

Two-tier doctors and psychologists would not even consider a spiritual solution for what they believe is only a physical problem. They would argue that the "recovery" experienced by the three people mentioned above was only a remission of a physical disease. Some Christian doctors may pray for a physical healing, which is noble, but it is unlikely that such prayers would resolve psychosomatic illnesses. To say there is no spiritual basis for psychosomatic illnesses is biblically unwarranted. Psychosomatic problems originate in our thinking, and that is primarily where our spiritual battles take place, as I will explain later.

LIVING IN THE EXCLUDED MIDDLE

A Christian worldview must be derived from Scripture, and not from our culture or personal experiences, which are too limited in scope and time. When we observe that one-fourth of all the healings recorded in the Gospel of Mark were due to the expulsion of demons, it should cause us to rethink how best to handle some illnesses. The woman whom Jesus healed in Luke 13:11-12 had been the victim of a "sickness caused by a spirit" for 18 years. Whenever I sense an illness coming on, I verbally submit my body to God as a living sacrifice, ask the Lord to fill me with His Holy Spirit, and command Satan and his demons to leave my presence in the wonderful name of Jesus. I have missed only one ministry obligation around the world over the past 45 years because of illness, and that was due to a kidney stone. That was definitely physical!

During freedom appointments, people often complain of physical symptoms that disappear after they resolve their personal and spiritual conflicts. The most common symptoms I have seen are headaches, dizziness, and general pain throughout the body. Some people feel like they need to vomit. There are well-meaning but ill-informed deliverance ministries that encourage people to throw up demons, which, of course, is ludicrous.

Some problems are clearly physical, such as a broken leg. In the case of physical ailments, go see your doctor, then have your church pray for a speedy recovery. Other problems, by contrast, are clearly spiritual, such as bitterness, guilt, and shame. Go see your pastor and get right with God.

The difficulty lies with the "twilight" in-between problems when the doctors can observe physical symptoms but can't find any physical cause for the illness. Several years ago, it seemed like everybody was struggling with hypoglycemia. I confess that as a pastor, I got caught up in this. It seemed like I was recommending a glucose tolerance test to every fourth person I met with. Most came back and said they were borderline glucose-intolerant! I would ask if they had taken the five-hour test, or the more conclusive seven-hour test. Eventually, the problem seemed to go away. What happened to hypoglycemia? Has our national diet changed such that low blood sugar is no longer a problem? Then came a wave of people supposedly afflicted by chronic fatigue syndrome, and that was followed by attention deficit disorder (ADD or ADHD).

I have a great appreciation for the medical profession and the proper use of medication when warranted. My uncle was the head engineer at the famed Mayo Clinic in Rochester, Minnesota. My brother taught at the University of Minnesota Medical School for 32 years as a biochemist. Two of my aunts were nurses, as was my sister, and my daughter is an LPN. I was admitted to medical school but chose seminary instead. So as I write all this, know that I respect what doctors and medicine have done for our well-being. The problem, however, is that when people have symptoms, we have been conditioned in our Western way of thinking to look for a natural or physical explanation first, and if that doesn't work, we say, "There is nothing left to do but pray."

Jesus said that in all things, we should "seek first His kingdom and His righteousness" (Matthew 6:33). Why don't we first submit to God and resist the devil (James 4:7)? The *first* thing a Christian should do about anything is pray. Why not submit our bodies to God as living sacrifices, which we have been urged to do (Romans 12:1)? "If the Spirit of Him who raised Jesus from the dead dwells in you, He who raised Christ Jesus from the dead will also give life to your mortal bodies through His Spirit who dwells in you" (Romans 8:11). You have nothing to lose by leading someone through the Steps, or taking yourself through them. At minimum, that means you will truly be ready to take communion the next Sunday, which is always a good thing. When is repentance ever wrong?

GETTING SPIRITUAL WITHOUT GOD

Over the past four decades, people in the West have begun to think there is more to life than what science can explain and what they can discern through their five physical senses. On the surface that may sound encouraging, but in fact, many of the same people who are disillusioned with the materialistic world are also disillusioned with established religion. Instead of turning to Christ and His church, they are filling their spiritual void with old-fashioned occultism dressed in the modern garb of parapsychology, holistic health, Eastern mysticism, and numerous cults. The center of their worldview is self: What will *I* get out of this? What about *my* needs? I'm doing *my* thing with my iPhone and iPad. The problem with pride is that it has *I* as its center.

The apostle Peter was confronted by Jesus for setting his interests on self rather than of God. Moments after confessing the fundamental truth that Jesus Christ is the Messiah, the Son of the living God (Matthew 16:13-16), Peter found himself in league with the powers of darkness. Having just blessed Peter for his noble confession, Jesus announced to him and the other disciples the suffering and death that awaited Him in Jerusalem. "Peter took Him aside and began to rebuke Him, saying, 'God forbid it, Lord! This shall never happen to You'" (verse 22). Jesus responded, "Get behind Me, Satan! You are a stumbling block to Me; for you are not setting your mind on God's interests, but man's" (verse 23).

Jesus's memorable rebuke seems mercilessly severe, but the fact that He identified Satan as the source of Peter's words describes precisely and appropriately the character of the advice Peter tried to give. Peter's comment was satanic in principle, for Satan's primary aim is to promote self-interest as the chief end of man. Satan is called the prince of this world because self-interest rules this world. He is called the accuser of the brethren because he does not believe that even a child of God has a higher motive than self-service. The evil one is whispering, "Save yourself at all costs. Sacrifice duty to self-interest, the cause of Christ to personal convenience. All men are selfish at heart and have their price. Some may hold out longer than others, but in the end, every man will prefer his own things to the things of God."

Such is Satan's creed, and unfortunately, the lives of all too many people validate his claim. Satan has deceived these people into thinking they are serving themselves when, in fact, they are serving the world, the flesh, and the devil.

The Christian worldview has a different center. Jesus confronts our self-sufficiency and offers a different perspective—one from the cross. Only when you live from God's perspective can you escape the bondage of the one whose intent is "to steal and kill and destroy" (John 10:10).

THE VIEW FROM THE CROSS

Adam and Eve were the first mortals tempted to "be like God" (Genesis 3:5). They were not the last to think they were God, act like God, or try to play the role of God in other people's lives. There is only one Creator God, and we are privileged to be created in His image and likeness. Adam became a living being when God breathed into him the breath of life. Adam was physically and spiritually alive, but he was not God. God told Adam that if he ate of the tree of the knowledge of good and evil, he would surely die. Satan questioned God's word and urged Adam, through Eve, to eat the forbidden fruit and unlock his godlike potential. Adam ate and died—not physically at first, but spiritually. His choice to sin separated him from God, and he was expelled from the Garden of Eden. Satan became the god of this world, and by the time we reach Genesis 6:5, God saw that "the wickedness of man was great on the earth, and that every intent of the thoughts of his heart was only evil continuously."

From the fall onward, everyone has been born physically alive but spiritually dead (Ephesians 2:1). We are physically alive as long as our souls remain in union with our bodies. For those who are born again, to be absent from the body is to be present with the Lord. We are spiritually alive when our souls are in union with God. The church fathers understood salvation to be union with God. What Adam and Eve lost in the fall was life, and what Jesus came to give us was life. Being separated from God, fallen humans sought to make a name for themselves and determine their own destiny. The diabolical idea that people are their own gods is the mantra of this fallen world and the primary link in the chain of spiritual bondage to the kingdom of darkness.

God never designed the soul to function as its own master. We lack the necessary attributes to determine our own destiny. Even the sinless and spiritually alive Adam in the Garden of Eden wasn't equipped to be his own god, much less his fallen descendants. If you desire to live in freedom from the bondage of the world, the flesh, and the devil, this primary link in the chain must be smashed. The self-centered worldview that Satan and his emissaries are promoting must be replaced by the perspective that Jesus introduced to His disciples in the wake of Peter's self-preserving rebuke:

> If anyone wishes to come after Me, he must deny himself, and take up his cross and follow Me. For whoever wishes to save his life will lose it; but whoever loses his life for My sake will find it. For what will it profit a man if he gains the whole world and forfeits his soul? Or what will a man give in exchange for his soul? For the Son of Man is going to come in the glory of His Father with His angels, and will then repay every man according to his deeds (Matthew 16:24-27).

This passage is the pivotal message in all four Gospels. Self-sufficiency is the number one dam that is holding back the rivers of revival. We are trying to do God's work in our way with our resources, and we can't. The following six guidelines from Jesus's statement constitute the view from the cross. They are the foundational guidelines for those who want to be free from the bondage of the world system and the devil who inspires it. Stay within the light of the cross, and you will successfully find your way in this dark world.

Deny Yourself

Denying yourself is not the same as self-denial. Every student, athlete, and cult member practices self-denial, restricting themselves from substances and activities that will hinder them as they reach for their goals. But the ultimate purpose of that kind of self-denial is self-promotion: to receive the top grade, to break a record, to achieve status and recognition.

By contrast, to deny ourselves is to deny self-rule. The flesh scrambles for the throne, but only God can occupy the throne, and He graciously offers to share it with us. For some deceptive reason, we want to rule our own lives and be self-sufficient, and overcoming that desire was a great struggle for me. When I was teaching at Talbot School of Theology, my wife became seriously ill. For nearly a year and a half, I didn't know whether she was going to live or die. We lost everything we owned, including our house, to pay for medical expenses. I was at the peak of my learning experience and was seeing God set others free, while my family was going down. It seemed like there was nothing I could do to change our circumstances. God stripped us down to nothing.

Thankfully, when all you have is God, that's when you learn that God is all you need. The trial ended when the school was hosting a day of prayer. The undergraduate students were having communion, and I sat with them on the gym floor, feeling like a modern-day Job. If I have ever heard from God, I did that night. There were no visions or voices, but the thought was clear: *Neil, there is a price to pay for freedom. Are you willing to pay the price?*

I left the gym knowing that the ordeal was over, even though my circumstances hadn't changed. Within a week, Joanne had fully recovered. Why did we have to go through that? First, I became a much more caring person for others. Second, God brought me to the end of my resources so I could discover His. My natural resources can't set a captive free or heal the brokenhearted. Only God can do that. Without that experience, I don't think I would have ever understood that my stoic self-sufficiency was my greatest enemy to my sufficiency in Christ. Before, I wouldn't have seen it as sin. But now I realize that brokenness is and always will be the key to effective ministry. Every book, CD, and DVD that I have written and recorded was produced after all that. Dying to self is a magnificent defeat.

We were not created to function independently of God, nor were our souls designed to function as master. "No one can serve two masters" (Matthew 6:24). When you deny yourself, you invite God to take the throne of your life, and occupy what is rightfully His so that you may be an instrument in His hand—one who accomplishes His objective and builds His kingdom.

Pick Up Your Cross Daily

The cross we are to pick up on a daily basis is the cross of Christ. Paul wrote, "I have been crucified with Christ; and it is no longer I who live, but Christ lives in me; and the life which I now live in the flesh I live by faith in the Son of God, who loved me and gave Himself up for me" (Galatians 2:20). His cross provided forgiveness from what we have done and deliverance from what we were. We are forgiven because He died in our place; we are delivered because we died with Him. We are both justified and sanctified by the finished work of Christ.

To pick up the cross daily means to acknowledge every day that we belong to God. We have been purchased by the blood of the Lord Jesus Christ (1 Peter 1:18-19). When we pick up the cross we affirm that our identity is based not in our physical existence but in our relationship with God. We are children of God (1 John 3:1-3). Our life is in Christ, because He is our life (Colossians 3:3-4).

Follow Christ

Seeking to overcome self by self-effort is a hopeless struggle. Self will never cast out self because an independent self that is motivated by the flesh still wants to be god. "Now those who belong to Christ Jesus have crucified the flesh with its passions and desires" (Galatians 5:24). "We who live are constantly being delivered over to death for Jesus' sake, that the life of Jesus also may be manifested in our mortal flesh" (2 Corinthians 4:11).

This may sound like a dismal path to walk, but I assure you that it is not. It is a tremendous experience to be known by the Great Shepherd and to follow Him as His sheep (John 10:27). "For all who are being led by the Spirit of God, these are sons of God" (Romans 8:14).

Sacrifice the Lower Life to Gain the Higher Life

What you invest in this world will stay here when you leave. Shoot for this world, and that's all you'll get. But shoot for the next world, and God will throw in the benefits of knowing Him now. For some sad reason, we want to be happy as animals rather than be blessed as children of God. To say it another way: "Bodily discipline is only of little profit, but godliness is profitable for all things, since it holds promise for the present life and also for the life to come" (1 Timothy 4:8).

Sacrifice the Pleasure of Things to Gain the Pleasure of Life

What would you exchange for love, joy, peace, patience, kindness, goodness, faithfulness, gentleness, and self-control? A new car? A promotion at work? A bigger house? A cabin in the hills? A jug of wine? To think that worldly positions and possessions can give you the fruit of the Spirit is to believe the lies of this world. The fruit of the Spirit is the result of abiding in Christ, and not self-actualization.

Sacrifice the Temporal to Gain the Eternal

Possibly the greatest sign of spiritual maturity is the ability to wait patiently for rewards that are lasting. Hebrews 11:24-26 says, "By faith Moses, when he had grown up, refused to be called the son of Pharaoh's daughter, choosing rather to endure ill-treatment with the people of God than to enjoy the passing pleasures of sin, considering the reproach of Christ greater riches than the treasures of Egypt; for he was looking to the reward." It is far better to know that we are the children of God than to gain something in this world that we will eventually lose. Even if following Christ results in temporal hardships, He will make everything right in eternity.

Satan wants to usurp God's place in your life. Every temptation he brings before you is an endeavor to get you to live independently of God. Whenever you focus on yourself instead of Christ or prefer material and temporal rewards over spiritual and eternal rewards, the tempter has succeeded. The message of this fallen world is to inflate the ego while denying God the opportunity to take His rightful place as Lord. Satan couldn't be more pleased—that was his plan from the beginning.

CHAPTER THREE

YOU HAVE EVERY RIGHT TO BE FREE

The Lord came to the lost sheep. He made a recapitulation of a very comprehensive dispensation, and He sought after His own handiwork. Therefore, it was necessary for Him to save the very man who had been created after His image and likeness—that is, Adam...Man was created by God for life. However, he was injured by the serpent who had corrupted him. Now if man, after losing life, never returned to it but was utterly abandoned to death, God would have been conquered. The wickedness of the serpent would have prevailed over the will of God.

IRENAEUS (AD 130–202)

Lydia was a middle-aged woman who was dealt a bad hand. Memories of ritual and sexual abuse that she suffered as a young child had haunted her continually throughout her life. Her shattered self-perception was written all over her when she came to see me. As Lydia told me her story, she displayed little emotion, but her words reflected total despair.

"Lydia, who do you think you are? I mean, how do you perceive yourself?" I asked.

"I think I'm evil," she answered stoically. "I'm just no good for anybody. People tell me I'm evil, and all I do is bring trouble."

"As a child of God, you're not evil. You may have done evil things, but at the core of your very being is a desire to do what is right, or you wouldn't be here," I argued. I handed her the following list of scriptures describing who she is in Christ:[5]

IN CHRIST

I am accepted:

- John 1:12 — I am God's child.
- John 15:15 — I am Christ's friend.
- Romans 5:1 — I have been justified.
- 1 Corinthians 6:17 — I am united with the Lord and one with Him in spirit.
- 1 Corinthians 6:20 — I have been bought with a price—I belong to God.
- 1 Corinthians 12:27 — I am a member of Christ's body.
- Ephesians 1:1 — I am a saint.
- Ephesians 1:5 — I have been adopted as God's child.
- Ephesians 2:18 — I have direct access to God through the Holy Spirit.
- Colossians 1:14 — I have been redeemed and forgiven of all my sins.
- Colossians 2:10 — I am complete in Christ.

I am secure:

- Romans 8:1-2 — I am free from condemnation.
- Romans 8:28 — I am assured that all things work together for good.
- Romans 8:31-34 — I am free from any condemning charges against me.

- Romans 8:35-39   I cannot be separated from the love of God.

- 2 Corinthians 1:21-22 I have been established, anointed, and sealed by God.

- Colossians 3:3   I am hidden with Christ in God.

- Philippians 1:6   I am confident the good work God has begun in me will be perfected.

- Philippians 3:20   I am a citizen of heaven.

- 2 Timothy 1:7   I have not been given a spirit of fear but of power, love, and a sound mind.

- Hebrews 4:16   I can find grace and mercy in time of need.

- 1 John 5:18   I am born of God and the evil one cannot touch me.

I am significant:

- Matthew 5:13-16   I am the salt and light of the earth.
- John 15:1-5   I am a branch of the true vine, a channel of His life.

- John 15:16   I have been chosen and appointed to bear fruit.

- Acts 1:8   I am a personal witness of Christ's.
- 1 Corinthians 3:16   I am God's temple.
- 2 Corinthians 5:17-20 I am a minister of reconciliation.
- 2 Corinthians 6:1   I am God's coworker.
- Ephesians 2:6   I am seated with Christ in the heavenly realm.

- Ephesians 2:10   I am God's workmanship.

- Ephesians 3:12   I may approach God with freedom and confidence.
- Philippians 4:13   I can do all things through Christ, who strengthens me.

"Would you read these statements out loud right now?" I asked. Lydia took the list and tried to read the first statement: "I am G-G-God's ch-ch…" Suddenly her whole demeanor changed, and she sneered, "No way, you dirty *bleep!*"

It is never pleasant to see the evil one reveal his ugly presence through a victim like Lydia. I calmly exercised Christ's authority and led Lydia through The Steps to Freedom in Christ. She was able to gain a new understanding of who she really was in Christ. Realizing that she was not just a product of her past, but rather, a new creation in Christ, she was able to throw off the chains of spiritual bondage and begin living according to who she really was, a child of God.

Later, Lydia told me that the list I asked her to read appeared to go blank when she started to read it. Satan didn't want her to know the truth of who she was in Christ, nor how Jesus meets her needs for life, identity, acceptance, security, and significance. He knew that God's truth would disarm his lie just as surely as light dispels darkness. The last thing the devil wants you to know is who you are in Christ.

YOU ARE A CHILD OF GOD

Nothing is more foundational to your freedom from Satan's bondage than understanding and affirming what God has done for you in Christ and who you are as His child. Your attitudes, actions, responses, and reactions to life's circumstances are greatly affected by what you believe about yourself. If you see yourself as a helpless victim of Satan and his schemes, you will probably live like a victim and be in bondage to his lies. But if you see yourself as a dearly loved and accepted child of God, you will likely start living like one. That is what John said in

1 John 3:1-3: "See how great a love the Father has bestowed on us, that we would be called children of God; and such we are…Beloved, now we are children of God…and everyone who has this hope fixed on Him purifies himself, just as He is pure."

Every defeated Christian I have worked with has had one thing in common. None of them have known who they were in Christ nor understood what it means to be a child of God. Scripture is very clear: "As many as received Him, to them He gave the right to become children of God" (John 1:12). "The Spirit Himself testifies with our spirit that we are children of God, and if children, heirs also, heirs of God and fellow heirs with Christ…so that we may also be glorified with Him" (Romans 8:16-17). Our identity and position in Christ is not only the basis for living a liberated life in Christ, but the foundation upon which we minister to others. We can't impart to others what we don't possess ourselves.

YOU ARE SPIRITUALLY AND THEREFORE ETERNALLY ALIVE

God created us to have a material self and an immaterial self, or an outer nature and an inner nature (2 Corinthians 4:16). The material self is your physical body, and the immaterial self is your soul/spirit. Because we are created in the image of God, we have the ability to think, feel, and choose (the combination of mind, emotions, and will are usually identified as the soul), and the ability to relate to God (if we are spiritually alive). As a Christian, your soul/spirit comes into union with God at the moment of your conversion, and that makes you spiritually alive. (Note: I use the terminology *soul/spirit* because conservative theologians don't unanimously agree about whether the human soul and the spirit are the same or separate entities.)

As a believer, you are no longer "in Adam," you are "in Christ." For every verse that says Christ is in you, there are many more saying you are "in Christ" or "in Him." Because the life of Christ is eternal, the spiritual life you now have in Christ is eternal. Eternal life is not something you get when you die physically; it is something you receive the moment you are born again! "He who has the Son has the life; he who does not have the Son of God does not have the life" (1 John 5:12).

Contrary to what Satan would like you to believe, he can't separate you from God, who has promised to never leave you nor forsake you (Hebrews 13:5). You don't have to physically die to get rid of tormenting spirits, which is a lie that deceived people commonly believe. You can submit to God and resist the devil, and he will flee from you (James 4:7).

YOU ARE A NEW CREATION IN CHRIST

If you don't fully understand your identity and position in Christ, you will likely believe there is little distinction between yourself and nonbelievers. Every verse in the list at the beginning of the chapter is true about every believer, and none of the verses are true about the natural person. The accuser will seize that opportunity, pour on the guilt, and question your salvation if you don't know who you are. Defeated Christians confess their sins and strive to do better, but inwardly they think, *I'm just a sinner saved by grace, hanging on until the rapture. Having my sins forgiven was the only thing that happened at salvation. I am still the same person I was before.*

Read how Paul describes who you were *before* you came to Christ: "You were dead in your trespasses and sins, in which you formerly walked according to the course of this world, according to the prince of the power of the air…and were by nature children of wrath" (Ephesians 2:1-3). As a believer you have become a partaker "of the divine nature, having escaped the corruption that is in the world by lust" (2 Peter 1:4).

As a born-again child of God, you are no longer "in the flesh"; you are now "in Christ." "You are not in the flesh but in the Spirit, if indeed the Spirit of God dwells in you" (Romans 8:9). "You were formerly darkness, but now you are Light in the Lord; walk as children of Light"

(Ephesians 5:8). "From now on we recognize no one according to the flesh…If anyone is in Christ, he is a new creature" (2 Corinthians 5:16-17). Paul doesn't identify believers by their flesh patterns. We are not alcoholics, addicts, codependents, pedophiles, or victims. We may struggle with some of those flesh patterns, but that is not who we are.

The New Testament refers to the person you were before you received Christ as your old self (old man). At salvation, your old self, which was motivated to live independent of God and was therefore characterized by sin, died (Romans 6:6); and your new self, united with Christ, came to life (Galatians 2:20). Because your soul is in union with God, you are identified with Him:

- In His death   Romans 6:3; Galatians 2:20; Colossians 3:1-3

- In His burial   Romans 6:4

- In His resurrection   Romans 6:5,8,11

- In His ascension   Ephesians 2:6

- In His life   Romans 5:10-11

- In His power   Ephesians 1:19-20

- In His inheritance   Romans 8:16-17; Ephesians 1:11-12

Your old self had to die in order to sever your relationship with sin, which dominated it. Being a saint or a child of God doesn't mean that you are sinless (1 John 1:8). But because your old self has been crucified and buried with Christ, you no longer *have* to sin (1 John 2:1). You sin when you choose to believe a lie or act independently of God.

You Can Be Victorious over Sin and Death

Death is the end of a relationship, not the end of existence. Sin is still a reality and appealing, but the power and authority it had over you has been broken. "Therefore there is now no condemnation for those who are *in Christ Jesus*. For the law of the Spirit of life *in Christ Jesus* has set you free from the law of sin and of death" (Romans 8:1-2).

The law of sin and the law of death are still present, and that is why Paul used the word "law." You cannot do away with a law, but you can overcome it with a greater law, which is the "law of the Spirit of life in Christ Jesus."

Furthermore, flesh patterns are still present. These learned habit patterns of thought and previously conditioned responses prompt you to focus on your own interests. However, you are no longer *in the flesh* as your old self was; you are now *in Christ*. But you can still choose to *live according to the flesh* (Romans 8:12-13), complying with those old urges that were conditioned to respond independently of God.

Paul teaches in Romans 6:1-11 that what is true of the Lord Jesus Christ is true of us in terms of our relationship to sin because we are alive "in Christ." God the Father "made Him who knew no sin to be sin on our behalf, so that we might become the righteousness of God *in Him*" (2 Corinthians 5:21). When He died on the cross, our sins were placed on Him. But when He rose from the grave, there was no sin on Him. When He ascended to the Father, there was no sin on Him. And today, as He sits at the Father's right hand, there is no sin on Him. Because we are seated in the heavenlies in Christ, we too have died to sin.

When we find a promise in the Bible, the only appropriate response is to claim it. When we find a commandment in Scripture, we should obey it. And when the Bible tells us the truth about who we already are and what Christ has already done, again, there is only one appropriate response—to believe it. I point this out only because the verses in Romans 6:1-10 are not commandments to be obeyed; they are truths to be believed. Christ has already died to sin, and because you are in Him, you also have died to sin. You cannot do for yourself what Christ has already done for you. Notice the use of the past tense in Romans 6:1-10:

- "We who *died* to sin" (verse 2).

- "All of us who *have been baptized* into Christ Jesus *have been baptized* into His death" (verse 3).

- "We *have been buried* with Him" (verse 4).

- "Our old self *was crucified* with Him, in order that our body of sin might be done away with, so that we would no longer be slaves to sin" (verse 6).

- "For he who *has died* is freed from sin" (verse 7).

- "If we *have died* with Christ, we believe that we shall also live with Him" (verse 8).

The verbs in these verses are past tense, indicating what is already true about us. The only right response is for us to believe.

Those first ten verses teach what Christ has already done for us, but we have a responsibility as well. "Even so consider yourselves to be dead to sin, but alive to God in Christ Jesus" (verse 11). Paul uses a present-tense verb because we are to continuously believe this truth. Believing it doesn't make it true. It is true whether we believe it or not. You may not feel dead to sin, but you are to *consider* it so because it *is* so. Some ask, "What experience must I have for this to be true?" The only necessary experience is that of Christ on the cross, which has already happened; and the only way to appropriate that truth is to believe it. Others try to put the old self to death and can't because the old self has already been crucified.

We don't make anything true by our experiences. Rather, we are to choose to believe what God says is true, then live accordingly by faith. Then the truth works out in our experience. It is not what we do that determines who we are. It is who we are that determines what we do. We don't labor in the vineyard hoping that God may one day accept us. God has already accepted us, and that is why we labor in the vineyard. We don't do the things we do with the hope that God may one day love us. God loves us, and that is why we do the things we do.

We can't do what Christ has already done for us, but we have to assume our responsibility to keep ourselves from sinning. Paul tells us how, in Romans 6:12-13: "Do not let sin reign in your mortal body so that you obey its lusts, and do not go on presenting the members of your body to sin as instruments of unrighteousness; but present yourselves to God as those alive from the dead, and your members as instruments of righteousness to God." You are dead to sin, but you can still serve it by putting your body at sin's disposal. It's up to you to choose whether you're going to use your body, which includes your brain, for sin or for the sake of righteousness.

Because of Christ's victory over sin, you are free to choose not to sin. It is your responsibility to not let sin reign in your mortal body. That is why the apostle Paul wrote, "I urge you, brethren, by the mercies of God, to present your bodies a living and holy sacrifice, acceptable to God, which is your spiritual service of worship" (Romans 12:1).

Having helped hundreds and hundreds of people through The Steps to Freedom in Christ, I can scarcely think of one who didn't have some kind of sexual problem. If you commit a sexual sin, you have used your body as an instrument of unrighteousness, and consequently, you have allowed sin to reign in your mortal body. If you commit a sexual sin with another person, the two of you become one flesh, according to 1 Corinthians 6:15-16.

Simple confession probably will not resolve the conflict. There is a prayer in the Steps asking God to reveal to people's minds every sexual use of their bodies as an instrument of unrighteousness, and God does. He usually starts with their first experience and works forward. As He brings those experiences to their mind, people are encouraged to renounce that use of their bodies; ask God to break the spiritual, mental, and emotional bond between themselves and the other persons; and finally, give their bodies to God as living sacrifices. Then they can be transformed by the renewing of their minds (Romans 12:2).

You Can Be Free from the Power of Sin

If you have allowed sin to reign in your mortal body, you know how hard the battle is. I've faced it myself. So did the apostle Paul. In Romans 7:15-25, he wrote about struggling with the same feelings of frustration. This passage clearly shows that the law is incapable of setting us free. I believe it also reveals what the struggle is like when we allow sin to reign in our mortal bodies. (Some believe this passage refers to Paul's preconversion experience. I disagree because every disposition of Paul's heart in this passage is toward God. In addition, the natural man does not "joyfully concur with the law of God" [verse 22] and "[confess] that the Law is good" [verse 16].)

I invite you to listen in as I walk through this passage with Dan, who had been struggling to overcome the power of sin in his life:

> *Neil:* Dan, let's look at a passage of Scripture that seems to describe what you are presently experiencing. Romans 7:15 reads, "For what I am doing, I do not understand; for I am not practicing what I would like to do, but I am doing the very thing I hate." Would you say that this verse describes you?

> *Dan:* Exactly! I desire to do what God says is right, but sometimes I find myself doing just the opposite.

> *Neil:* You probably identify with verse 16 as well: "If I do the very thing I do not want to do, I agree with the Law, confessing that the Law is good." Dan, how many personalities or players are mentioned in this verse?

> *Dan:* There is only one person, and it is clearly "I."

> *Neil:* It is very defeating when we know what we want to do, but for some reason can't do it. How have you tried to resolve this in your own mind?

> *Dan:* Sometimes I wonder if I'm even a Christian. It seems to work for others, but not for me. Often I wonder if the Christian life is even possible or if God is really here.

> *Neil:* If you and God were the only players in this scenario, it would stand to reason that you would either blame God or yourself for your predicament. But now look at verse 17: "So now, no longer am I the one doing it, but sin which dwells in me." How many players are there now, Dan?

> *Dan:* Apparently two, but I don't understand.

Neil: Let's read verse 18 and see if we can make some sense out of it: "I know that nothing good dwells in me, that is, in my flesh; for the willing is present in me, but the doing of the good is not."

Dan: I know that I'm no good.

Neil: That's not what it says, Dan. In fact, it says the opposite. *Whatever it is that is dwelling in you* is not *you.* If I had a splinter in my finger, it would be "nothing good" dwelling in me. But the "nothing good" isn't me; it's the splinter. It is also important to note that this "nothing good" is not even my flesh, but it is dwelling *in* my flesh. If we saw only ourselves in this struggle, it would be hopeless to live righteously. These passages are going to great lengths to tell us that there is a second party involved in our sin struggles whose nature is different from ours.

You see, Dan, when you and I were born, we were born under the *penalty* of sin. And we know that Satan and his emissaries are always working to keep us under that penalty. When God saved us, Satan lost that battle, but he didn't curl up his tail or pull in his fangs. He is now committed to keeping us under the *power* of sin. We also know that he is going to work through the flesh, which remains with us after salvation.

Let's read on to see if we can learn more about how this battle is being waged: "The good that I want, I do not do; but I practice the very evil that I do not want. But if I am doing the very thing I do not want, I am no longer the one doing it, but sin which dwells in me. I find then the principle that evil is present in me, the one who wants to do good" (verses 19-21).

Dan, can you identify from these passages the nature of that "nothing good" which indwells you?

Dan: Sure, it is clearly evil and sin. But isn't it just my own sin? When I sin I feel so guilty.

Neil: There is no question that you and I sin, but we are not "sin" as such. Evil is present in us, but we are not evil per se. This does not excuse us from sinning, however, because Paul wrote earlier that it is our responsibility to not let sin reign in our mortal bodies (Romans 6:12). Do you ever feel so defeated that you want to strike out at someone or yourself?

Dan: Almost every day!

Neil: But when you cool down, do you again entertain thoughts that are in line with who you are in Christ?

Dan: Always, and then I feel terrible about lashing out.

Neil: Verse 22 explains this cycle: "For I joyfully concur with the law of God in the inner man." When we act out of character with who we really are, the Holy Spirit immediately brings conviction because of our union with God, and we often take it out on ourselves. But soon our true nature expresses itself again and we are drawn back to God. It's like the frustrated wife who announces that she has had it with her husband. She wants out and couldn't care less about the bum. But after she acknowledges her pain and expresses her emotions, she softens and says, "I really do love him, and I don't want a divorce. But I just don't see any other way out." That's the inner person, the true self, being expressed.

Verse 23 describes the nature of this battle with sin: "I see a different law in the members of my body, waging war against the law of my mind and making me a prisoner of the law of sin which is in my members." According to this passage, Dan, where is the battle being fought?

Dan: The battle appears to be in the mind.

Neil: That's precisely where the battle rages. Now if Satan can get you to think you are the only one in the battle, you will get down on either yourself or God when you sin. Let me put it this way: Suppose there is a talking dog on the other side of a closed door and the dog is saying, "Come on, let me in. You know you want to. Everybody is doing it. You will get away with it. After all, who would know?" So you open the door, and the dog comes in and clamps his teeth around your leg. On the other side of the door, the dog plays the role of the tempter, but once you let the dog in, he plays the role of the accuser. "You opened the door! You opened the door!" And what do you do?

Dan: I usually end up confessing because I feel so guilty. But in my struggle with sin, nobody has ever told me about this tempting and accusing dog! I usually end up beating on myself.

Neil: I think you should beat on the dog. People eventually get tired of beating on themselves, so they walk away from God under a cloud of defeat and condemnation. On the other hand, just beating on the dog is not enough either. You were right to confess to God, which means you agreed with Him that you did open the door, but that is not enough. Confession is only the first step in repentance. Christians who only do that get caught up in the sin-confess-sin-confess-sin-confess cycle and eventually give up. You submitted to God when you agreed with Him that you opened the door; now you should resist the devil, and he will flee from you (James 4:7). Finally, go back and close the door and don't get suckered into opening it again. Repentance isn't complete until you have truly changed.

Paul expressed this feeling of unresolved conflict in verse 24: "Wretched man that I am! Who will set me free from the body of this death?" Note he did not say, *"Wicked* or *sinful* man that I am"; he said, *"Miserable* man that I am." There is nobody more miserable than the person who knows what is right and wants to do what is right, but for some reason can't. He is defeated because he is in bondage.

His attempts to do the right thing are met with defeat. He wonders, *Is there any victory?*

The answer is in verse 25: "Thanks be to God through Jesus Christ our Lord! So then, on the one hand I myself with my mind am serving the law of God, but on the other, with my flesh the law of sin." Now let's read Romans chapter 8 and see how Paul overcomes the law of sin by the law of life in Christ Jesus.

Dan: I think I'm getting the picture. I've been feeling guilty for my inability to live the Christian life without really understanding how to live it. I have tried to overcome this sin by myself, and I have never really understood the battle for my mind.

Neil: You're on the right track. Condemning yourself won't help because there is no condemnation for those who are in Christ Jesus (Romans 8:1-2). Let's see if we can resolve your conflict with genuine repentance and faith in God. With your permission, I would like to walk you through these Steps to Freedom. Then we can talk about how to win that battle for your mind and see if we can learn to walk by faith in the power of the Holy Spirit. Then you will not carry out the desires of your flesh (Galatians 5:16).

CHAPTER FOUR

YOU CAN WIN THE BATTLE FOR YOUR MIND

The devil, however, as he is the apostate angel, can only go to this length, as he did at the beginning, to deceive and lead astray the mind of man into disobeying the commandments of God, and gradually to darken the hearts.

IRENAEUS (AD 130–202)

He rescued us from the domain of darkness, and transferred us to the kingdom of His beloved Son, in whom we have redemption, the forgiveness of sins" (Colossians 1:13-14).

"If anyone is in Christ, he is a new creature; the old things passed away; behold, new things have come" (2 Corinthians 5:17).

"You have died and your life is hidden with Christ in God" (Colossians 3:3).

"If those verses are true, then how come I still struggle with the same thoughts and feelings I did before I became a Christian?" I suspect that every honest Christian has asked that question or at least thought about it. There is a very logical reason why you still think, feel, and too often act as you did before you were born again.

During the early and formative years of your life, you had neither the presence of God in your life nor the knowledge of His ways. Consequently, you learned to live independently of God. This learned independence from God is a major characteristic of what Scripture calls the flesh. When you became a new creation in Christ, nobody pushed the delete button in your memory bank. Everything you learned before Christ (including all the accompanying feelings) is still recorded in your memory. That is why Paul said, "Do not conform to the pattern of this world, but be transformed by the renewing of your mind" (Romans 12:2 NIV). Even as believers we can still be conformed to this world by listening to the wrong programs or reading the wrong material.

MENTAL STRONGHOLDS

In our natural state, we learned many mentally and emotionally unhealthy ways to cope with life or defend ourselves. Psychologists refer to these unhealthy patterns of living as defense mechanisms, and they are not congruent with a liberated life in Christ. For instance, if you got in trouble, or thought you would, for telling the truth, you probably learned to lie to protect yourself. Other common defense mechanisms include

- denial (conscious or subconscious refusal to face the truth)
- fantasy (escaping from the real world)
- emotional insulation (withdrawing to avoid rejection)
- regression (reverting to less-threatening times)
- displacement (taking out frustrations on others)
- projection (blaming others)
- rationalization (making excuses for poor behavior)

Defense mechanisms are similar to what Paul called strongholds. He wrote, "Though we walk in the flesh, we do not war according to the flesh, for the weapons of our warfare are not of the flesh, but divinely powerful for the destruction of fortresses. We are destroying speculations and every lofty thing raised up against the knowledge of God, and we are taking every thought captive to the obedience of Christ" (2 Corinthians 10:3-5).

Fortresses ("strongholds" NIV) are fleshly thought patterns that were programmed into your mind when you learned to live independently of God. Your worldview was shaped by the environment you were raised in. But when you became a Christian, nobody pressed the CLEAR button. Your old fleshly habit patterns of thought weren't erased.

What was learned has to be unlearned. If you have been trained wrong, can you be retrained? If you believed a lie, can you renounce that lie and choose to believe the truth? Can your mind be reprogrammed? That is what repentance is: a change of mind. We are transformed by the renewing of our minds. That is possible because "we have the mind of Christ" (1 Corinthians 2:16), and the Holy Spirit will lead us into all truth. But the world system we were raised in and our independent flesh patterns are not the only enemies of our sanctification. The good news is that we can reprogram our minds, but we still need to check for "viruses."

SATAN'S SCHEMES

Satan's strategy is to infiltrate your mind with his thoughts and to promote his lie in the face of God's truth. If he can control your thoughts, he can control your life. That is why Paul continued in the present tense with the statement, "And we are taking every thought captive to the obedience of Christ" (2 Corinthians 10:5). In this passage, the word "thought" is the Greek word *noema*. How Paul used this word elsewhere in the second letter to the Corinthian church is very revealing.

Paul instructed the church to forgive an offender after they had carried out church discipline. "One whom you forgive anything, I forgive also; for indeed what I have forgiven, if I have forgiven anything, I did it for your sakes in the presence of Christ, so that no advantage would be taken of us by Satan, for we are not ignorant of his schemes [*noema*]" (2 Corinthians 2:10-11). "Schemes" comes from the same root word, *noema*. Satan takes advantage of those who will not forgive. After helping thousands find their freedom in Christ, I can testify that unforgiveness is the major reason people remain in bondage to the past.

Concerning evangelism, Paul wrote, "If our gospel is veiled, it is veiled to those who are perishing, in whose case the god of this world has blinded the minds [*noema*] of the unbelieving so that they might not see the light of the gospel of the glory of Christ, who is the image of God" (2 Corinthians 4:3-4). How are we going to reach this world for Christ if Satan has blinded the minds of unbelievers? The answer is prayer.

Paul wrote, "I am afraid that, as the serpent deceived Eve by his craftiness, your minds [*noema*] will be led astray from the simplicity and purity of devotion to Christ" (2 Corinthians 11:3). My conversation with a 55-year-old undergraduate student illustrates how a mind could be led astray. Jay came into my office one day and said, "Dr. Anderson, I'm in trouble."

"What's the problem, Jay?"

"When I sit down to study, I get prickly sensations all over my body, my arms involuntarily rise, my vision gets blurry, and I can't concentrate. If this keeps up, I'm going to flunk all my classes. I can't even read my Bible."

"Tell me about your walk with God," I probed.

"I have a very close walk with God," Jay boasted.

"What do you mean by that?" I asked.

"Well, when I leave school at noon each day, I ask God where He wants me to go for lunch. If Burger King comes to mind, I go to Burger King. At the counter I ask God what He wants me to eat. If the thought comes to order a Whopper, I order a Whopper."

"What about your church attendance?" I continued.

"I go every Sunday wherever God tells me to go. For the last three Sundays, God has told me to go to a Mormon church."

Jay sincerely wanted to do what God desired for him to do, but he was being deceived. God was not directing him to a Mormon church, and we shouldn't fall into thinking that a spontaneous thought about Whoppers is guidance from God. Jay was listening to his own subjective thoughts as if they were God's voice instead of "taking every thought captive to the obedience of Christ" (2 Corinthians 10:5). In so doing, he had opened the door to Satan, with the result that his theological studies were being sabotaged. Deceiving thoughts had convinced him that God was preparing him to be one of the two prophets mentioned in the book of Revelation who were slain in the streets of Jerusalem. Jay even tried to convince his college roommate that he was the other prophet! Tears of gratitude flowed from his eyes when he found his freedom, and he returned to his right mind.

SATAN AND OUR MINDS

Scripture teaches that Satan is capable of putting thoughts into our minds. In the Old Testament, we read that "Satan rose up against Israel and incited David to take a census of Israel" (1 Chronicles 21:1 NIV). What is wrong with taking a census? Shouldn't David know how many troops he has for combat? Satan knew that David had a whole heart for God and would not knowingly defy the Lord. The strategy was to get David to put his confidence in his resources rather than God's. The same David wrote, "A horse is a false hope for victory" (Psalm 33:17). He knew the battle belonged to the Lord, but suddenly he had this "thought" to take a census against the protests of his military commander, Joab, who knew that to do this was sin. Tragically, 70,000 men of Israel fell as a result of David's sin.

How did Satan incite David? Did he talk audibly to David? No, these were David's thoughts. At least he thought they were. Therein lies the deception. Deceptive thoughts come first person singular in such a way that we think they're our own thoughts. I began to realize this years ago while helping others find their freedom in Christ. Thoughts like, *I'm stupid, I'm dumb, I'm ugly, I am no good* may be more than "self-talk."

Judas also listened to the devil. "During supper, the devil having already put into the heart of Judas Iscariot, the son of Simon, to betray him…" (John 13:2). We may be tempted to dismiss this as just a bad decision prompted by the flesh, but Scripture clearly says that the origin of those thoughts was Satan. When Judas realized what he had done, he took his own life, illustrating that "the thief comes only to steal and kill and destroy" (John 10:10).

I noted earlier that Satan filled the heart of Ananias to lie to the Holy Spirit (Acts 5:3). The word "filled" is the same word Paul used when he admonished believers to be "filled" with the Spirit (Ephesians 5:18). Whatever we yield ourselves to, to that we will be filled (controlled).

Martin Luther wrote, "The Devil throws hideous thoughts into the soul—hatred of God, blasphemy, and despair." Concerning himself he reported, "When I awake at night, the Devil tarries not to seek me out. He disputes with me and makes me give birth to all kinds of strange thoughts. I think that often the Devil, solely to torment and vex me, wakes me up while I am actually sleeping peacefully. My night time combats are much harder for me than in the day. The Devil understands how to produce arguments that exasperate me. Sometimes he has produced such as to make me doubt whether or not there is a God."[6] (For other references to the devil putting thoughts into the minds of noted saints, see the book *The Life of the Devil.*[7])

David Powlison, though opposed to the view that demons can invade believers, acknowledges that Satan can put thoughts into one's mind. " 'Voices' in the mind are not uncommon: blasphemous mockeries, spurts of temptation to wallow in vile fantasy or behavior, persuasive lines of unbelief. Classic spiritual warfare interprets these as coming from the evil one."[8] I am curious as to why he doesn't see that as an invasion! Thomas Brooks, in his discussion about Satan's devices, continually spoke of Satan presenting thoughts to the soul of believers.[9]

"NOT AGAINST FLESH AND BLOOD"

I have counseled hundreds of believers who were struggling with their thought life. Some have difficulty concentrating and reading their Bible, while others say they hear voices or struggle with accusing and condemning thoughts. With few exceptions, these struggles have proven to be a spiritual battle for their minds. This shouldn't surprise us since we have been warned in 1 Timothy 4:1 (NIV): "The Spirit clearly says that in later times some will abandon the faith and follow deceiving spirits and things taught by demons."

Why isn't the Christian community more aware of this battle for our minds? For one, I can't read your mind, and you can't read mine. Thus we don't have any idea what is going on in the minds of other people unless they have the courage to share about it with us. In many cases they won't because in our society, most people would assume they are mentally ill. Consequently, they might tell you about their negative experiences; but only with the right person will they dare to share what is going on inside. Are they mentally ill, or is there a battle going on for their mind? If we are "ignorant of [Satan's] schemes" (2 Corinthians 2:11), we will likely come to the conclusion that any problem in the mind must be the result of a chemical imbalance or a flesh pattern.

Psychologists and psychiatrists routinely see patients who are hearing voices: chemical imbalance is the standard diagnosis. I believe our body chemistry can get out of balance and cause discomfort, and hormonal problems can throw our systems off. But I also believe that other legitimate questions need to be asked, such as, "How can a chemical produce a personality and a thought?" "How can our neurotransmitters involuntarily and randomly fire in such ways that they create thoughts that we are opposed to thinking?" Are there natural explanations? We should remain open to any legitimate answers and explanations, but I don't think we will discover comprehensive answers unless we take into account the reality of the spiritual world.

When people say they are hearing voices, what are they actually hearing? The only way we hear audible sounds with our ears is when there is a sound source. Sound waves move from the source through the medium of air and strike our eardrums, which send a signal to our brains. Physically speaking, that is how we hear. But "voices" that people hear or the "thoughts" that they struggle with are not coming from sound sources if others around them are not hearing the same sounds.

In a similar fashion, when people say they see things that others don't, what are they actually seeing? The only way that we can see something visually is to have a light source reflecting from a material object to our eyes, which then sends a signal to our brain. Satan and his demons are spiritual beings; they do not have material substance, so we cannot see them or any spiritual being with our physical eyes, nor hear them with our ears. "Our struggle is not against *flesh and blood*, but against the rulers, against the authorities, against the powers of this dark world and against the spiritual forces of evil in the heavenly realms" (Ephesians 6:12 NIV).

BRAIN VERSUS MIND

There is a fundamental difference between our brains and our minds. Brains are organic matter. When we die physically, we are separated from our bodies, and our brains return to dust. At that moment, we will be absent from our bodies and present with the Lord (2 Corinthians 5:8). But we won't be mindless because our minds are a part of our souls.

Our ability to think is similar to how a computer functions. Both involve two separate components: One is the hardware, which is the actual physical computer (the brain); the other is the software (the mind), which is programmable. The software is not material. If it is removed from the hardware, the hardware still weighs the same. Likewise, if the spirit is removed from the body, the body also remains the same weight. A computer is worthless without the software, but neither will the software work if the hardware shuts down.

If something is not functioning correctly between the ears, the medical profession would first consider it to be a hardware problem. If your only reference point is Scripture, you would think otherwise. Of course one can have a neurological problem, or brain damage or dementia, and for the latter, the prognosis is not good. According to Romans 12:1-2, we should submit our bodies to God (which includes our brain), but we are transformed by the renewing of our minds.

After hearing my presentation on this subject, a dear lady wanted some clarification. She said, "I recently visited my daughter on the mission field, and I contracted malaria. I got so sick that I almost died. At the height of my fever, I started to hallucinate. Are you telling me that those hallucinations were demonic?"

"What were you hallucinating about?" I asked.

"Mostly about Pluto, Mickey Mouse, Donald Duck, and Daisy," she replied.

"Did you stop at Disneyland on your way to the mission field?" I inquired, and she responded, "Well yes, I did. How did you know?"

There was nothing demonic about her experience. Her visit to Disneyland was fresh on her mind. When we go to sleep, our physical brains continue to function, but there are "no hands on the keyboard." If you are mentally active and pounding away on the keyboard of your mind, you are not asleep. You go to sleep when you relax and let your thoughts drift away. While you are sleeping, your brain continues to function, and it can randomly access whatever has been stored in your memory. Consider the content of your dreams. Don't they almost always relate to people you know, things you have seen, or places you have been to? The stories in your dreams can be rather creative, but the people and places have already been programmed into your memory. Suppose a child watches a horror movie, then goes to sleep and has a nightmare. Chances are the players in the nightmare will be the same ones as in the movie.

But when someone has grotesque nightmares with images not previously seen or heard, then I would suspect that the origin of the dream is demonic. When we take people through The Steps to Freedom in Christ, those kinds of nightmares stop.

THE BATTLE IS REAL

We need to expose this spiritual battle for our minds for what it is so that we can have a comprehensive answer for those who experience it. Let me illustrate why: What typically happens when frightened children come into their parents' bedroom and say they saw or heard something in their room? One of the parents will probably go into the child's room, look in the closet or under the bed, then say, "There is nothing in your room, honey—now go back to sleep!"

Yet if you as an adult saw something in *your* room, would you just forget about it and go back to sleep? "But I looked in the room. There was nothing there," you respond, and you would be correct. There never was anything in the room that could be observed by your natural senses. "Then it's not real," says the skeptic. Oh yes it is! What your child saw or heard was in his or her *mind*, and it was *very real*.

I can't explain the means by which people pay attention to deceitful spirits. Neither do I know how the devil is able to invade our minds, but I don't have to know how he does it in order to protect myself according to Scripture's instructions. The spiritual battle for our minds does not operate according to the laws of nature, which we can comprehend. There are no physical barriers that can confine or restrict the movements of Satan. The frightened face of a child testifies that the battle is real. Why not respond to your child as follows?

"Honey, I believe you saw or heard something. I didn't hear or see anything, so that helps me understand. You may be under a spiritual attack, or you could be having bad memories of a movie you saw. Sometimes we can't tell the difference between what is real and a dream we just had. Before I pray for your protection, I want you to know that Jesus is much bigger and more powerful than anything you see or hear that frightens you. The Bible teaches us that greater is Jesus who is living in us than any monsters in the world. Because Jesus is always with us, we can tell whatever it is that is frightening us to leave in Jesus's name. The Bible tells us to submit to God and resist the devil, and he will flee from us. Can you do that, honey? Do you have any questions? Then let's pray together."

Much of what is being passed off today as mental illness is actually a battle for our minds. Proverbs 23:7 says, "As he thinks within himself, so he is." In other words, you don't do anything without first thinking it. All behavior is the product of what we choose to think or believe. We can't see what people think. We can only observe what they do. Trying to change behavior without changing what we believe—and therefore what we think—will never produce lasting results.

Because we can't read another person's mind, we have to learn to ask the right questions. Consider the following examples:

Five-year-old Danny was sent to the office of his Christian school for hurting several other children on the playground. He had been acting aggressively toward others and was restless in class. His teacher said, "I'm puzzled by his recent behavior—it isn't like Danny to act this way!" Danny's mother was a teacher at the school. When she asked her son about Jesus, he covered his ears and shouted, "I hate Jesus!" Then he grasped his mother and laughed in a hideous voice!

We asked Danny whether he ever heard voices talking to him in his head. He looked relieved at the question and volunteered that voices were shouting at him on the playground to hurt other kids. The thoughts were so loud that the only way to quiet them was to obey, even though he knew he would get into trouble. We told Danny that he didn't have to listen to the voices anymore. We led Danny through the children's version of the Steps to Freedom, and had him pray the prayers along with us. When we were done, we asked him how he felt. A big smile came across his face, and with a sigh of relief, he said, "Much better!" His teacher noticed new calmness in Danny the next day as though he were a different child. He did not repeat his aggressive behavior in school.

A committed Christian couple adopted a young boy and received him into their home with open arms. Their innocent little baby turned into a monster before he was five. Their home was in turmoil when I was asked to talk to him. After some friendly chatting, I asked him if it ever seemed like someone was talking to him in his head.

"Yes," he said, "all the time."

"What are they saying?"

"They're telling me that I'm no good."

I then asked him if he had ever invited Jesus into his life. He replied, "Yes, but I didn't mean it."

I told him that if he really did ask Jesus to come into his life, he could tell those voices to leave him. Realizing that, he gave his heart to Christ.

A medical doctor and his wife heard thumping on the wall of their son's room. He had stabbed the wall several times with a pair of scissors. They never caught him doing it, nor did they find the scissors. Then the child began to cut up every piece of clothing in the house. Again they never actually caught their son doing it. Huge medical and counseling bills piled up as they desperately tried to find a solution. Finally, the parents were introduced to our material and began to consider that this might be a spiritual problem. They asked their son if he ever had thoughts telling him to do what he was doing. He said, "Yes, and if I don't do what they tell me to do, they say they will kill you [the father]!" The little boy thought he was saving his father's life!

One of my students, who was a staff member at his church, led the church's children's director through the Steps. She shared the following testimony, which illustrates the frustration that many face as they try to find the help they need:[10]

> I thought my story was unique, but I often wondered if anyone else had the spiritual conflicts I was suffering with. My problem began a couple of years ago. I was experiencing terribly demonic nightmares and had nights during which I felt the presence of something or someone in my room. One night I woke up feeling like someone was choking me, and I could not speak or say the name of Jesus. I was terrified.

> I sought help from church leaders and pastors. They had no idea how to encourage me. Eventually fear turned into panic anxiety disorder, and my thoughts were so loud, destructive, and frightening that I visited my primary care provider. I thought for sure she would understand my belief that this was a spiritual battle. When I expressed the idea that the enemy was attacking me, she responded by diagnosing me with bipolar disorder, and told me that I

would be on medication for the rest of my life. She also gave me a prescription for antidepressants and antianxiety meds. I was devastated.

I told my husband the diagnosis, and he assured me that it wasn't true. I decided not to take the medication. I just didn't have any peace about doing that. My pastors prayed over me, but nothing changed. I began Christian counseling, which helped a bit, but it was nowhere near worth the $400 per month that I paid. When I told my Christian counselor about what was happening in my mind, and about my fears, she too said, "I think it is time for medication." It seemed like everyone thought I was crazy. No one believed that my problem was spiritual.

Thankfully, I came across one of your books and read stories of people I could relate to. I knew there was an answer. It was in that book that I first heard of The Steps to Freedom in Christ. Honestly, I was afraid of the Steps at first. I didn't know what to expect, but one of our pastors had recently met Dr. Anderson and was learning how to lead people through the Steps. He offered to help me, and I accepted.

Going through the Steps was one of the most difficult yet incredible things I've ever done. I experienced a lot of interference, such as a headache and confusion, but having the Holy Spirit reveal to me all that I needed to renounce was incredible. When I prayed and asked God to bring to my mind the sins of my ancestors, I was shocked at all that came up. I don't even know my ancestors! I later asked my mother about the things that came to my mind during the session, and she confirmed that my family had been involved in those things. I was amazed by how the Holy Spirit brought out the truth.

After going through the Steps, my mind was completely silent. It was amazing. There were no nagging thoughts. I was totally at peace. I wanted to cry with joy. After that, I wasn't afraid of being alone, and the nightmares were gone. I didn't have to play the radio or television to drown out the terrible thoughts. I could sit in silence and be still.

TAKING EVERY THOUGHT CAPTIVE

How do we know whether those negative, lying, and condemning thoughts are from the evil one or just our own flesh patterns? In one sense, it doesn't make any difference. We are to take *every* thought captive to the obedience of Christ. If a thought isn't true, don't believe it. Ask yourself: "Did I want to think that thought or those thoughts? Did I make a conscious decision to think those thoughts?" If not, why do you think those thoughts are yours?

One person laminated a card that she kept with her at all times. The card read, "Where did that thought come from? A loving God?" You will know that condemning, blasphemous, and tempting thoughts or voices did not originate from you if you work through the Steps to Freedom and those thoughts are no longer present. On the other hand, you can't tell flesh patterns to leave. They are slowly replaced or overcome as we renew our minds. Paul said we are not to be anxious (double-minded) about anything. Rather we are to turn to God in prayer, "and the peace of God, which surpasses all comprehension, will guard your hearts and your minds [*noema*] in Christ Jesus" (Philippians 4:7). The next verse says we are to let our minds dwell on those things that are true, pure, lovely, and right.

Our relationship with God is personal, and as in any relationship, there are certain issues that have to be resolved in order for the relationship to work. We can't expect God to bless us if we are living in open rebellion against Him. "Rebellion is like the sin of divination, and arrogance like the evil of idolatry" (1 Samuel 15:23 niv). If we are proud, God is opposed to us (James 4:6). If we are bitter and unwilling to forgive, God will turn us over to the torturers (Matthew 18:34) as a disciplinary effort. These issues have to be resolved first. Then we can experience the peace our Lord purchased for us on the cross.

Perhaps a testimony from a veteran missionary will illustrate this point. She was seeing her psychiatrist, psychologist, and pastor once a week just to hold her life together. The next step was hospitalization. I spent one Friday afternoon with her and her pastor, who was a former student of mine. Two-and-a-half months later, I received this letter:

> I've been wanting to write to you for some time, but I've waited this long to confirm to myself that this is truly "for reals" (as my four-year-old daughter says). I'd like to share an entry from my journal, which I wrote two days after our meeting.
>
> *Since Friday afternoon I have felt like a different person. The fits of rage and anger are gone. My spirit is so calm and full of joy. I wake up singing praise to God in my heart.*
>
> *That edge of tension and irritation is gone. I feel so free. The Bible has been really exciting and stimulating and more understandable than ever before. There was nothing dramatic that happened during the session on Friday, yet I know in the deepest part of my being that something has changed. I am no longer bound by accusations, doubts, and thoughts of suicide or murder, or other harm that comes straight from hell into my head. There is a serenity in my mind and spirit, a clarity of consciousness that is profound.*
>
> *I've been set free!*
>
> *I'm excited and expectant about my future now. I know I'll be growing spiritually again and will be developing in other ways as well. I look forward happily to the discovery of the person God has created and redeemed me to be, as well as the transformation of my marriage.*
>
> *It is so wonderful to have joy after so long a darkness.*

It's been two-and-a-half months since I wrote that, and I'm firmly convinced of the significant benefits of finding freedom in Christ. I'd been in therapy for several months, and while I was making progress, there is no comparison with the steps I'm able to make now. My ability to "process" things has increased manifold. Not only is my spirit more serene, my head is actually clearer! It's easier to make connections and integrate things now. It seems like everything is easier to understand now.

My relationship with God has changed significantly. For eight years I felt that He was distant from me. Shortly before I met you, I was desperately crying out to Him to set me free—to release me from this bondage I was in. I wanted so badly to meet with Him again, to know His presence was with me again. I needed to know Him as friend, as companion, not as the distant authority figure He had become in my mind and experience. Since that day two-and-a-half months ago, I have seen my trust in Him grow. I've seen my ability to be honest with Him increase greatly. I really have been experiencing the spiritual growth I'd anticipated in my journal. It's great!

CHAPTER FIVE

CONFRONTING THE REBEL PRINCE

The grace bestowed upon the holy apostles is worthy of all admiration. But the bountifulness of the Giver surpasses all praise and admiration. He gives them, as I said, His own glory. They receive authority over the evil spirits. They reduce to nothing the pride of the devil that was so highly exalted and arrogant. They render ineffectual the demon's wickedness. By the might and efficiency of the Holy Spirit, burning them as if they were on fire, they make the devil come forth with groans and weeping from those whom he had possessed.

CYRIL OF ALEXANDRIA (AD 376–444)

Mary was a 26-year-old flower child from the 1960s. She was a Christian and a university graduate, but she had severe mental and emotional problems that developed after her father divorced her mother. Within a period of five years, Mary had been institutionalized three times and was diagnosed paranoid schizophrenic. After about three weeks of counseling, Mary finally told me about her struggle with snakes.

"What about the snakes?" I asked.

"They crawl on me at night when I'm in bed," she confessed.

"What do you do when the snakes come?"

"I run to my mother. But they always come back when I'm alone."

"Why don't you try something different next time?" I continued. "When you're in bed and the snakes come, say out loud, 'In the name of Jesus Christ, I command you to leave me.'"

"I couldn't do that," Mary protested. "I'm not mature or strong enough."

"It's not a matter of your maturity; it's a matter of your position in Christ. You have as much right to submit to God and resist the devil as I do."

Mary squirmed at the prospect, and I could tell she was afraid. She finally agreed to at least try, since she had nothing to lose. The next week when Mary walked in, she said, "The snakes are gone!"

"Great! Why didn't you tell me about them sooner?"

"Because I was afraid you would get them too."

Thinking I would get them was just another part of the deception. If her problem had been neurological, then taking authority over the snakes in Jesus's name wouldn't have worked. In Mary's case, the problem was predominately spiritual, and five years of hospitalization and chemical treatment hadn't worked.

CARRYING JESUS'S BADGE OF AUTHORITY

After watching Jesus heal the sick and cast out demons, it was time for the disciples to try their hand at it. "He called the twelve together, and gave them power and authority over all the demons and to heal diseases. And He sent them out to proclaim the kingdom of God and to perform healing" (Luke 9:1-2). They preached the gospel and healed the sick (verse 6), but when the 12 came back, Luke made no mention of them casting out demons. Later a father brought his demon-harassed son to see Jesus, saying, "'I begged Your disciples to cast it out, and they could not.' And Jesus answered and said, 'You unbelieving and perverted generation, how long shall I be with you and put up with you? Bring your son here'" (Luke 9:41). Jesus rebuked the spirit and healed the boy (verse 42).

Jesus didn't spare the disciples' feelings when He pointed out their deficiencies. Most believers today will pray for the sick, then conclude, "If it be God's will." It doesn't take much faith to pray that way because it puts the onus on God. It takes a different level of faith to confront a demon and be confident about the outcome. One of the disciples' perversions was pride, which would render them ineffective. A few verses later, we see them arguing amongst themselves as to who was the greatest, and Jesus knew their hearts (verses 46-47).

Jesus confronted the disciples about several kingdom-killing perversions before appointing 70 others and sending them out on a similar mission. These perversions included self-sufficiency (verses 10-25), being ashamed of Jesus (verses 26-36), unbelief (verses 37-45), pride (verses 46-48), possessiveness (verses 49-50), ministering in the wrong spirit (verses 51-56), false confidences (verses 57-58), and lame excuses (verses 59-62).

The seventy "returned with joy, saying, 'Lord, even the demons are subject to us in Your name'" (Luke 10:17). Jesus quickly warned them about another possible perversion: "I have given you authority to tread on serpents and scorpions, and over all the power of the enemy, and nothing will injure you. Nevertheless do not rejoice in this, that the spirits are subject to you, but rejoice that your names are recorded in heaven" (verses 19-20). The words "serpents" and "scorpions" do not refer to snakes and bugs, because reptiles and insects are not our enemies. Jesus was metaphorically referring to the devil and his angels. He was telling His disciples, "You may think that the demons are subject to you, but in reality they are in subjection to Me, because of My authority and My power. The only reason you were effective was because your names are written in the Lamb's book of life." In other words, don't be an arrogant rich kid because your daddy has money. Nevertheless, Jesus "rejoiced greatly in the Holy Spirit" (verse 21) because the 70 were ready to go on to the next level of discipleship.

Understanding the power and authority believers have over the kingdom of darkness could lead some to abuse their position in Christ and step out on their own and "get thrashed." We have no spiritual power or authority apart from our identity and position in Christ. *Who we are* must always take precedence over *what we do*; and we cannot accomplish anything apart from Christ. Even Jesus was tempted by the devil to use His divine attributes independently of His heavenly Father.

The Right and the Ability to Rule

Authority is *the* issue in spiritual warfare. Two opposing sovereigns cannot rule in the same sphere at the same time. That issue was settled by the crucifixion and resurrection of Jesus. He Himself said, "All authority has been given to Me in heaven and on earth. Go therefore and make disciples of all the nations" (Matthew 28:18-19). Therefore, Satan has no spiritual authority in heaven or on earth.

Authority is the *right* to rule; it is based on a legal position. A policeman has the right to stop traffic at an intersection because he has been commissioned by the state, which vested that civil authority in him (see Romans 13:1-5). Power is the *ability* to rule. A policeman may have the authority to stop traffic, but he doesn't have the physical ability to stop a terrorist driving a truck with the intention to kill, unless he pulls out his police revolver and shoots him. Believers have both the authority to do God's will because of their position in Christ, and the power to do God's will as long as they walk by the Spirit: "Finally, be strong in the Lord and in the strength of His might" (Ephesians 6:10).

No good manager would delegate *responsibility* without the *authority* to carry out his directions. Nor would he send his workers on an assignment without enabling them to do it. Even secular leaders talk about the need to empower their employees. Issuing a command that cannot be obeyed undermines the authority of the manager. Jesus charged His disciples with the *responsibility* to proclaim the kingdom of God. Had He not also given them *authority* and *power* over the kingdom of darkness, the demons would have scoffed at their feeble attempts and sent them running for cover as they did the seven sons of Sceva in Acts 19:13-16:

Some of the Jewish exorcists, who went from place to place, attempted to name over those who had the evil spirits the name of the Lord Jesus, saying, "I adjure you by Jesus who Paul preaches." Seven sons of one Sceva, a Jewish chief priest, were doing this. And the evil spirit answered and said to them, "I recognize Jesus, and I know about Paul, but who are you?" And the man, in whom was the evil spirit, leaped on them and subdued all of them and over-powered them, so that they fled out of that house naked and wounded.

In the flesh, you don't have the power to resist Satan and his demons, but *in Christ, you do.* The Israelites looked at Goliath fearfully and said, "We can't fight him." But young David looked at Goliath and said, "Who is this uncircumcised Philistine, that he should taunt the armies of the living God?" (1 Samuel 17:26), then killed him with his sling. The army saw Goliath in relation to themselves and trembled; David saw Goliath in relation to God and triumphed. When you encounter the spiritual enemies of your soul, remember: You plus Jesus equal a majority. A newly converted child of God has the same authority in the spiritual world that the highest-ranking church official does. We are to "glory in Christ Jesus and put no confidence in the flesh" (Philippians 3:3).

Pulling Rank

"Subject" (Greek, *hupotasso*) is a military term meaning "to arrange under." It pictures a group of soldiers snapping to attention and following precisely the orders of their commanding officer. That is how we should all respond to our Lord. For our spiritual protection, "every person is to be in subjection to the governing authorities" (Romans 13:1). God is saying to His children, "You are living in a fallen world ruled by Satan. Get in rank and follow Me."

Spiritually defeated Christians see God and His kingdom on one side of the battlefield, and Satan and his kingdom on the other side as equal and opposites. They are stuck in the middle between the two, stretched out like the rope in a game of tug-of-war. On some days, God seems to be winning, and on other days, the devil appears to have the upper hand. They feel like pawns in the battle between good and evil.

The 70 disciples in Luke 10 came back from their mission with a different perspective, a correct perspective. Spiritual authority is not a tug-of-war on a horizontal plane; it is a vertical chain of command. Jesus Christ has all authority in heaven and on earth (Matthew 28:18); He's at the top of the chain of command. He has given His authority and power to His servants to be exercised in His name (Luke 10:17); we're under His authority, and we share it for the purpose of doing His will. And Satan and his demons? They're at the bottom, subject to the authority Christ has placed in us. They have no more right to rule your life than a private has the right to order a general to clean the latrine.

Why, then, does the kingdom of darkness continue to exert such negative influence in the world and in the lives of Christians? Because Satan has deceived the whole world, and therefore, the whole world lies in the power of the evil one (1 John 5:19). However, Satan is not an equal power with God; he is a disarmed and defeated foe (Colossians 2:15). But if he can deceive you into believing that he has more power and authority than you do, you will live as if he does! You have been given authority over the kingdom of darkness, but if you don't believe it and live accordingly, it's as if you didn't have it.

I was thankful for our authority in Christ when ministering to a severely demonized woman. During the session, the woman—who was physically imposing—suddenly rose from her chair and walked toward me with a menacing look. I was glad that the weapons of our warfare are not of the flesh, because I would have had a difficult time defending myself against a demonized person of her size.

Instead, I spoke these words based on 1 John 5:18—not to the woman, because she was blanked out at the time, but to the evil spirit controlling her: "I'm a child of God, and the evil one can't touch me. Sit down right now." She stopped in her tracks and returned to her chair. Had I not exercised my authority in Christ, fear would have controlled me, and some kind of power encounter would have ensued. By taking a stand in Christ's name, I neutralized the demon's hollow show of power and was able to minister to the woman.

It is important to realize that you don't "shout out the devil." Authority doesn't increase with volume. Shouting or screaming at the devil is an impulsive response motivated by fear. It is no different than with parental authority. If you are shouting and screaming at your children in an attempt to control their behavior, you are not properly exercising your God-given authority as a parent; you are undermining it. You are living according to the flesh.

The episode with the woman was merely a scare tactic from the enemy, who was hoping I would respond in fear. Fear of anything (other than the fear of God) is mutually exclusive to faith in God. When Satan tries to incite fear, we are to maintain our position in Christ and exhibit the fruit of the Spirit, which includes self-control (Galatians 5:23).

A family of four were out for a drive when a bee flew in the back window of their vehicle. The two children screamed, "Daddy, there is a bee in the car!" The father reached back and grabbed the bee in his hand. The stinger went deep into his palm, and then he released the bee. The children started screaming again until their father showed them his hand with the stinger in it. Jesus is saying to us, "Look at My hand. Look at My feet and side. I took the stinger. Satan no longer has one."

THE RICHES OF OUR INHERITANCE IN CHRIST

We may have an even greater advantage in spiritual warfare than the first disciples did. They were *with* Christ (Mark 3:14-15), but we are *in* Christ. That was Paul's great news in the opening lines of his letter to the church at Ephesus. Notice how many times he mentions our position in Christ:

> Blessed be the God and Father of our Lord Jesus Christ, who has blessed us with every spiritual blessing in the heavenly places *in Christ*, just as He chose us *in Him* before the

foundation of the world...To the praise of the glory of His grace, which He freely bestowed on us *in the Beloved. In Him* we have redemption through His blood...He made known to us the mystery of His will, according to His kind intention which He purposed *in Him* with a view to an administration suitable to the fullness of the times, that is, the summing up of all things *in Christ...In Him* also we have obtained an inheritance...to the end that we who were the first to hope *in Christ* would be to the praise of His glory. *In Him,* you also, after listening to the message of truth, the gospel of your salvation—having also believed, you were sealed *in Him* with the Holy Spirit of promise (Ephesians 1:3-13).

Paul wanted to make sure that nobody missed his point. He tells us ten times in verses 3-13 that we are "in Christ." Everything we have is the result of our intimate, personal relationship with the resurrected Christ and His indwelling Spirit. The problem is, we don't see it. So Paul continues:

I pray that the eyes of your heart may be enlightened, so that you will know what is the hope of His calling, what are the riches of the glory of His inheritance in the saints, and what is the surpassing greatness of His power toward us who believe. These are in accordance with the working of the strength of His might which He brought about in Christ, when He raised Him from the dead and seated Him at His right hand in the heavenly places (verses 18-20).

We have the authority to do God's will. We don't have the authority to do our will. If we exceed God's authority, we are operating in the flesh and will be defeated. If we fail to exercise our authority, we will likewise be defeated, and we will not be able to fulfill our delegated responsibilities.

The Depth and Breadth of Authority

In Ephesians 1:19-23, Paul explained that the source of Christ's authority was the same power that raised Him from the dead and seated Him at the Father's right hand. That power source is so dynamic that Paul used four different Greek words in verse 19 to describe it: "power" (*dunameos*), "working" (*energeian*), "strength" (*kratous*), and "might" (*ischuos*). Behind the resurrection of the Lord Jesus Christ lies the mightiest work of power recorded in the Word of God. And the same power that raised Christ from the dead and defeated Satan is the power available to us as believers.

Paul also wants to open our eyes to the expansive scope of Christ's authority, which is "far above all rule and authority and power and dominion, and every name that is named, not only in this age but also in the one to come" (Ephesians 1:21). Think about the most powerful and influential political or military leaders in the world, good and bad. Imagine the most feared terrorists, crime kingpins, and drug barons. Think about the notorious figures of the past and present who have blighted society with their diabolical ways. Think about Satan and all the powers of darkness marshaled under his command. Jesus's authority is not only above all these human and spiritual authorities past, present, and future—He is *far* above them.

Authority Conferred

Paul was saying that Christ's power and authority has been conferred on "us who believe" (Ephesians 1:19). Paul had already explained that God's supreme act of power and authority occurred when He raised Christ from the dead and seated Him in the heavenlies far above all other authorities (verses 19-21). After parenthetically alluding to the sinful state in which we existed prior to salvation (2:1-3), Paul continued his central theme of Christ's authority as it relates to us: "God, being rich in mercy, because of His great love with which He loved us, even when we were dead in our transgressions, made us alive together with Christ (by grace you have been saved), and raised us up with Him, and seated us with Him in the heavenly places in Christ Jesus" (verses 4-6).

Paul wants us to see that when Christ was raised from the dead (1:20), those of us who have believed in Him were also resurrected from our condition of spiritual death and made alive "together with Christ" (2:5-6). The resurrection of Christ from the tomb and our resurrection from spiritual death happened at the same time. It's only logical that the head (Christ) and the body (His church) should be raised together.

Furthermore, when God seated Christ at His right hand and conferred on Him all authority (Ephesians 1:20-21), He also seated us at His right hand (2:6) because we are "together with Christ" (2:5). The moment you receive Christ, you are seated with Him in the heavenlies. Your identity as a child of God and your authority over spiritual powers are not things you *are* receiving or *will* receive at some time in the future; you have them right now. You are a spiritually alive child of God *right now*. You are seated in the heavenlies with Christ *right now*. You have power and authority over the kingdom of darkness and are able to do His will *right now*.

Paul also related this empowerment and life-changing truth in his letter to the Colossians: "In Him [Christ] you have been made complete, and He is the head over all rule and authority" (Colossians 2:10). Notice the verb tense: We *have been* made complete. When? At the death, resurrection, and ascension of Jesus Christ. Because Christ is the God-appointed head over all rule and authority, and because we are seated with Him in the heavenlies, we have the power and authority to do His will.

Paul mentioned something else in Colossians that we need to know: "He...disarmed the rulers and authorities, [and] He made a public display of them, having triumphed over them through Him" (2:15). Not only were you made alive in Christ, but Satan was disarmed and defeated some 2,000 years ago. His defeat is not pending, nor is it future; it has already happened. It is not our responsibility to defeat the devil. Jesus has already done that.

If Satan is already disarmed, why don't we experience more victory in our lives? Because the father of lies has deceived the whole world. Satan roams around like a hungry lion, looking and sounding ferocious. A lion roars to paralyze its prey in fear, and they are consumed. But Satan's fangs have been removed and he has been declawed, and we have to believe that or we will be consumed.

God's ultimate purpose for conferring His authority on the church is given in Ephesians 3:8-12:

> To me, the very least of all saints, this grace was given, to preach to the Gentiles the unfathomable riches of Christ, and to bring to light what is the administration of the mystery which for ages has been hidden in God who created all things; so that the manifold wisdom of God might now be made known through the church to the rulers and authorities in the heavenly places. This was in accordance with the eternal purpose which He carried out in Christ Jesus our Lord, in whom we have boldness and confident access through faith in Him.

It is the eternal purpose of God to make His wisdom known through the church to "the rulers and authorities in the heavenly places." When it comes to fulfilling this "eternal purpose," how is the church doing? Some are still asking, "What rulers and authorities?" I pray that God would open the eyes of all His children so that the church would come alive in Christ and fulfill its purpose.

Qualified for Kingdom Work

I believe there are four qualifications for living in the authority and power of Christ:

1. *Belief.* Paul talks about "His power toward us who *believe*" (Ephesians 1:19). Imagine a rookie traffic cop approaching a busy intersection to direct traffic for the first time. His instructors at the academy told him that all he had to do was step into the street and hold up his hand, and cars would stop. But because he's insecure, he stands on the curb, tweets his whistle weakly, and sort of waves at an oncoming car, which roars by him. His authority is diminished by his lack of confidence.

Now imagine a seasoned officer of the law at the same intersection. He sizes up the situation, steps into the street carefully but confidently, blows his whistle, and stretches out his hand—and the cars stop. He is exercising his authority in self-control.

In the spiritual realm, if you don't believe you have Christ's authority over the kingdom of darkness, you're not likely to exercise it. I will explain in later chapters how to help people without losing control. A few years back, I was helping a young lady who was having a hard time staying focused. Suddenly her countenance changed, and a voice other than her own said, "Who the [*bleep*] do you think you are?" I calmly said, "I'm a child of God, and you have no authority to speak." Immediately the young lady came back to her right mind, and we finished the session. You must know who you are in Christ to ensure victory!

2. *Humility*. Humility is confidence properly placed. Humility is like meekness, which in the case of Christ, was great strength under great control. In exercising our authority, humility is placing confidence in Christ, the source of our authority, instead of in ourselves. Like Paul, we "glory in Christ Jesus and put no confidence in the flesh" (Philippians 3:3). Jesus didn't shrink back from exercising His authority, and He showed humility by doing everything according to what His Father told Him to do.

Pride says, "I can do it." Humility says, "I can do all things through [Christ], who strengthens me." Apart from Christ, we can do *nothing* of lasting significance (John 15:5). We humbly exercise His authority—in His strength and in His name.

3. *Boldness*. It is the mark of a Spirit-filled Christian to be strong and courageous. Joshua was challenged four times to be strong and courageous (Joshua 1:6,7,9,18). "The wicked flee when no one is pursuing, but the righteous are bold as a lion" (Proverbs 28:1). When the early church prayed about their mission of sharing the gospel in Jerusalem, "the place where they had gathered together was shaken, and they were all filled with the Holy Spirit and began to speak the word of God with boldness" (Acts 4:31). Spirit-inspired boldness is behind every successful advance in the church. "God has not given us a spirit of timidity, but of power and love and discipline" (2 Timothy 1:7).

We are living in an age of anxiety. If you are struggling with any kind of anxiety disorder, I encourage you to read the book that I coauthored with my colleague Rich Miller, *Letting Go of Fear* (Harvest

House Publishers, 2018). The fear of God is not only the beginning of wisdom, it is the one fear that can expel all others. The opposite of boldness is cowardice, fear, and unbelief. Notice what God thinks about these characteristics:

> I am the Alpha and Omega, the beginning and the end. I will give to the one who thirsts from the spring of the water of life without cost. He who overcomes will inherit these things, and I will be his God and he will be My son. But for the cowardly and unbelieving and abominable and murderers and immoral persons and sorcerers and idolaters and all liars, their part will be in the lake that burns with fire and brimstone, which is the second death (Revelation 21:6-8).

Most of us would not expect to see the cowardly and unbelieving headlining a list that includes murderers, sorcerers, and idolaters! Obviously God is not pleased with a cowardly church that limps along in unbelief.

After I conducted a major conference in the Philippines, a missionary shared her testimony. She had been warned about going to a certain village because a quack doctor was too powerful for her and the whole village was under his spell. She had believed this deception, but after she came to the conference, she realized this was just a lie. She went to the village and ended up leading this deceived man to Christ, and within six months, those in the village had become Christians.

4. *Dependence.* The authority we're talking about is not an independent authority. We have the authority to do God's will—nothing more, and nothing less. We don't charge out on our own initiative like evangelical ghostbusters to hunt down the devil and engage him in combat. God's primary call is for each of us to focus on the ministry of the kingdom: loving, caring, preaching, teaching, praying, and so on. However, when demonic powers challenge us in the course of doing ministry, we can deal with them on the basis of our authority in Christ and our dependence on Him. Then we carry on with our primary task.

Nor is the spiritual authority of the believer an authority to be exercised over other believers. We are to be "subject to one another in the fear of Christ" (Ephesians 5:21). Also, there is a God-established authority on earth that governs the civil and social structures of government, work, home, and church (Romans 13:1-7). It is critically important that we submit to these governing authorities—unless, of course, they exceed their God-given authority or command us to do something that is sinful. Then we must obey God rather than man.

FREE FROM FEAR

When we boldly and humbly exercise the authority that Christ has conferred upon us over the spiritual realm, we experience the freedom we all have in Christ. After the first edition of this book was published, I received the following testimony:

> For the past 35 years, I have lived from one surge of adrenaline to the next. My entire life has been gripped by paralyzing fears that seem to come from nowhere and everywhere—fears that made very little sense to me or anyone else. I invested four years of my life obtaining a degree in psychology, hoping it would enable me to understand and conquer those fears. Psychology only perpetuated my questions and insecurity. Six years of professional counseling offered little insight and no change in my level of anxiety.
>
> After two hospitalizations, trips to the emergency room, repeated EKGs, a visit to the thoracic surgeon, and a battery of other tests, my panic attacks only worsened. By the time I came to see you, full-blown panic attacks had become a daily occurrence.
>
> It has been three weeks since I've experienced a panic attack! I have gone to malls, church services, played for an entire worship service, and even made it through Sunday

school with peace in my heart. I had no idea what freedom meant until now. When I came to see you, I had hoped that the truth would set me free, and now I know it has! Friends have told me that even my voice is different, and my husband thinks I'm taller!

When you live in a constant state of anxiety, most of life passes you by because you are physically/emotionally/mentally unable to focus on anything but the fear, which is swallowing you. I could barely read a verse of Scripture in one sitting. It was as though someone snatched it away from my mind as soon as it entered. Scripture was such a fog to me. I could only hear the verses that spoke of death and punishment. I had actually become afraid to open my Bible. These past weeks I have spent hours a day in the Word, and it makes sense. The fog is gone. I am amazed at what I am able to hear, see, understand, and retain.

Before *The Bondage Breaker,* I could not say "Jesus Christ" without my metabolism going berserk. I could refer to "the Lord" with no ill effect, but whenever I said "Jesus Christ," my insides went into orbit. I can now call upon the name of Jesus Christ with peace and confidence…and I do it regularly.

CHAPTER SIX

JESUS HAS YOU COVERED

> From what we read of the Lord our Savior throughout the
> Scriptures, it is manifestly clear that the whole armor of Christ
> is the Savior Himself. It is He whom we are asked to "put
> on." It is one and the same thing to say, "Put on the whole
> armor of God" and say, "Put on the Lord Jesus Christ."
>
> **JEROME (AD 347–419)**

Can one ever feel safe living in this fallen world? Is there a physical location you can escape to when your life is in constant turmoil? Is there a drug you can take? Is there a person who can help that isn't getting paid to do so? Is going to church the answer? Which church? Where's God? Consider those questions and try to empathize with the woman who wrote the following letter during our weeklong conference Resolving Personal and Spiritual Conflicts:

Dear Dr. Anderson:

I attended your Sunday sessions, but while waiting to talk to you after the Sunday evening meeting I suddenly felt ill. I was burning up like I had a fever, and I got so weak I thought I was going to faint. So I went home.

I need help. I've had more trouble in my life since I became a Christian. I've overdosed on alcohol and drugs so many times I can't count them. I've cut myself several times with razor blades, sometimes very seriously. I have thoughts, feelings, and ideas of suicide weekly, like stabbing myself through the heart. I'm a slave to masturbation; I'm out of control, and I don't know how to stop.

On the outside I appear very normal. I have a good job, and I live with an outstanding family in our community. I even work with junior high students at my church. I can't really explain my relationship with God anymore. I've been seeing a psychiatrist for two years. Sometimes I think I'm this way because of a messed-up childhood, or maybe I was born this way.

How can I tell if my problems are in my mind, or the result of sin and disobedience against God, or the evidence of demonic influence? I would like to talk to you during the conference. But I don't want to try another thing that doesn't work.

Frances

I met with Frances that week, and she was as miserable, frustrated, and defeated as she sounded in her letter. There is a place that we can go and feel safe, but it is not a physical location. Our only sanctuary is "in Christ." Taking a pill to cure your body is commendable, but taking prescription medication, street drugs, or alcohol to cure your soul is deplorable. Frances did finally come to the right church. Once she began to realize that she was not a powerless or defenseless pawn in a spiritual battle, she made choices that changed her situation, and her chains fell off. A year later she wrote,

> I was hesitant to write you because I could not believe that my life would be changed or different for any length of time. I'm the girl who tried to kill herself, cut herself, and destroy herself in every possible way. I never believed that the pain in my mind and soul would ever leave so that I

could be a consistent and productive servant of the Lord Jesus Christ.

I have given it more than a year, and it was the best year I've ever had. I have grown in so many different ways since the conference. I feel stable and free because I understand the spiritual battle going on for my life. Things come back at me sometimes, but I know how to get rid of them right away.

GOD'S PROTECTION

Wouldn't it be great if every Christian knew "how to get rid of them right away"? If we understood the spiritual battle and knew the protection we have in Christ, there wouldn't be so many casualties.

Satan's first goal is to blind the mind of unbelievers (2 Corinthians 4:3-4). But the battle doesn't stop when you become a Christian. He doesn't curl up his tail and pull in his fangs when he fails to keep you from coming to Christ. He is still committed to fouling up your life and "proving" that Christianity doesn't work, that God's Word isn't true, and that nothing changed when you were born again.

Some Christians are a little paranoid about evil powers lurking around every corner looking for someone to devour. That's an unfounded fear. Your relationship to demonic powers in the spiritual realm is a lot like your relationship to germs in the physical realm. You know that germs are all around you: in the air, in the water, in your food, in other people, and even in you. Should you live in constant fear of them? If you did, you would be a hypochondriac. The only appropriate response to the swarm of germs around you is to eat the right foods, get enough rest and exercise, and keep yourself and your possessions clean. Your immune system will protect you. However, if you didn't believe in germs, you would be less likely to take those protective measures. Before the medical profession discovered the reality and nature of microbes, doctors and nurses saw no need to wear masks, scrub up before surgery, or use antibiotics—which is why some patients died.

It's the same in the spiritual realm. Demons are like invisible germs looking for someone to infect. We are never told in Scripture to be afraid of them. You just need to be aware of their existence and commit yourself to knowing the truth and living a righteous life. The only real sanctuary you have is your position in Christ, and in Him, you have all the protection you need.

In Ephesians 6:10-18, Paul describes the armor of God, which He has provided for our protection. The first fact you should understand about God's protection is that our role is not passive. Notice how often we are commanded to take an active role:

> *Be strong* in the Lord and in the strength of His might. *Put on* the full armor of God, so that you will *be able* to *stand firm* against the schemes of the devil. For our struggle is not against flesh and blood, but against the rulers, against the powers, against the world forces of this darkness, against the spiritual forces of wickedness in the heavenly places. Therefore, *take up* the full armor of God, so that you will *be able* to *resist* in the evil day, and having done everything, to *stand firm* (verses 10-13).

Some Christians ask, "If the Lord has disarmed the enemy and fitted me with armor, why can't I just trust in that?" That's like a person joining the military asking, "Our country has the most advanced tanks, planes, missiles, and ships in the world. Why should I go through basic training and learn how to stand guard?" They had better learn the essentials because soldiers, sailors, and airmen are the ones who maintain and use military weapons and hardware, which are useless without them, and only as good as the ones operating them.

Our "commanding officer" has provided everything we need to remain victorious over the forces of darkness. He says, in effect, "I've prepared a winning strategy and designed effective weapons. But if you don't do your part by staying on active duty, you're likely to become a casualty of war." In her classic book *War on the Saints*, Jessie Penn-Lewis wrote, "The chief condition for the working of evil spirits in a human being, apart from sin, is passivity, in exact opposition to the condition which God requires from His children for His working in them."[11] You can't expect God to protect you from demonic influences if you don't take an active part in your own defense.

DRESSED FOR BATTLE

Because we are in an ongoing spiritual battle, Paul chose to explain our protection in Christ by using the imagery of armor:

> Stand firm therefore, having girded your loins with truth, and having put on the breastplate of righteousness, and having shod your feet with the preparation of the gospel of peace; in addition to all, taking up the shield of faith with which you will be able to extinguish all the flaming missiles of the evil one. And take the helmet of salvation, and the sword of the Spirit, which is the word of God (Ephesians 6:14-17).

When we put on the armor of God, we are putting on the armor of light, which is the Lord Jesus Christ (Romans 13:12-14). When we put on Christ, we take ourselves out of the realm of the flesh, where we are vulnerable to attack, which is why we are instructed to "make no provision for the flesh" (Romans 13:14). Satan has nothing in Christ (John 14:30), and to the extent that we put on Christ, the evil one cannot touch us (1 John 5:18).

Armor You Have Already Put On

It would appear from the verb tenses in Ephesians 6:14-15 that the first three pieces of the armor—belt, breastplate, and shoes—are already on you: "having girded," "having put on," "having shod." You strapped on those three pieces of armor the moment you received Jesus Christ as your Lord and Savior. The past tense of the verb, "having," signifies that the action it refers to was completed before we were instructed to stand firm. That's the logical way a soldier would prepare for action: He would make sure his protective armor is on before engaging the enemy.

The belt of truth. Jesus said, "I am...the truth" (John 14:6). Because Christ is in you, the truth is in you. The belt of truth is our defense against Satan's primary weapon, which is deception. "Whenever he [Satan] speaks a lie, he speaks from his own nature, for he is a liar and the father of lies" (John 8:44). You gird your loins with truth by standing firm in your faith.

Lying may be the number one social problem in America, and believing lies is what keeps people in bondage. Ironically, most people lie to protect themselves, but in reality *truth* is our first line of defense. Truth is never an enemy—it is a liberating friend. Facing the truth is the first step in any recovery program, because all addicts lie. Many want out of their addiction because they are tired of living a lie. We have to speak the truth in love (Ephesians 4:15) if we want to live free in Christ and have meaningful relationships.

The only thing a Christian ever has to admit to is the truth. If a thought comes to mind that contradicts God's truth, dismiss it. If an opportunity comes along to say or do something that compromises or conflicts with truth, avoid it. Adopt a simple rule for living: If it's the truth, I'm in; if it's not the truth, count me out.

When Jesus was about to leave this planet and depart from the 11, He offered what is called the High Priestly Prayer, and it reveals what His primary concern is for the church. "I do not ask You to take them out of the world, but to keep them from the evil one" (John 17:15). How? "Sanctify them in the truth; Your word is truth" (verse 17). You overcome the father of lies with divine revelation, not human reasoning or research.

The breastplate of righteousness. When you put on Christ at salvation, you are justified before our holy God (Romans 5:1)—not with *your* righteousness, but Christ's righteousness (1 Corinthians 1:30; Philippians 3:8-9). Putting on the breastplate of righteousness is your defense against the accuser of the brethren. So when Satan aims an arrow at you by saying, "You're not good enough to be a Christian," you can respond, with Paul, "Who will bring a charge against God's elect? God is the one who justifies" (Romans 8:33).

Even though we stand on our righteous position in Christ, we should be aware of any deeds of unrighteousness. We are saints who sin. Putting on the armor of light means we walk in the light as He is in the light (1 John 1:6-8). Walking in the light is not sinless perfection. It means living in continuous agreement with God. It is part of our growth process. "If we confess our sins, He is faithful and righteous to forgive us our sins and to cleanse us from all unrighteousness" (1 John 1:9). Confession is not saying, "I'm sorry." It is saying, "I did it" the moment you sense the conviction of sin. Many people are sorry, but usually they are sorry they got caught, and even then they will only acknowledge as little as they have to. To confess (Greek, *homologeo*) means to acknowledge or to agree. It is the same as walking in the light. Covering up anything is walking in darkness.

You can walk in the light because you're already forgiven. Why not be honest with God, who already knows everything you have done and thought? Because of His grace, believers are the righteousness of God in Christ (2 Corinthians 5:21). Your eternal destiny is not at stake when you sin, but your daily victory is. Confession of sin clears the way for the fruitful expression of righteousness in your daily life. Follow Paul's example: "I also do my best to maintain always a blameless conscience both before God and before men" (Acts 24:16).

The shoes of peace. When you receive Christ, you are united with the Prince of Peace. "Having been justified by faith, we have peace with God through our Lord Jesus Christ" (Romans 5:1). "Let the peace of Christ rule in your hearts" (Colossians 3:15), and you do that by letting "the Word of Christ richly dwell within you" (verse 16).

The shoes of peace become protection against the divisive schemes of the devil when you act as a peacemaker among believers (Romans 14:19). Peacemakers encourage fellowship and have a ministry of reconciliation. Fellowship and unity in the body of Christ are based on our common spiritual heritage. True believers are children of God, and that's enough to bring us together in peace. If you are withholding fellowship with someone until you agree perfectly on every point of doctrine, you'll be the loneliest Christian on earth. We need to make a concerted effort to be "diligent to preserve the unity of the Spirit in the bond of peace" (Ephesians 4:3). "Blessed are the peacemakers, for they shall be called sons of God" (Matthew 5:9). Be assured that "the God of peace will soon crush Satan under your feet" (Romans 16:20).

The Rest of the Armor

Paul mentions three more pieces of armor that we must "take up" to protect ourselves from Satan's attack: the shield of faith, the helmet of salvation, and the sword of the Spirit, which is the Word of God. The first three are established by our position in Christ; the last three we "take up" to win daily battles.

The shield of faith. The object of our faith is God and His Word. The more you know about them, the more faith you will have. The less you know, the smaller your shield will be, and the easier it will be for one of Satan's fiery darts to reach its target. If you want your shield of faith to grow large and protective, your knowledge of God and His Word must increase (Romans 10:17).

These flaming missiles from Satan are nothing more than smoldering lies, burning accusations, and fiery temptations bombarding our minds. Whenever you discern a deceptive thought, accusation, or temptation, defuse it with truth. Jesus withstood Satan's temptation by quoting Scripture. Every time you memorize a Bible verse, listen to a good sermon, or participate in a Bible study, you enlarge your shield of faith.

The helmet of salvation. Every defeated Christian I have met with has doubted their salvation. Paul wrote in 1 Thessalonians 5:8, "Since we are of the day, let us be sober, having put on the breastplate of faith and love, and as a helmet, the hope of salvation." Salvation delivers us from the penalty of sin, but even more it protects us from the power of sin, and someday from the presence of sin. Without this hope, the Christian can easily be wounded in battle. In 2 Peter 1:2-11, we are told how to have the assurance of salvation:

Grace and peace be multiplied to you in the knowledge of God and of Jesus our Lord; seeing that His divine power has granted to us everything pertaining to life and godliness, through the true knowledge of Him who called us by His own glory and excellence. For by these he has granted to us His precious and magnificent promises, so that by them you may become partakers of the divine nature, having escaped the corruption that is in the world by lust. Now for this very reason also, applying all diligence, in your faith supply moral excellence, and in your moral excellence, knowledge, and in your knowledge, self-control, and in your self-control, perseverance, and in your perseverance, godliness, and in your godliness, brotherly kindness, and your brotherly kindness, love. For if these qualities are yours and are increasing, they render you neither useless nor unfruitful in the true knowledge of our Lord Jesus Christ. For he who lacks these qualities is blind or short-sighted, having forgotten his purification from his former sins. Therefore, brethren, be all the more diligent to make certain about His calling and choosing you; for as long as you practice these things, you will never stumble; for in this way the entrance into the eternal kingdom of our Lord and Savior Jesus Christ will be abundantly supplied to you.

The sword of the Spirit. The Word of God is the only offensive weapon in the armor of God. Paul used *rhema* instead of *logos* for "word" in Ephesians 6:17 because he wanted to emphasize the spoken word of God. There is only one Word of God, but the Greek word *rhema* carries with it the idea of proclamation. The emphasis of *logos* is more on the content than the proclamation. For instance, Paul said in Romans 10:17, "Faith comes from hearing, and hearing by the word [*rhema*] of Christ." It is appropriate to use *rhema* in this context because the emphasis is on preaching the good news and hearing it.

Our defense against direct attacks by the evil one is to speak aloud God's truth because Satan is not omniscient, and he doesn't perfectly know what you're thinking. By observing you, he can get a pretty good idea of what you are thinking, just as any student of human behavior can. Magicians and mentalists refer to that as "cold readings." But he doesn't know what you're going to do before you do it. If you pay attention to a deceiving spirit (see 1 Timothy 4:1), he will know whether you believe his lie by how you behave. In addition, if he gave you the thought, then he will know what you are thinking.

You are ascribing too much power to Satan if you think he can read your mind perfectly and know the future perfectly. Occultic practices may attempt to read your mind or predict the future, but only God perfectly knows what is on your mind, and only He perfectly knows the future. You should never ascribe to Satan the divine attributes of God. The good news is you can communicate silently with God in your mind, and carry on unspoken communion with your heavenly Father.

Paul wrote, "With the heart a person believes, resulting in righteousness, and with the mouth he confesses, resulting in salvation" (Romans 10:10). That raises a question: If you know your own thoughts and God also knows them, then why does verbal confession result in salvation? Saving faith is not complete until the will is exercised, but Paul could also be implying the need for the god of this world to hear our commitment to Christ.

It should surprise no one that most spiritual attacks happen when you are alone, and usually at night. One of Job's friends had such an encounter (Job 4:12-17):

> Now a word was brought to me stealthily, and my ear received a whisper of it. Amid disquieting thoughts from the visions of the night, when deep sleep falls on men, dread came upon me, and trembling, and made all my bones shake. Then a spirit passed by my face; the hair of my flesh bristled up. It stood still, but I could not discern its appearance; a form was before my eyes; there was silence, then I heard a voice: "Can mankind be just before God? Can a man be pure before his Maker?"

"A word" was not a word from the Lord. God doesn't come to us "stealthily." That was a visit by the accuser of the brethren, who had a message for Job: *You are suffering because of your sin*. In truth, however, Job was suffering because "there is no one like him on the earth, a blameless and upright man, fearing God and turning away from evil" (Job 1:8). Good people do suffer for the sake of righteousness. Christians all over the world are having demonic visitations at night, similar to that described in Job. Deep sleep is suddenly aroused by an overwhelming sense of fear that makes their hair stand up. Some report a sensation of pressure on their chest, and when they try to respond physically, they seemingly can't, as though something was grabbing their throats and holding them down. At such times, the presence of evil is all you sense, but God is also present.

Please don't assume that every time you awaken at night it is because you are under attack. You are probably waking up because of the pickle you ate, or a noise in the house, or just as a natural occurrence. However, if it does happen repeatedly at a precise time of night, like 3:00 a.m., it likely is a spiritual attack, and it is not necessarily because you are doing something wrong. It is not a sin to be under attack. You may be experiencing spiritual opposition because you are doing something *right*. In fact, if you are *not* experiencing some spiritual opposition to your ministry, there is a good chance that Satan doesn't see you as any threat to his plans.

While conducting conferences, I have asked the following question of those in attendance: "How many of you have awakened suddenly at night with an overwhelming sense of fear at a precise time, like 3:00 a.m.?" I have never seen less than a third of the people raise their hands. I was doing a conference for 250 leaders of a megachurch, and 95 percent of the attendees raised their hands. When I first started doing a conference we called Resolving Personal and Spiritual Conflicts, I was attacked the night before every conference at 3:00 a.m., and this continued for four years, then stopped. I quickly learned how to stop the attacks and go back to sleep. If I did nothing, I would toss and turn until 4:00 a.m.

How do we call upon the name of the Lord and be saved if we can't speak? First, these encounters are not a physical battle that requires a physical effort on our part, because "the weapons of our warfare are not of the flesh, but divinely powerful for the destruction of fortresses" (2 Corinthians 10:4). Because of the overwhelming sense of fear, we naturally respond in the flesh because it is not God we are fearing. Second, notice the order in which the following commands are stated in Scripture: "Submit therefore to God. Resist the devil and he will flee from you" (James 4:7). You can always submit to God inwardly because He knows the thoughts and intentions of the heart (Hebrews 4:12). The moment you call upon the name of the Lord, you will be free to verbally resist the devil. All you have to say is "Jesus," but you would have to say it. God may be allowing this in order to test your faith. Remembering this has certainly made me more dependent upon Him.

PRAYING BY THE SPIRIT

After instructing us to put on the armor of God, Paul wrote, "With all prayer and petition, pray at all times in the Spirit, and with this in view, be on the alert with all perseverance and petition for all the saints" (Ephesians 6:18). "The Spirit also helps our weakness; for we do not know how to pray as we should, but the Spirit Himself intercedes for us" (Romans 8:26). The word "helps" (Greek, *sunantilambano*) in this verse is two prepositions before the word "take." The Holy Spirit comes alongside, picks us up, and takes us to the throne of grace. Any prayer that God the Holy Spirit prompts us to pray is a prayer that God our heavenly Father will always answer.

Combating Spiritual Blindness

There are specific needs we should consider for prayer in spiritual warfare. One need relates to the condition of blindness that Satan has inflicted on unbelievers (2 Corinthians 4:3-4). People cannot come to Christ unless their spiritual eyes are opened. Theodore Epp wrote, "If

Satan has blinded and bound men and women, how can we ever see souls saved? This is where you and I enter the picture. Spoiling the goods of the strong man has to do with liberating those whom Satan has blinded and is keeping bound...This is where prayer comes in."[12]

Prayer is a primary weapon in combating spiritual blindness. The apostle John wrote, "If we ask anything according to His will, He hears us. And if we know that He hears us in whatever we ask, we know that we have the requests which we have asked from Him" (1 John 5:14-15). That assurance of answered prayer is followed by the instruction for believers to ask God to bring life to unbelievers (verse 16).

Because the field is white and ready for harvest, we should pray for workers (Matthew 9:37-38). Paul asked, "How will they hear without a preacher?" (Romans 10:14). When the Holy Spirit lays concern for an unbeliever on my heart, I always pray that God would send a messenger to that person and that God would give that person life. You can also pray that the eyes of lost people would be opened to the truth that will set them free in Christ.

We can also pray as Paul did in Ephesians 1:18-19, that the eyes of believers may be enlightened to understand spiritual power, authority, and protection, which is their inheritance in Christ. As long as Satan can keep us in the dark about our position and authority in Christ, he can keep us stunted in our growth and ineffectual in our witness and ministry. We need to pray for each other continually that Satan's smoke screen of lies will be blown away and that our vision will be crystal clear.

Binding the Strong Man

Another purpose for authoritative prayer is binding the "strong man" mentioned in Matthew 12:29. Jesus said, "How can anyone enter the strong man's house and carry off his property, unless he first binds the strong man?" He was saying that you cannot rescue people from the bonds of spiritual blindness or demonic influence unless you first overpower their captors. Satan is disarmed, but he will not let go of anything he thinks he can keep until we exercise the authority delegated to us by the Lord Jesus Christ. By faith we lay hold of the property in Satan's clutches that rightfully belongs to God, and we hold on until Satan turns loose. C. Fred Dickason, who taught systematic theology at Moody Bible Institute for years, gives several helpful suggestions for how to pray for someone who is being harassed by demons:[13]

1. Pray that the demons may be cut off from all communication and help from other demons and Satan.

2. Pray that the demons would be confused and weakened in their hold on the person.

3. Pray that the person would be strengthened in his faith to understand his position in Christ and to trust and obey God's Word.

4. Pray that the person may be able to distinguish between his thoughts and feelings and those of Satan.

5. Pray that the person might recognize the demonic presence and not be confused, but willingly seek godly counsel and help.

6. Pray that God would protect and guide His child and set angelic forces at work to break up every scheme of the enemy.

When I was on the staff of a large church, I joined the secretary and custodial staff for lunch. As I entered the room, I noticed a tall man in his mid-twenties alone at the other end of the room. He was a total stranger to us, and was standing at the chalkboard writing tiny words and then erasing them. "Who's that?" I asked my coworkers.

"We don't know. He just walked in."

Amazed that someone hadn't already greeted the man, I walked over and said, "Hi, my name is Neil. Can I help you?"

"Oh, I don't know," he answered rather distantly as he put down the chalk. He looked and sounded like his mind had been blown by drugs, so I walked him outside to talk. He told me that he worked at a local car wash, and I invited him to attend church. After an hour of conversation, he left.

A couple days later, Bill came back, and we talked some more. Two weeks later on a Sunday afternoon, I was in my office getting ready for the evening service when my intercom buzzed. "There's a guy down here named Bill who wants to see you."

"Send him up," I answered.

I didn't have much time to spend with Bill, but I didn't want to ignore him either. So I got right to the point. "I'm glad you're here, Bill," I began. "May I ask you a personal question?" Bill nodded. "Have you ever trusted in Christ to be your Lord and your Savior?"

"No."

"Would you like to?"

"I don't know," Bill answered with a troubled expression.

I reached for a salvation tract and read through it with him. "Do you understand this, Bill?"

"Yes."

"Would you like to make that decision for Christ right now?"

"Yes."

I wasn't sure he could read, so I said, "I'll pray a simple prayer of commitment, and you can repeat it after me phrase by phrase, okay?"

"Okay."

"Lord Jesus, I need You," I began.

Bill started to respond, "Lor-r-r..." Then he locked up completely. I could sense the oppression in the room.

"Bill, there's a battle going on for your mind," I said. "I'm going to read some Scripture and pray out loud for you. I'm going to bind the enemy and stand against him. As soon as you can, you just tell Jesus what you believe."

His eyes revealed that the battle was raging. I started reading Scripture and praying aloud. I was still very new at dealing with demonic powers at the time, so I was grasping at straws.

After about 15 minutes of prayer and Scripture, Bill suddenly groaned, "Lord Jesus, I need You." Then he slumped back in his chair as if he had just completed ten rounds of a boxing match against the world heavyweight champion. He looked at me with tear-filled eyes and said, "I'm free." I had never mentioned the word *freedom* with him. But he was free. He knew it, and I could see it.

Understanding the spiritual nature of our world should have a profound effect on our evangelistic strategy. All too often we proclaim the virtues of Christianity to unbelievers as if we were standing outside a prison compound proclaiming to the inmates the benefits of living in the outside world. But unless someone overpowers the prison guards and opens the gates, how can the prisoners experience the freedom we're telling them about?

PART TWO

STAND FIRM!

He [Satan] invented heresies and schisms to undermine faith,
pervert the truth and break unity. Unable to keep us in the
dark ways of former error, he draws us into a new maze of
deceit. He snatches men away from the church itself and, just
when they think they have drawn near to the light and escaped
the night of the world, he plunges them unawares into a
new darkness. Though they do not stand by the gospel and
discipline and law of Christ, they call themselves Christians.
Though they are walking in darkness, they think they are in
the light, through the deceitful flattery of the adversary who,
as the apostle said, transforms himself into an angel of light
and adorns his ministers as ministers of righteousness. They
call night day...cunningly to frustrate truth by their lying.

CYPRIAN (AD 200–258)

CHAPTER SEVEN

MANIPULATING SPIRITS

Who is it who tests the spirits, and how can they be tested? Our Lord shows this in the Gospels, where he predicted that evil spirits of the kind John had experienced would come. Jesus said, "Beware of false prophets, who come to you in sheep's clothing but inwardly are ravenous wolves. You will know them by their fruits. Are grapes gathered from thorns, or figs from thistles?" These therefore are the fruits by which the evil spirits who speak by false prophets can be discerned; the thorns of schisms and terrible thistles of heresy which sting all those who go anywhere near them.

BEDE (AD 673–735)

I first met Sharon Beckmann when she attended one of my conferences. Several years prior to our meeting, Sharon was a licensed professional counselor who was living a rather normal life. She was married with one child and lived comfortably in the suburban foothills of Denver, but she sensed a spiritual void in her life. Unfortunately she got drawn into the New Age movement, and for the next seven years was trained to become a channel for spirit guides. Becoming a medium eventually led to divorce, and her life began to deteriorate.

She finally came to the conclusion she was losing her mind. She didn't want to be a channel anymore for those voices in her mind, but when she wouldn't play ball with those "friendly" spirit guides, they turned against her. She found herself housebound and unable to function. Somehow she knew that the only way to get rid of the voices was to become a Christian. Sharon's story, as told in her book *Enticed by the Light* (Zondervan), reveals a sad commentary on the church in America. She couldn't find a church that would help her become a Christian. After hearing her story, one pastor suggested that she wouldn't feel very comfortable in his congregation.

She finally found a good evangelical pastor who led her to the Lord, but he didn't know how to help her resolve the spiritual conflicts that continued to plague her. She found another church that helped those who were dealing with spiritual warfare, and they worked with her for two years. They would call up the spirits and try to cast them out. They would have some successes, but there was never any complete resolution.

One day Sharon realized these well-intentioned Christians were just trying to manipulate the spirits, which was what she had tried to do when she was a spiritist or medium, although for different purposes. Shortly afterward, she drove to my conference and learned a completely different approach to resolving personal and spiritual conflicts. I was privileged to write the foreword in her book.

Not very many churches are equipped to help people like Sharon, and I think we had better get ready for a flood of requests. The coming apostasy is going to leave a lot of people in bondage to the god of this world.

THE REBEL AUTHORITY

Let's refresh our minds as we start from the beginning again. God originally created Adam and Eve to rule over the birds of the sky, the beasts of the field, the fish of the sea, and over all the earth (Genesis 1:26). But Adam forfeited his position of authority when he sinned, and Satan became the rebel holder of authority—whom Jesus referred to as "the ruler of this world" (John 12:31; 14:30; 16:11). When the devil tempted Jesus, he offered Him "all the kingdoms of the world and their glory" (Matthew 4:8) in exchange for Jesus's worship. Satan said that the earth "has been handed over to me, and I give it to whomever

I wish" (Luke 4:6). Satan could say this because Adam had abdicated dominion over God's creation at the fall, and Satan ruled from the fall to the cross. The death, resurrection, and ascension of Christ secured forever Jesus's authority over all things (Matthew 28:18). This authority was extended to all believers in the Great Commission so that we may continue His mission of destroying the works of the devil (1 John 3:8).

We all were born spiritually dead and subject to the ruler of this world, whom Paul called "the prince of the power of the air" (Ephesians 2:2). But when we received Christ, God "rescued us from the domain of darkness, and transferred us to the kingdom of His beloved Son" (Colossians 1:13). We are now citizens of heaven, not earth (Philippians 3:20). Satan is the ruler of this world, but he is no longer *our* ruler. Rather, Christ is our Lord.

Yet as long as we remain on planet Earth, we are still on Satan's turf. He will try to rule our lives by deceiving us into believing we are still under his authority. As aliens in a hostile world, we need protection from this evil tyrant. Christ has not only provided protection, but in Christ we have authority over the kingdom of darkness. We also have the indwelling Holy Spirit, who is the Spirit of truth (John 14:17), and He will guide us into all truth (John 16:13).

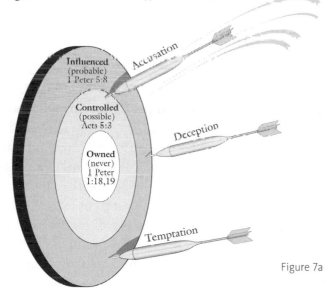

Figure 7a

Degrees of Vulnerability

Even though we are secure in Christ and have all the protective armor we need, we are still vulnerable to Satan's accusations, temptations, and deceptions (see Figure 7a). The fact that we have been instructed to put on the armor of God reveals that we are vulnerable to some degree. Therefore, it is *probable* that Satan will have some *influence* over every believer if we let him. It is *possible* that he can gain some measure of *control* over our lives if we are deceived and believe his lies. I have seen countless numbers of believers who are almost paralyzed by what Satan tells them. The oppression is so overwhelming that some can't seem to make the right choices and live responsible lives. They actually *can* make choices, but they don't *think* they can, so they don't.

Ownership is never at stake, however. We belong to God, and Satan can't touch who we are in Christ. We may be demon-oppressed, but we are always Holy Spirit-possessed. As long as we are living in these natural bodies in this fallen world, we are targets for Satan's fiery darts. The answer is not to stick our heads in the sand like an ostrich. That would still leave us exposed to Satan's attacks.

The Powers That Be

Belief in a personal devil has always been a creed of the church. That doesn't mean we have our own personal devil, but that the devil is an actual personage rather than merely an impersonal force. The tendency in our culture is to depersonalize Satan. It is common to hear someone say of another, "He has his own personal demons." They don't mean that literally. They mean the person has his own personal problems. Mass killings are referred to as evil, but people don't attribute them to the evil one. Contributing to the problem is the Western translation of the Lord's prayer: "Deliver us from evil." The original Greek text has a definite article before "evil." Many foreign translations render the passage "deliver us from the evil one," making it consistent with the High Priestly Prayer in John 17, where the Lord prayed that we be kept "from the evil one" (verse 15).

Satan is a created being. He is not omnipresent, omniscient, or omnipotent, and yet he is the ruler of this world. He can't be everywhere in the world tempting and deceiving billions of people at the same time. He rules through an army of emissaries (demons or fallen angels) who propagate his lies around the world.

Neither disbelief in demonic activity nor an inordinate fear of demons is healthy. In *The Screwtape Letters*, C.S. Lewis wrote, "There are two equal and opposite errors into which our race can fall about the devils. One is to disbelieve their existence. The other is to believe and feel an unhealthy interest in them. They themselves are equally pleased by both errors and hail a materialist or a magician with the same delight."[14]

Paul gave a description of the demonic hierarchy in Ephesians 6:12: "Our struggle is not against flesh and blood, but against the rulers, against the powers, against the world forces of this darkness, against the spiritual forces of wickedness in the heavenly places." Some liberal "scholars" argue that the "rulers" and "powers" mentioned in this verse refer to ungodly human structures of authority instead of a hierarchy of demons under Satan's headship. Some references to rulers and powers in Scripture do designate human authorities (see Luke 12:11; Acts 4:26). However, in Paul's epistles, these terms are used in reference to supernatural powers (Romans 8:38-39; Colossians 1:16; 2:15). It is clear from the context of Ephesians 6:12 that the rulers, powers, and forces that oppose us are spiritual entities in the heavenlies—that is, the spiritual world. (For a scholarly treatment of this subject, I would encourage you to read *Powers of Darkness* by Dr. Clinton Arnold, which is subtitled *Principalities & Powers in Paul's Letters* and published by Inter-Varsity Press.)

THE PERSONALITY OF DEMONS

The Bible does not attempt to prove the existence of demons any more than it attempts to prove the existence of God. It simply reports on their activities knowing its first readers believed in their existence.

When Jesus performed miraculous deeds, those who opposed Him charged Him with having a demon (John 8:48-49,52; 10:20-21). Because Jesus knew what was on their minds, they thought He was getting His information from demons (spirit guides). Nor did the church fathers have a problem accepting the reality of demons, as Origen noted:

> In regard to the devil and his angels and opposing powers, the ecclesiastical teaching maintains that the beings do indeed exist; but what they are or how they exist is not explained with sufficient clarity. This opinion, however, is held by most: that the devil was an angel; and having apostatized, he persuaded as many angels as possible to fall away with himself; and these, even to the present time, are called his angels.[15]

Luke gave us a helpful view into the personality and individuality of evil spirits. After Jesus cast out a demon who had rendered a man dumb, His detractors accused Him of casting out demons by the power of "Beelzebul, the ruler of the demons" (Luke 11:15). During the discussion that followed, Jesus said,

> When the unclean spirit goes out of a man, it passes through waterless places seeking rest, and not finding any, it says, "I will return to my house from which I came." And when it comes, it finds it swept and put in order. Then it goes and takes along seven other spirits more evil than itself, and they go in and live there; and the last state of that man becomes worse than the first (verses 24-26).

Several deductions about evil spirits can be gleaned from this passage:

1. *Demons can exist outside or inside organic bodies.* Demons
   are dismembered spirits that find a measure of rest in
   organic beings, preferring even swine over nothingness
   (Mark 5:12). To affect the physical realm, they have to

work through willing or deceived subjects. The puppet master of this world has no arms or mouth except for those under his domain. Hierarchical spirits may claim territorial rights and associate with certain geographical locations, such as the prince of the kingdom of Persia (Daniel 10:13-21).

2. *They are able to travel at will.* Being spiritual entities, demons are not subject to the barriers of the natural world. The walls of your church building do not establish it as a sanctuary from demonic influence. Remember, the only real sanctuary we have is our position "in Christ."

3. *They are able to communicate.* From the Luke 11 passage, we learn that evil spirits can communicate with each other. They can also speak to humans through a human subject, such as they did through the Gadarene demoniacs (Matthew 8:28-34). Such extreme cases reveal a takeover of the central nervous system.

4. *Each one has a separate and personal identity.* Notice the use of personal pronouns in the passage: "I will return to my house from which I came" (Luke 11:24). Evil spirits are thinking personalities as opposed to impersonal forces. Secular methods of research are not going to reveal their existence. Divine revelation is the only authoritative source on the reality and personality of evil spirits.

5. *They are able to remember and make plans.* The fact that evil spirits can leave a place, come back, remember their former state, and plan reentry with others shows their ability to think and plan.

6. *They are able to evaluate and make decisions.* The evil spirit found its human target "swept and put in order" (verse 25), indicating that it can evaluate its intended victim.

7. *They are able to combine forces.* Notice that one spirit joined

with a group of seven others, making the victim's last state worse than his first. In the case of the Gadarene demoniacs, the number of demons was "legion" (Mark 5:9). I have heard many people identify a number of different voices in their mind, often describing them as a committee in their head.

8. *They vary in degrees of wickedness.* The first demon in the passage brought back seven other spirits "more evil than itself" (Luke 11:26). Jesus indicated a different degree of wickedness when He said, "This kind cannot come out by anything but prayer" (Mark 9:29). The concept of variations in power and wickedness fits the hierarchy that Paul lists in Ephesians 6:12. I can personally attest that some cases are more difficult than others.

People can start feeling phantom symptoms when they talk about germs and viruses. The same can happen when talking about evil spirits. So keep this truth in mind as you read this book: "You are from God, little children, and have overcome them; because greater is He who is in you than he who is in the world" (1 John 4:4). If you continue walking in the light, you won't be afraid of the darkness.

RUNNING THE GAUNTLET OF EVIL

Imagine that you just walked through the door of life, and ahead of you is a narrow street lined on both sides with two-story apartments. At the far end of the street—which gets broader and broader—stands Jesus Christ, saying, "Come to Me; I am the Author and Finisher of your faith." There is nothing in the street that can keep you from walking toward Jesus. So when you receive Christ, you fix your eyes on Him, and start walking by faith in the power of the Holy Spirit.

But because this fallen world is still under the dominion of Satan, the apartments on either side are inhabited by beings who are committed to keeping you from reaching your goal. They have no power or authority to block your path or even slow your step, so they hang out of the windows and call to you, hoping to turn your attention away from your goal and disrupt your progress. They are like pimps who are trying to lure you into their houses of ill repute.

Some will tempt you by saying, "Hey, look over here! I've got something you really want. It tastes good, feels good, and is a lot more fun than your boring walk down the street. Come on in and take a look."

Others will accuse you by saying, "Who do you think you are? God doesn't love you. You will never amount to anything. Surely you don't believe that bit about being saved." Satan's emissaries are masters at accusation, especially after they have distracted you through temptation. One minute they're saying, "Try this; there's nothing wrong with it." Then when you yield to the temptation, they immediately accuse you: "See what you did? How can you call yourself a Christian when you behave like that?"

Some of those fiery darts are very deceptive because they come to our minds in the first person singular: *I don't need to go to church today. I'll pray about it later. I don't have time to read the Bible right now. I don't see anything wrong with having a few drinks after work.* Such self-talk may not be self-talk at all.

RUNNING THE RACE

There are three ways we can respond to mental assaults. First, the most spiritually defeated Christians are those who pay attention to deceiving spirits (see 1 Timothy 4:1). They give in to the temptations, believe the lies and accusations. Some people hear the gospel, but "the evil one comes and snatches away what has been sown in his heart" (Matthew 13:19). Others have stepped through the door, but are immediately bombarded with doubts and accusations. They are stopped in their tracks. They could actually keep on walking, but they don't know that, so they sit down and make no progress in their walk toward God. To combat that, the early church would have new converts face the west and say out loud, "I renounce you, Satan, in all your works and all your ways." Then the new converts would be told to face the east and make their profession of faith in God. There are very few, if any, evangelical churches who offer a well-defined repentance process to new believers. That is the strategy I share in my book *Becoming a Disciple-Making Church* (Bethany House Publishers, 2017).

A young couple went to their pastor for marriage counseling. In the process, the pastor led the husband to Christ one Sunday afternoon. The husband was then encouraged to go to a Living Free in Christ conference that evening. He learned who he was in Christ, and he was made aware of the battle for his mind and how to win it. Later, he become one of my seminary students, and he told me that week was the most incredible week of his life. Every morning he would wake up with doubting thoughts, and then he would recall what he had just learned the evening before. By the end of the week, he was totally free. I have never seen a new convert take off and continue growing like he did.

The second response is to argue with the tormentors. It may appear that doing this means fighting the good fight, but in reality, engaging the tormentors means being distracted by them. Instead of arguing with demons, we should be marching forward, keeping our focus on Jesus. When we allow ourselves to get distracted, we end up playing whack-a-mole, which is a carnival game in which you use a mallet to whack a mole that emerges from one of several possible holes. It doesn't make any difference whether the negative or lying thoughts (that is, the distracting moles) come from the world, the flesh, or the devil. We are to take *every* thought captive in obedience to Christ. Trying *not* to think negative thoughts doesn't work. Rather, we are told in Philippians 4:8 to think upon that which is true, right, and honorable. We are not called to dispel the darkness; we are called to turn on the light.

Don't pay attention to the voices of this world is the third and right response. In answer to every arrow of temptation, accusation, or deception the world and the devil shoots at us, we are to simply raise the shield of faith, deflect the attack, and walk on. We are to tune out the noises of this world and tune in to the voice of God. One goal in leading people through The Steps to Freedom in Christ is equipping them to get rid of their negative thoughts and experience the peace of God, which surpasses all comprehension and will guard their hearts and minds in Christ Jesus (Philippians 4:7).

While I was teaching at Talbot School of Theology, an undergraduate student made an appointment with me. She was researching satanism and wanted to ask me some questions. I answered some, but then I stopped. "I don't think you should be researching satanism," I said.

"Why not?" she asked.

"Because you are not experiencing your freedom in Christ," I responded.

"What do you mean by that?" she protested.

I told her, "I suspect that you struggle with your Bible classes just trying to pay attention. I would guess that your devotional and prayer life are virtually nonexistent. I'm sure your self-esteem is down in the mud somewhere, and you probably entertain a lot of suicidal thoughts."

That student later told a friend, "That man read my mind!" I didn't read her mind; rather, I have been helping people long enough to discern what is going on with them. That summer, she was given permission to take my graduate-level class Resolving Personal and Spiritual Conflicts, and this is what she wrote me two weeks later:

> What I've discovered this last week is this feeling of control. Like my mind is my own. I haven't sat and had these strung-out periods of thought and contemplation—that is, conversations with myself. My mind just simply feels quieted. It really is a strange feeling. My emotions have been stable. I haven't felt depressed once this week. My will is mine. I feel like I have been able to choose to live my life abiding in Christ. Scripture seems different. I have a totally different perspective. I actually understand what it is saying. I feel left alone. Not in a bad way. I'm not lonely; just a single person.
>
> For the first time, I believe I actually understand what it means to be a Christian, who Christ is, and who I am in

Him. I feel capable of helping people and handling myself. I've been a codependent for years, but this last week I haven't had the slightest feeling or need for someone. I guess I'm describing what it is like to be at peace. I feel this quiet, soft joy in my heart. I have been more friendly with strangers and comfortable. There hasn't been this struggle to get through the day. And then there is the fact that I have been participating actively in life and not passively, critically watching it. Thank you for lending me your hope—I believe I have my own now in Christ.

CHAPTER EIGHT

THE LURE OF KNOWLEDGE AND POWER

As we have already suggested, there is hardly a human being who is unattended by a demon. And it is well known to many that premature and violent deaths (which men ascribe to accidents) are in fact brought about by demons...For in cases of exorcisms, [the evil spirits] sometimes claim to be one of the relatives of the persons possessed by him...The situation is similar in the other kind of sorcery that is supposed to bring up from Hades the souls now resting there.

TERTULLIAN (AD 160–220)

I was listening to one of my fellow doctoral students give a presentation on the future of education as it related to the mind. Present in the class were principals of schools, educational administrators, teachers, and a variety of community leaders. The presenter, a principal of an elementary school, was excitedly describing such phenomena as astral projection, telekinesis, clairvoyance, and telepathy. That would be less surprising in present-day graduate programs, since parapsychology and metaphysics have gained acceptance in secular institutions. But this was 1980, the dawning of the New Age, and such subjects weren't typically addressed in doctoral programs.

His New Age presentation piqued the curiosity of my fellow students. They enthusiastically interacted with the lecturer and asked many questions. The lure of special knowledge and power has always caught the fancy of those who think there is something out there that their natural senses can't pick up. I'm not talking about the knowledge gained from disciplined study or research. *Esoteric* knowledge is perceived through a sixth sense (or spiritual sense) and is intended only for the initiated (or anointed ones). Psychics supposedly have special powers that are not available to all. There are even licensed or accredited psychics so that the so-called true mediums can be separated from the charlatans.

Two of our country's former first ladies have consulted psychics. Police have enlisted the help of psychics in their attempts to find missing people or even solve crimes. Almost every public newspaper and airline magazine offers a daily horoscope. Spiritism is the dominant religious orientation in this world—it's particularly strong in Brazil, where one missionary told me at least 85 percent of the population are practicing spiritists.

Near the end of the class, I asked this fellow doctoral student, "While you were doing your research, did you ever ask yourself whether this new frontier of the mind was good or bad? Is there anything morally wrong with what you presented?"

"No," he replied, "I'm not interested in that."

"I think you should be," I said. "Because nothing you have shared is new. It is as old as biblical history, and God strictly forbids His people from being involved with it."

That brought a swift end to the class, and a number of fellow students gathered around me, wondering what could possibly be wrong with what the presenter had said.

A TRAP AS OLD AS THE BIBLE

The lure of the occult is almost always on the basis of acquiring special knowledge and power. Actually, knowledge is power. For example, *precognition* means to know about something before it happens. Imagine the power you would have if you knew what events would take place before they happened. You could become a billionaire just by betting at the racetrack. To know something ahead of time means that you have connected with some kind of power that can arrange future events.

Satan has a limited capacity to do that by manipulating deceived people. Everything he does is a counterfeit of Christianity: Clairvoyance is a counterfeit of divine revelation; precognition is a counterfeit of prophecy; telepathy is a counterfeit of prayer; psychokinesis is a counterfeit of God's miracles; and spirit guides counterfeit the Holy Spirit. Why would someone want to have a spirit guide when they could have the Holy Spirit as their guide?

The spiritual death that Adam suffered left a spiritual void in all his descendants—a void that left them longing for knowledge and power yet can only be filled through an intimate relationship with the Lord and Savior Jesus Christ. "For in Him all the fullness of Deity dwells in bodily form, and in Him you have been made complete, and He is the head over all rule and authority" (Colossians 2:9-10). However, Satan is trying to pass off his counterfeits as the real thing. He will gain a foothold in your life if he can lure you into the deceptive world of psychic knowledge and power. The so-called New Age is certainly not new. On the eve of the Israelites' invasion of the Promised Land, Moses commanded the people,

> When you enter the land which the LORD your God gives you, you shall not learn to imitate the detestable things of those nations. There shall not be found among you anyone who makes his son or his daughter pass through the fire, one who uses divination, one who practices witchcraft, or one who interprets omens, or a sorcerer, or one who casts a spell, or a medium, or a spiritist, or one who calls up the dead. For whoever does these things is detestable to the LORD; and because of these detestable things the LORD your God will drive them out before you. You shall be blameless before the LORD your God (Deuteronomy 18:9-13).

This command is as viable for us today as it was for the Israelites. We live in a contemporary Canaan where it is socially acceptable to consult spiritists, mediums, palm readers, psychic counselors, and horoscopes for guidance and esoteric knowledge. Unfortunately, this is true among Christians also. In 1990 we surveyed 1,725 professing Christian teenagers in evangelical churches and schools, asking if they ever participated in the following:[16]

OCCULT ACTIVITY	NUMBER OF THOSE SURVEYED WHO WERE INVOLVED*
Astral projection	44
Table lifting	149
Fortune telling	180
Astrology	321
Dungeons & Dragons	286
Crystals or pyramids	72
Ouija board	416
Automatic writing	35
Tarot cards	99
Palm reading	192
Spirit guides	37
Blood pact	100
Total number involved	861
Total with no involvement	864
Total number surveyed	1725

Almost 50 percent of these Christian teenagers indicated some type of involvement, and that was before smart phones, sexting, and the Internet! We never asked about witchcraft or sorcery, which Moses also mentioned in Deuteronomy 18. We wanted to redo the research 20 years later, but half the churches and schools we contacted wouldn't permit us.

Police departments are telling parents today, "Wake up! Drugs and illicit sex aren't the only things your kids are into. They're into *satanism*. We've seen the blood and the mutilated animals." The head of campus security at Biola University—where I taught—belonged to an organization for security officers from campuses across Southern California. This secular group met once a month. When it was our school's turn to host the meeting, he asked me to speak to the group about spiritual phenomena in our culture. "There aren't many Christians in the group," he said, "but they'll be on our campus, so I want you to speak to them." I agreed to do so.

It was a veteran group that included former military personnel and police officers. When I started talking about the rise of satanism in our community, there wasn't a doubter or scoffer in the bunch. Every one of them had a story to share about finding grisly evidence of satanism being active on their own campus. They were told by their administrators to cover up what was going on. School officials don't want the public to know about such things for the same reason they don't like to report rapes.

Every cult or occult practice that Moses warned the Israelites to avoid in Canaan—from "harmless" horoscopes to unthinkable atrocities involving animal and human sacrifice—is present in our culture today.

KNOWLEDGE FROM THE DARK SIDE

Two conferences, both open to the public, were held in Pasadena, California. One was a major world conference on international missions, and about 600 people attended. At the same time, a New Age conference was taking place in the Pasadena Civic Center, and more than 40,000 people showed up! That's the world we live in. People don't want to hear from God, who will convict them of their sin. Like the principal I mentioned earlier, they are not interested in morality, and postmoderns resent any authority telling them what is right or wrong, especially the church. "This is the judgment, that the Light has come into the world, and men loved the darkness rather than the Light, for their deeds were evil" (John 3:19). So people go to shamans, psychics, mediums, palm readers, and astrologers rather than God.

God strictly forbade His covenant people from consulting any source other than Himself for guidance. "Do not turn to mediums or spiritists; do not seek them out to be defiled by them...As for the person who turns to mediums and to spiritists, to play the harlot after them, I will also set My face against that person and will cut him off from among his people...A man or a woman who is a medium or a spiritist shall surely be put to death" (Leviticus 19:31; 20:6,27). Those who pursued false guidance were to be cut off from the rest of the community, and those who gave false guidance were to be put to death.

Today, we do almost the opposite. We make celebrities out of mediums and spiritists and put them on TV and radio. More women consult with psychics or New Age practitioners than licensed professional counselors. You can attend a psychic fair in practically any city in our land and pay for a personal spiritual "reading." The reader is either a fake or a spiritual medium who enters a trance and becomes a channel for some demonic spirit. Far from being seen as a blight on society, these people are often revered as highly as ministers and doctors for their "expertise." Some even profess belief in Jesus and speak of His "psychic power," and believe Him to be an avatar (an incarnation in human form).

Charlatans and Real Mediums

Where do mediums and spiritists get their "amazing" information and insights? Many of them are "paying attention to deceitful spirits" (1 Timothy 4:1), but some so-called psychic phenomena are clever illusions. These so-called spiritists give what are called "cold readings." These charlatans ask the naïve a few simple leading questions, and they observe their clients' speech, mannerisms, appearance, and dress. Based on the answers clients give and personal observations, these spiritists make general statements that would appear to be fairly accurate.

The gullible are so impressed with the accuracy of these "revelations" that they start giving more information, which these charlatans then fabricate into a "reading." This is not demonic; it's just verbal sleight of hand.

But the kinds of mediums and spiritists whom God warned against in Leviticus and Deuteronomy are not con artists. Rather, they possess and pass on knowledge that doesn't come through natural channels of perception. These people have opened themselves up to the spirit world and serve as spiritual channels. The charlatan who gives phony cold readings is only interested in bilking you of your money. But the false knowledge and direction that comes from Satan through a medium is intended to bilk you of your spiritual vitality and freedom.

Rory was the victim of a medium. A sharp-looking man in his late forties who had just gone through a divorce, Rory came into my office and told me his incredible story. One day he took a new lady friend named Bernice on a date to a Southern California theme park. While they were walking through the shops, they came to a little store advertising a resident psychic. The sign read, "Come in and receive instructions for your life."

Rory and Bernice went inside, and the psychic astounded them with her esoteric knowledge. Whether she was a true medium receiving her information from a familiar spirit or a clever con artist, I don't know. But the effect on the couple was profound. "If you have this kind of power," Rory exclaimed, "what else can you do for me?" The psychic promised that she could help him become a success at his job and in all the other areas of life.

Rory fell for it, and he and Bernice began seeing the psychic on a regular basis. The psychic advised them to marry each other, which they did. They continued to seek and follow the psychic's advice as a couple.

Four years later, Rory was in my office. His marriage to Bernice was a disaster, and the successful job the psychic had promised never materialized. When I asked him how much money he had poured down the drain in his pursuit of this psychic's knowledge, Rory answered, "I personally gave her almost 15,000 dollars, but Bernice lost more than 65,000 dollars."

There's big money in these psychic/con artist operations, and a lot of them are raking it in. Many people crave to know something extra about their lives and future, and they will pay handsomely for the inside information they desire. I received the following email from a former psychic:

> I just finished your DVD based on *The Bondage Breaker*, in which you discuss deception and the lure of knowledge and power. As a former channeler, let me share how psychics work. They only know what they are told by demons, and demons only know that which they have observed or what has been spoken out. For example, if my husband and I were talking about going to Hawaii for a vacation and I went to see a psychic, they might say something like, "I see you on vacation somewhere warm. There is a beach and sand. You're with a tall dark man—your husband. I believe it is Hawaii."
>
> Of course anyone would be impressed (deceived) by that apparent knowledge of the unknown. I worked as a psychic and ran in circles with those who were very "gifted" in that area. I got hooked at an early age. They were always able to tell me what had been spoken out and even some things that looked like they might happen. For example, I have always been a writer (and musician), and they would tell me that I was talented and would succeed in both areas, but everyone (even nonchannelers) told me that because of my passion for writing. It was an obvious gift, and I was persistent. So of course I would naturally find ways to get published, and eventually that happened. It did not happen in the time frame they had predicted because that information was unknown to them—so they bluffed their way through. Some of their predictions about the future happened, and some of them didn't. What I noticed was

that a psychic could give intimate details about a person's past, but not their future. They were always vague and often incorrect about unfolding events.

I was constantly told the key to becoming a good psychic is submitting to "the spirit." I had the "gift," but it would be stronger/better if I submitted more. I was told I was rebelling from my "gift" when I resisted. God is gracious and merciful. There was always something (the Lord no doubt) that held me back from fully committing, and even though I was not yet a believer. I eventually saw the inconsistencies and deception, and slowly stepped away. After becoming a believer and going through your Steps to Freedom, I was set free from my involvement in these areas and saw the entire deception clearly.

The Down Side of Seeking the Dark Side

Not much is known about the Hebrew biblical terms translated "medium" and "spiritist." Because "medium" (*ob*, meaning "witch" or "necromancer") is feminine, and "spiritist" (*yidd oni*, from the root "to know") is masculine, some students of the Bible think that they are male and female counterparts of the same role.

The Old Testament abounds with illustrations of kings, false prophets, and mediums who led the nation of Israel in rebellion against God. One of the more well-known cases was Israel's first monarch, King Saul, who was appointed by the prophet Samuel (1 Samuel 9). Saul served well until his infamous rebellion against God's will (1 Samuel 15), a sin that God equated with the sin of divination (verse 23). Why did Saul sin and reject the word of the Lord? Because he feared the voice of the people more than the voice of God—a problem all too evident in our world today.

Although Saul said he was sorry that he had sinned, there was no evidence that suggested he was truly repentant. So "the Spirit of the LORD departed from Saul, and an evil spirit from the LORD terrorized him" (1 Samuel 16:14).

There are two important takeaways for us in this passage. First, it seems to imply that when a person is disobedient, he can lose the Holy Spirit. In the Old Testament era, the Holy Spirit's presence in God's people was selective and temporary. The Spirit's presence in Saul was like the Spirit's presence in David in 1 Samuel 16:13: a special equipping of the Spirit for God's anointed king. This unique equipping is not the same as the personal relationship God's children enjoy with the Spirit today. "In Him, you also, after listening to the message of truth, the gospel of your salvation—having also believed, you were sealed in Him with the Holy Spirit of promise, who is given as a pledge of our inheritance" (Ephesians 1:13-14).

After the cross, those who comprise the church have been identified by the indwelling presence of the Holy Spirit, who unites the children of God with their heavenly Father (Ephesians 1:13-14). Jesus promised that no one will snatch us out of His hand (John 10:28), and Paul assured us that nothing can separate us from God's love (Romans 8:35-39). We are secure in Christ and indwelt by His Spirit through faith in the finished work of Christ.

Second, it may seem contradictory that an evil spirit could be sent by God. Yet He is the Lord of the universe and can use whatever instruments He chooses to accomplish His work. He can use Satan and his emissaries to discipline His people, as He did with Saul. God used the godless nation of Assyria as "the rod of My anger" to discipline His people (Isaiah 10:5-6). Even the church is advised to turn a grossly immoral member over to Satan "for the destruction of his flesh, that his spirit may be saved in the day of the Lord Jesus" (1 Corinthians 5:5).

Whenever the evil spirit came upon Saul, David (the heir apparent to Israel's throne) would play his harp, and the evil spirit would depart (1 Samuel 16:23). I don't think I can overstate the prominent role that music plays in the spiritual realm. When Elisha was about to inquire of God, he said, " 'Now bring me a minstrel.' And it came about, when the minstrel played, that the hand of the LORD came upon him" (2 Kings 3:15). During David's reign, more than 4,000 musicians were assigned to sing in the temple night and day (1 Chronicles 9:33;

23:5). It is the mark of Spirit-filled Christians to sing and make melody in their hearts to the Lord and speak to each other in psalms, hymns, and spiritual songs (Ephesians 5:18-20).

On the other side of the truth lies the destructive power of some secular music. I led a satanist to the Lord, and he showed me numerous symbols on popular record albums identifying the groups' association with satanism. He said that about 85 percent of today's heavy metal and punk music groups are "owned" by satanists. They have knowingly or unwittingly sold themselves to satanism in exchange for fame and fortune. They might not actually practice satanism, but most are hopelessly lost and lead others astray through the godless message in their music.

After the prophet Samuel died, Saul's twisted thirst for spiritual knowledge led him to seek guidance from a medium. Having previously purged the nation of mediums and spiritists (1 Samuel 28:3), Saul decided to pay a visit to the witch of Endor, who had somehow escaped the purge. Coming to the witch in disguise, Saul persuaded her to call up Samuel (verses 8-19). But the scheme backfired when God permitted Samuel himself to return, terrifying the medium (who was expecting a counterfeit spirit). Samuel's message to Saul was nothing but bad news, foretelling the imminent capture of Israel by the Philistines and the deaths of Saul and his sons (verse 19).

God expressly forbids necromancy. "When they say to you, 'Consult the mediums and the spiritists who whisper and mutter,' should not a people consult their God? Should they consult the dead on behalf of the living? To the law and to the testimony! If they do not speak according to this word, it is because they have no dawn" (Isaiah 8:19-20).

The story of the rich man and Lazarus teaches the present-day impossibility of communicating with the dead (Luke 16:19-31). When psychics claim to have contacted the dead, don't believe them. When psychologists claim to have regressed clients back to a former existence through hypnosis, don't believe them. When New Age mediums purport to channel a person from the past into the present, realize that the "person" is nothing more than a demonic spirit or the fraudulent work of a con artist.

An Old Idea in New Clothing

The New Age movement cloaks the occultic message of enlighten-ment: "You don't need God; you *are* God. You don't need to repent of your sins and depend on God to save you. Sin isn't a problem; you just need to turn off your mind and tune in to the great cosmic oneness through harmonic convergence." The New Age pitch is the oldest lie of Satan: "You will be like God" (Genesis 3:5).

People all around the world are ignoring the God who loves them and wants to guide their lives, and are instead seeking fulfillment in the kingdom of darkness. "Is it because there is no God in Israel that you are sending to inquire of Baal-zebub, the god of Ekron?" Elijah lamented (2 Kings 1:6). We may well ask with Jehu, "What peace, so long as the harlotries of your mother Jezebel and her witchcrafts are so many?" (9:22). Peace can be found only in the Prince of Peace, not in the prince of darkness.

People such as the devotees of Simon in Acts 8:9-10 will continue to be astonished by those who practice sorcery. Others, such as the customers of the demon-possessed slave girl in Acts 16:16-18, will con-tribute to the profit of those who exercise a spirit of divination. As in these examples from the early church, those who seek knowledge and power from the dark side will greatly interfere with the work of God, deceiving many by the counterfeit forces they employ. Other people will thirst after power to such an extent that they will sacrifice to the "goat demons" (Leviticus 17:7) and even sacrifice their own children to demons (Psalm 106:36-38).

Let these words from Scripture sober us to the reality that even believers are vulnerable to being lured away from the knowledge and power of God by the enemy, who exaggerates our sense of indepen-dence and importance apart from God:

> Jeshurun grew fat and kicked—you are grown fat, thick, and sleek—then he forsook God who made him, and scorned the Rock of his salvation. They made Him jealous with strange gods; with abominations they provoked Him

to anger. They sacrificed to demons who were not God, to gods whom they have not known, new gods who came lately, whom your fathers did not dread. You neglected the Rock who begot you, and forgot the God who gave you birth (Deuteronomy 32:15-18).

CHAPTER NINE

TEMPTED TO DO IT YOUR WAY

What can the reason be that with each temptation the devil adds, "If you are the Son of God"? He is acting just like he did in the case of Adam, when he disparaged God by saying, "In the day you eat, your eyes will be opened." So he does in this case, intending thereby to signify that our first parents had been beguiled and outsmarted and had received no benefit. So even in the temptation of Jesus he insinuates the same thing, saying, "In vain God has called you 'Son' and has beguiled you by his gift. For, if this is not so, give us some clear proof that you are from that power."

JOHN CHRYSOSTOM (AD 347–407)

A Catholic high school invited me to speak to their religion class about Protestant Christianity. I was greeted by the monsignor, and I asked him to hold me accountable for anything I said about the Catholic Church that was incorrect. He agreed, and introduced me to the class. I started with the Reformation, explained justification by faith, and shared how we could have a personal relationship with God. Then I handed out a gospel tract, and invited the students to ask questions.

A young man asked, "Do you have a lot of *don'ts* in your religion?"

I said, "I don't think I have any that God doesn't. At least I hope I don't, but what you are really asking me is, Do I have any freedom?"

"Okay," he said. "Do you have any freedom?"

I said, "Sure, I can do whatever I choose to do."

I paused for a moment, and I could tell the students wondered if I really meant that.

"Well, can't I? I suppose I can rob a bank, but I would have to spend the rest of my days looking over my shoulder, wondering if I was going to be caught. I suppose I can tell a lie, but I would have to remember who I told the lie to and what I told them. Freedom doesn't reside in the exercise of choice; it is always related to the consequences of those choices. Jesus set me free to make the right choices and live a liberated life in Him. 'It was for freedom that Christ set us free' [Galatians 5:1]. The freedom we have in Christ is not a license to live independently of God, which has many unintended consequences. We will all be tempted by Satan to make sinful choices leading to bondage and death.

"By the way," I said, "are you free to be the person God created you to be?" The class left when the bell rang, and the monsignor said to me, "That was terrific!" I was tempted to ask, "Which part?"

Some believers question their salvation when they are bombarded by Satan's temptations, but it is not a sin to be tempted. Jesus was "tempted in all things as we are, yet without sin" (Hebrews 4:15). As long as we are physically alive in this present world, we will be tempted just like Jesus was, but He didn't sin, and we don't have to sin either. Temptation is an enticement to live independently of God. What Jesus modeled was a life dependent upon the heavenly Father: "I can do nothing on My own initiative" (John 5:30). "I live because of the Father" (John 6:57). "I have not even come on My own initiative" (John 8:42). "Now they have come to know that everything You have given Me is from You" (John 17:7).

THE BASIS OF TEMPTATION

Have you noticed that what may tempt you may not tempt another person, and vice versa? Temptations from without lack power unless there is a corresponding desire within. Jesus said, "The ruler of the world is coming, and he has nothing in Me" (John 14:30). What is there within us that makes us a target, and how did we get that way? Recall that we were born physically alive, but spiritually dead (i.e., separated from God), and we lacked the knowledge of His ways. Consequently we learned to live independently of God, and we all learned differently. Rather than having our needs met through a living relationship with our loving heavenly Father, we strove to meet our needs on our own. We developed habits and patterns of thought that centered our interests on ourselves.

When we were born again, our self-centered flesh patterns came into conflict with the leading of God's Holy Spirit. Paul wrote, "I say, walk by the Spirit, and you will not carry out the desire of the flesh. For the flesh sets its desire against the Spirit, and the Spirit against the flesh; for these are in opposition to one another, so that you may not do the things that you please" (Galatians 5:16-17). They are in opposition because the flesh was programmed to live independently of God, and like Jesus, the Holy Spirit will not act independently of the Father.

With every temptation comes a choice to live by the Spirit or walk by the flesh, and the consequences of that choice are either the fruit of the Spirit (verses 22-23) or the deeds of the flesh (verses 19-21). "Those who belong to Christ Jesus have crucified the flesh with its passions and desires. If we live by the Spirit, let us also walk by the Spirit" (verses 24-25). The choice is easier when you believe that "God will supply all your needs according to His riches in glory" (Philippians 4:19).

Too Much of a Good Thing

Most believers won't often be tempted to commit overt sins such as killing, stealing, and destroying. Satan is too clever and subtle for that. He knows that we will recognize the flagrant wrong in such temptations and that we are unlikely to act on them. That is not to say such thoughts won't pop into our minds. But rather than act on them, the uninformed will wonder what is wrong with them because such thoughts are surfacing in their minds.

Usually the tempter's strategy is to entice us to take or do that which is good and blow it out of proportion. One piece of pie is okay, but not the whole pie in one sitting. Heresy often begins with truth that's taken out of balance. Satan treats us like the proverbial frog in the pot of water, gradually turning up the heat of temptation and hoping we don't notice that we are approaching the boundary of God's will and thus jumping out before something good becomes sin.

Paul wrote, "All things are lawful for me, but not all things are profitable. All things are lawful for me, but I will not be mastered by anything" (1 Corinthians 6:12). He saw nothing but green lights in every direction of the Christian life. Everything is good and lawful for us because we are free from sin and no longer under the condemnation of the law. However, Paul also knew that if we irresponsibly floorboard our lives in any of these good and lawful directions we will eventually run the red light of God's will and fall into sin. Here are some examples:

- physical rest becomes laziness
- quietness becomes noncommunication
- ability to profit becomes avarice and greed
- enjoyment of life becomes intemperance
- physical pleasure becomes sensuality
- admiring what others possess becomes covetousness
- enjoyment of food becomes gluttony
- self-care becomes vanity
- self-respect becomes conceit
- communication becomes gossip
- cautiousness becomes unbelief
- positiveness becomes insensitivity
- anger becomes rage and bad temper
- lovingkindness becomes overprotection
- judgment becomes criticism
- same-sex friendship becomes homosexuality

- sexual freedom becomes immorality
- conscientiousness becomes perfectionism
- generosity becomes wastefulness
- self-protection becomes dishonesty
- carefulness becomes fear

Sin Versus Growth

First John 2:12-14 describes three levels of maturity. The first level is "little children" (verse 12). Their sins are forgiven and they have some knowledge of God. They have overcome the *penalty* of sin. Level-two believers are "young men" (verses 13-14) who "have overcome the evil one," and John repeats that for emphasis. It is unlikely that believers will make it to level two in their spiritual growth if they are ignorant of Satan's schemes. In a practical sense, level-two believers have overcome the *power* of sin, and they are no longer in bondage to uncontrollable appetites and habits. They have successfully overcome the temptations of this world.

Finally, those who mature to level three are considered "fathers" (verses 13-14) who have an intimate and long-standing relationship with their heavenly Father.

CHANNELS OF TEMPTATION

After describing three levels of maturity, John mentioned three channels through which Satan will entice us to act independently of God (1 John 2:15-17):

> Do not love the world nor the things in the world. If anyone loves the world, the love of the Father is not in him. For all that is in the world, the lust of the flesh and the lust of the eyes and the boastful pride of life, is not from the Father, but is from the world. The world is passing away, and also its lusts; but the one who does the will of God lives forever.

The three channels of temptation are "the lust of the flesh," "the lust of the eyes," and "the boastful pride of life." The lust of the flesh refers to our physical appetites and seeks gratification in this world. The lust of the eyes is our self-serving interests. The pride of life relates to self-promotion and self-exaltation. Satan confronted both the first Adam and the last Adam through the same three channels of temptation. Each channel questions God's supremacy and destroys our dependence upon, confidence in, and obedience to God (see below).

CHANNELS OF TEMPTATION 1 John 2:15-17			
	Lust of the Flesh (Appetites and cravings)	Lust of the Eyes (Self-interest)	Pride of Life (Self-promotion)
Eve	"The woman saw that the tree was good for food" (Genesis 3:6)	"and that it was a delight to the eyes" (Genesis 3:6)	"and that the tree was desirable to make one wise" (Genesis 3:6)
Satan	"Indeed, has God said, 'You shall not eat from any tree of the garden'?" (Genesis 3:1)	"You surely will not die!" (Genesis 3:4)	"You will be like God" (Genesis 3:5)
Questions	The will of God (Ephesians 5:17)	The Word of God (Matthew 16:24-26)	The worship of God (1 Peter 5:5-11)
Destroys	Dependence upon God	Confidence in God	Obedience to God
Jesus	"Man does not live by bread alone, but man lives by everything that proceeds out of the mouth of the LORD" (Deuteronomy 8:3)	"You shall not put the LORD your God to the test" (Deuteronomy 6:16)	"You shall fear only the LORD your God; and you shall worship Him" (Deuteronomy 6:13)

The Lust of the Flesh

Satan first appealed to the lust of the flesh in Eve. He planted doubt in her mind about the fruit of the tree when he said, "Has God said, 'You shall not eat from any tree of the garden'?" (Genesis 3:1). Eve answered, "God has said, 'You shall not eat from it or touch it'" (verse 3). Notice that Eve added to God's Word when she said "or touch it." Satan had piqued her appetite for the forbidden fruit, and she "saw that the tree was good for food" (verse 6).

There is no record of Satan pursuing Jesus to tempt Him, because there was nothing in Jesus to tempt. It was the Holy Spirit who led Jesus "into the wilderness to be tempted by the devil" (Matthew 4:1). To make the temptations real, Jesus fasted for 40 days and 40 nights and was hungry. He was on the verge of starvation. His circumstances aptly describe when we are most vulnerable: depleted, isolated, and alone.

Satan tempted Jesus by appealing to the lust of the flesh: "If You are the Son of God, command that these stones become bread" (Matthew 4:3). This strikes at the very heart of temptation. Satan wanted Jesus to use His divine attributes independently of His heavenly Father to save Himself. That is what Peter wanted Jesus to do, bringing a swift rebuke: "Get behind Me, Satan! You are a stumbling block to me; for you are not setting your mind on God's interests, but man's" (Matthew 16:23). Yielding to the lust of the flesh draws us away from the will of God. Note that there is nothing sinful about eating. Hunger is a legitimate physical sensation, and God supplies food to meet that need.

Jesus replied, "Man shall not live on bread alone, but on every word that proceeds out of the mouth of God" (Matthew 4:4). What Jesus said is important, but what is often overlooked is the fact He said it. Remember, Satan has no obligation to obey our thoughts. Knowing this has been extremely helpful for me when I travel for ministry purposes. I am most vulnerable when I'm tired at night after a full day of ministry, alone in my hotel room, and tempted to watch what I shouldn't on television. I have learned to pray out loud, submit myself and my body to God, renounce any past use of the room in ways that didn't please God, exercise the authority every believer has in Christ over the evil one by telling him to leave, and ask God for a hedge of protection around me and the room.

The Lust of the Eyes

God told Adam that he would surely die if he ate from the tree of the knowledge of good and evil (Genesis 2:17). But Satan said to Eve, "You surely will not die!" (Genesis 3:4). "When the woman saw that the tree was good for food, and that it was a delight to eyes, and that the tree was desirable to make one wise, she took from its fruit and ate, and she gave also to her husband with her, and he ate" (verse 6).

The lust of the eyes subtly draws us away from the Word of God and eats away at our confidence in God. Naïve believers see what the world has to offer and tests the limits of God's grace. Instead of trusting God, they adopt a "prove it to me" attitude. That was the essence of Satan's second temptation of Jesus: "If You are the Son of God, throw Yourself down [from the pinnacle of the temple]; for it is written, 'He will command His angels concerning You'; and 'On their hands they will bear You up, so that You will not strike Your foot against a stone'" (Matthew 4:6). Jesus wasn't about to play Satan's "prove it to me" game. He replied, "It is written, 'You shall not put the Lord your God to the test'" (verse 7).

When I was a pastor, some of the members of our church unwittingly yielded to the temptation to put God to the test. I had a dear friend who was dying of cancer. His wife asked me not to pray for him if I included the words "if it be Your will" in the prayer. I told her that I bow to a higher will than mine. Word spread around the church that four independent "witnesses" all testified that Dick wasn't going to die because God had told them so. Several exclaimed, "Isn't it wonderful that God is going to heal Dick?!" Three weeks later, Dick was dead.

If God was the One who told these four people that Dick wasn't going to die, then what does that make God? A liar? The originator of this "good news" was obviously the father of lies, who wanted to create a false hope and destroy the congregation's confidence in God.

God is under no obligation to us; He is under obligation to Himself.

There is no way you can cleverly word a prayer so that God must capitulate to your will. That not only distorts the meaning of prayer, it is an attempt to manipulate God. The righteous will live by faith in the written Word of God and not demand that God prove Himself in response to their whims or wishes, no matter how noble they may appear to be. We are the ones being tested, not God.

The Pride of Life

The third channel of temptation is the desire to direct our own destiny, to rule our own world, to be our own god. Satan said, "God knows that in the day you eat from it your eyes will be opened, and you will be like God, knowing good and evil" (Genesis 3:5). "God doesn't want you to eat from the tree because He is holding out on you," says Satan. Eve saw that "the tree was desirable to make one wise" (verse 6). Their pride of life cost them their lives, and Satan usurped their role and became the god of this world.

Satan tried to tempt Jesus in this way as well: "The devil took Him to a very high mountain, and showed Him all the kingdoms of the world and their glory; and he said to Him, 'All these things I will give You, if You fall down and worship me'" (Matthew 4:8-9). Note that Jesus didn't challenge Satan's right to offer Him the kingdoms of the world. Because he was the god of this world, they were his to offer, but Jesus was not about to settle for anything less than the defeat of Satan. So He replied, "Go, Satan! For it is written, 'You shall worship the Lord your God, and serve Him only.' Then the devil left Him; and behold, angels came and began to minister to Him" (verses 10-11).

By appealing to the pride of life, Satan intends to steer us away from the worship of God and destroy our obedience to Him. When you manipulate others to get ahead of them, when you lie on your resume, when you compromise your convictions to accomplish a goal, when you smear another to make yourself look better, beware: That is the pride of life. Putting yourself on a pedestal is worshipping and serving Satan, and that is what he wants more than anything else because that has always been his goal:

How you have fallen from heaven, O star of the morning, son of the dawn! You have been cut down to the earth, you who have weakened the nations! But you said in your heart, "I will ascend to heaven; I will raise my throne above the stars of God, and I will sit on the mount of assembly in the recesses of the north. I will ascend above the heights of the clouds; *I will make myself like the Most High*" (Isaiah 14:12-14).

Instead of being "like God," as Satan promised, Adam and Eve became like Satan and fell as he did. Satan had to crawl on his belly like a snake in the presence of spiritually alive Adam, who had dominion over this earth. If he could trick Adam into believing that he could elevate his status, then Adam would fall. Think about it: Through humble submission to God, we are privileged to sit with Christ in the heavenlies.

When Freedom in Christ Ministries was growing rapidly during the early 1990s, the idea of setting up a radio ministry was discussed in a staff meeting. I sensed no leading to do that, and said at the time, "I know nothing about radio, and unless someone has a million dollars to give away, and unless a person with radio experience comes forward, I have no interest in doing it."

Then we had a staff retreat, and I talked about the extraordinary ministries of Elijah and Elisha and how deceptive forces derailed Elijah and tried to get Elisha off track. The very next week, a man flew out to meet with us. He didn't have a million dollars; he had a billion. He didn't have a radio ministry; he had a television ministry and a mail distribution center. They were ours to use if we wanted. My wife and I knew immediately that this was not from God. One member of our staff was baffled by our refusal, and we found out later that he had kept in touch with the wealthy man. It may seem odd that we would decline such an opportunity, but a couple years later, God very clearly confirmed that it was a good thing we had not moved forward in connection with that individual.

TWO OF OUR BIGGEST APPETITES

Let's be honest: There is something inside us that wants to respond to temptations. The flesh craves to be satisfied, but you can never satisfy the desires of the flesh. The more you feed your carnal desires, the more they grow. One beer leads to two. One kiss leads to petting, and so on. In contrast, "Blessed are those who hunger and thirst for righteousness, for they shall be satisfied" (Matthew 5:6). If you believed that, what would you be doing? If you aren't hungering and thirsting after righteousness, then you don't really believe that promise. People don't always live according to what they profess, but they do live according to what they actually believe.

Eat to Live or Live to Eat?

Food is the ultimate appetite because it is necessary for survival. So we eat to live, but when we begin to live to eat, food no longer satisfies. Instead, it consumes us, and millions of people feel powerless to control their appetite for food. When your body is deprived of necessary nutrients, you naturally crave those foods that will keep you healthy and your immune system functioning.

But when you turn to food to relieve stress and anxiety or to satisfy a lust for sweets, salt, etc., you only increase the power of temptation, and the more overweight you get. Obesity is the number one physical health problem in America, in spite of the fact that new diet programs regularly emerge promising great results. They are all law-based, listing the foods you cannot eat. The law (any law) has the capacity to stimulate the desire to do what it intended to prohibit (Romans 7:5,8). That's what prompted Paul to ask, "Is the Law then contrary to the promises of God?" (Galatians 3:21). Of course not, but the law is powerless to give life. If you don't think that is true, tell your child he can go here, but he can't go there. The moment you say that, guess where he wants to go? That is not a new concept. God told Adam he could eat from any tree in the garden except one (Genesis 2:17).

It is no coincidence that Paul mentioned misuse of food in conjunction with his sober warning that "in later times some will fall away from the faith, paying attention to deceitful spirits and doctrines of demons" (1 Timothy 4:1). One of the evidences of the last days will be people who "advocate abstaining from foods" (verse 3) that are intended to meet a legitimate need. Anorexia and bulimia are called eating disorders, but they have little to do with food. The primary issue for both is deception.

Why do some people cut themselves, binge and purge, or force themselves to defecate? They think there is evil present in them, and they want to get it out. Paul said, "I find then the principle that evil is present in me, the one who wants to do good" (Romans 7:21). Will cutting, purging, or defecating get rid of the evil in a person? Of course not. I encouraged one young lady (who was a Christian college graduate taking 75 laxatives a day) to say, "I renounce defecating as a means of cleansing myself; I trust only in the cleansing work of Christ." As soon as she said that, she began to cry and continued to do so uncontrollably for ten minutes. When she regained her composure, I asked, "What were you thinking during that time?" She said, "I can't believe the lies I have been deceived by!"

A pastor's wife wrote to me after a conference:

> I can't begin to tell you all that the Lord has done in my life through the truth you shared with us at the conference. I am now more aware of the deception of the enemy, and this makes my gratefulness for my powerful and gracious Savior real. I was bulimic for 11 years. But now I can be in the house alone all day with a kitchen full of food and be in peace. When a temptation or lie from Satan pops into my mind, I fend it off quickly with the truth. I used to be in bondage to those lies for hours and hours each day, always fearing food. Now I'm rejoicing in the freedom that the truth brings.

Sexual Passions Unleashed

Paul also mentioned deceivers who will forbid marriage in the last days (1 Timothy 4:3). Paul taught that celibacy was good, "but because of immoralities, each man is to have his own wife, and each woman is to have her own husband" (1 Corinthians 7:2). Sexual sins are in a class by themselves. "Every other sin that a man commits is outside the body, but the immoral man [fornicator] sins against his own body" (1 Corinthians 6:18). Almost every inquirer I have met with has confessed some kind of sexual aberration. Some were in bondage to uncontrollable lust. Others were the victims of sexual abuse.

Jesus said, "Everyone who looks at a woman with lust for her has already committed adultery with her in his heart" (Matthew 5:28). Lustfully looking at the opposite sex, viewing raunchy movies, and indulging in pornography are evidences that something isn't right in the core of our being. Remember, the power of temptation is related to the desire within. The Greek word translated "lust" is *epithumos*. The prefix *epi* means "to add to," signifying that something is being added to a normal drive. The problem only worsens when we pollute our minds with pornography and have sexual experiences outside of marriage. Notice in the following testimony how the young man developed his flesh patterns and how attempts to satisfy his flesh only led to further degradation:

> I was raised in what everyone would think was the perfect home. My parents were Christians and were very involved in church. They went out of their way to demonstrate their love. When I reached puberty, I was interested in sex just like every other red-blooded boy. My father and mother were not very good at sharing at an intimate level, so most of what I learned was from a book they had in the house.

> From that book I figured out how to masturbate. Pretty soon I was a slave to it. I soon found pornography and became a slave to that. It was available in stores, and they didn't seem to care about a junior high kid buying it. I was in my own private little world. On the outside I was this Christian kid—involved in the youth group, a counselor at Christian camp, and a member of the "perfect family" at

church. On the inside I was in complete bondage to pornography and lustful thinking.

I went to a Christian college, and there I continued to feed my lustful habits. I married my beautiful Christian girlfriend, and to everyone around us we were the "perfect couple." But I still had this private world that even my wife didn't know about. My job took me on the road, where I got closer and closer to the big one (adultery). I always thought I could dabble with pornography and not commit adultery, but it finally happened, and then it happened again and again. I would have guilt and remorse, but never true repentance.

Finally, events that I know were orchestrated by God led to my wife finding out, and I confessed my secret life of sexual addiction. With the help of your books *Winning the Battle Within*, *Victory Over the Darkness*, and *The Bondage Breaker*, I was able to discover my freedom in Christ. No more bondage! No more slavery to sin!

THE WAY OF ESCAPE

First Corinthians 10:13 says: "No temptation has overtaken you but such as is common to man; and God is faithful, who will not allow you to be tempted beyond what you are able, but with the temptation will provide the way of escape also, so that you will be able to endure it." That may sound like a hollow promise to those who are caught up in the tempted-sin-confess, tempted-sin-confess, tempted-sin-confess cycle and finally give up. The way out after having given in to temptation is to confess, repent, resist, and stand firm.

In Romans 6:1-10, believers are identified with Christ in His death, burial, resurrection, and life. That passage shares how the law of the Spirit of life in Christ Jesus has overcome the law of sin and death, and we share in that life because we are alive in Christ. But we have a responsibility as well. "Even so consider yourselves to be dead to sin, but alive to God in Christ Jesus. Therefore do not let sin reign in your mortal body so that you obey its lusts" (verses 11-12). It is our responsibility to not allow sin to reign in our mortal bodies, and the next verse tells us how: "Do not go on presenting the members of your body to sin as instruments of unrighteousness; but present yourselves to God as those alive from the dead, and your members as instruments of righteousness to God" (verse 13). You can't commit a sexual sin without using your body as an instrument of unrighteousness, and doing so allows sin to reign in your mortal body. Unless that is dealt with, there is sin within you that gives temptation its power.

In The Steps to Freedom in Christ, there is a prayer in which people are to ask God to reveal to their minds every sexual use of their bodies as instruments of unrighteousness, and God will do that. Usually He starts with the first sexual encounter and works forward. The inquirers are then encouraged to renounce that use of their bodies and ask God to break the sexual, mental, and emotional bond between themselves and their partners. Finally, they are exhorted to give their bodies to God as a living sacrifice, which we are urged to do according to Romans 12:1. Once they do that, then they can do what they are told in next verse: "Do not be conformed to this world, but be transformed by the renewing of your mind, so that you may prove what the will of God is, that which is good and acceptable and perfect" (12:2). Trying to win the battle for their minds without first dealing with the sin that is reigning in their mortal bodies will be nearly impossible.

"Do you not know that your bodies are members of Christ?" (1 Corinthians 6:15). "Or do you not know that your body is a temple of the Holy Spirit…?" (verse 19). Repentance cleans out the temple and makes room for Jesus. Then when temptation knocks at the door, all the devil will see is "Christ in you, the hope of glory" (Colossians 1:27).

Here is how one man cleaned out his temple and kept the door closed:

> I had been involved in, a user of, and addicted to pornography for many years. I hit bottom when my wife finally caught me. Shortly after I was caught, my wife and I were

in a restaurant that had a rack of Christian books. Among them was one of your books, *Discipleship Counseling* [Bethany House Publishers]. I knew it was for me. That began my recovery.

I had come to a place of doubting my salvation. Did God really love me? Was I beyond hope? That book and *The Bondage Breaker* and *Winning the Battle Within* helped me realize that I had been lied to and deceived by the enemy of my soul—and I went through The Steps to Freedom in Christ. I am free today. I believe I have "redemption and forgiveness of sins," that I am "dead to sin and alive to God." I am taking very seriously my responsibility to stay free. I meet weekly with an accountability group of men at my church. I now have a regular daily devotion with my Lord. God is doing for me what I could not do for myself.

CHAPTER TEN

ACCUSED BY THE FATHER OF LIES

God made another being, in whom the disposition of the divine origin did not remain. Therefore, he was infected with his own envy, as with poison. So he passed from good to evil. Through his own will, which had been given to him by God unfettered, he acquired for himself a contrary name. From this, it appears that the source of all evils is envy. For he envied his predecessor [the Son], who through His steadfastness is acceptable and dear to God the Father. This person, who from good became evil by his own act, is called by the Greeks *diabolos* [slanderer]. We call him the Accuser, for he reports to God the faults to which he himself entices us.

LACTANTIUS (AD 240–320)

Those who walk into a pastor's office seeking help for personal problems do not feel good about themselves. Not one person beginning treatment for substance abuse has a healthy self-image. No victim of abuse has a positive sense of worth, and ultimately, they are not in bondage to their abuse. Rather, they are in bondage to the lies they believe because of the abuse, such as, "It was my fault." "I'm no good." "God doesn't love me." The "accuser of our brethren" (Revelation 12:10) has a field day with those who have unresolved personal and spiritual conflicts. I don't recall one person whom I have led through The Steps to Freedom in Christ who didn't have a self-image problem. None of them knew who they were in Christ. Many times I have asked during the process, "Who do you think your worst enemy is?" Everyone has said, "Me," which isn't true. It was because of their worst enemy's lies that they thought they were their own worst enemy.

Not all accusations come directly to us from deceiving spirits. Some accusations come "by means of the hypocrisy of liars" (1 Timothy 4:2) who are being deceived. People's lives and reputations are being destroyed by false accusations. Those who listen to false accusations far outnumber those who hear the retraction.

I was asked by a district superintendent to help bring resolution to an accused pastor and his wife. A counselor had been working with their daughter, who was accusing her parents of being satanists. I met with the superintendent, the counselor, the pastor, and his wife. I asked the counselor to begin by sharing what her client (the couple's daughter) had accused them of doing. Tragically, the daughter had committed suicide prior to our meeting. The pastor and his wife denied that they were satanists. I said, "You have volunteered to come to this meeting to clear your name. Would you be willing to go through a portion of The Steps to Freedom with me?" They agreed. An appendix in the Steps has a page of satanic renunciations, and I asked them to read them out loud. They did so with no interference. Had they been satanists, there is no way they could have done that. The counselor then realized she had wrongly believed the story of a deceived client. I reminded the counselor of what 1 Timothy 5:19 says: "Do not receive an accusation against an elder except on the basis of two or three witnesses."

Satan uses temptation and accusation as a brutal one-two punch. He tempts us by saying, "Why don't you try it? Everybody does it. Besides, you can get away with it. Who's going to know?" Then the moment we fall for the temptation, he becomes the accuser: "What kind of Christian are you to do such a thing? You're a pitiful excuse for a child of God. You'll never get away with it. You might as well give up because God has already given up on you."

Satan is called "the accuser of our brethren...who accuses them before our God day and night" (Revelation 12:10). We have all heard his lying, hateful voice in our hearts and consciences. It seems as though he never lets up on us. Many Christians are perpetually discouraged because they believe his persistent lies about them. The last thing the devil wants you to know is who you are in Christ. One defeated Christian wrote,

> My old feelings that life isn't worth the trouble keep coming back. I'm scared, lonely, confused, and very desperate. I know deep down that God can overcome this, but I can't get past this block. I can't even pray. When I try, things get in my way. When I'm feeling good and I begin putting into action what I know God wants me to do, I'm stopped dead in my tracks by those voices and a force so strong I can't continue. I'm so close to giving in to those voices that I almost can't fight them anymore. I just want some peace.

PUTTING THE ACCUSER IN HIS PLACE

The Lord revealed to the prophet Zechariah a heavenly scene in which Satan's accusations of God's people are put into proper perspective:

> He showed me Joshua the high priest standing before the angel of the LORD, and Satan standing at his right hand to accuse him. The LORD said to Satan, "The LORD rebuke you, Satan! Indeed, the LORD who has chosen Jerusalem rebuke you! Is this not a brand plucked from the fire?" Now Joshua was clothed with filthy garments and standing before the angel (3:1-3).

The Lord Rebukes Satan

The cast of characters in this scene are assembled in a heavenly courtroom. The judge is God the Father. The prosecuting attorney is

Satan. The defense attorney is Jesus. The accused defendant is Joshua the high priest, who represents all of God's people. Historically, it was a very solemn occasion: Each year, on behalf of the people of Israel, the high priest was to enter the holy of holies on the Day of Atonement. Before doing so, he was to perform elaborate purification rites and ceremonial cleansings. Only then could he enter into God's presence. If he wasn't right before God, he could be struck dead on the spot. The high priest wore bells on the hem of his robe so that those who were outside the holy of holies could tell whether he was still alive and moving. A rope was tied around his ankle so he could be pulled out in case he was struck dead, for no other priest was permitted to go in to find out how the high priest was doing.

In the vision, Joshua, the high priest, is standing in God's presence with filthy garments that represent the sins of Israel. Not a good thing! Satan the accuser says, "Look at him, God. He's filthy. He deserves to be struck dead." At the same time, the defense attorney is standing there saying, "Look at My hands and My feet. I took the penalty for their sins." God the Father then pronounces the sentence, "Not guilty," and rebukes the accuser, putting him in his place. "You're not the judge, and you cannot pass sentence on My people. I have rescued Joshua from the flames of hell, and your accusations are groundless."

This courtroom scene continues night and day for every child of God. Satan persists in pointing out our faults and weaknesses to God and demands that He zap us for being less than perfect. In the meantime, God is saying to every believer, "My little children, I am writing these things to you so that you may not sin. And if anyone sins, we have an Advocate with the Father, Jesus Christ the righteous; and He Himself is the propitiation for our sins; and not for ours only, but also for those of the whole world" (1 John 2:1-2). Jesus "is able also to save forever those who draw near to God through Him, since He always lives to make intercession for them" (Hebrews 7:25). We have been invited to come into His presence with boldness and confidence (Ephesians 3:12), so "let us draw near with a sincere heart in full assurance of faith" (Hebrews 10:22).

The Lord Removes Our Filthy Garments

The reason Satan's accusations are groundless is because God has solved the problem of our filthy garments. Zechariah's description of the heavenly scene continues:

> He spoke and said to those who were standing before him, saying, "Remove the filthy garments from him." Again he said to him, "See, I have taken your iniquity away from you and will clothe you with festal robes." Then I said, "Let them put a clean turban on his head." So they put a clean turban on his head and clothed him with garments, while the angel of the LORD was standing by (3:4-5).

God has not only declared us forgiven, He has removed our filthy garments of unrighteousness and clothed us with His righteousness. Notice that the change of wardrobe is something that *God* does, not we ourselves. We don't have any garments of righteousness to put on that will satisfy God. Our armor against Satan's accusations is the breastplate of righteousness, which is placed on us when we put on the Lord Jesus Christ.

The Lord Admonishes Us to Respond

Now that we are forgiven and clothed in Christ's righteousness, there is work to be done. "If you will walk in My ways and if you will perform My service, then you will also govern My house and also have charge of My courts, and I will grant you free access among these who are standing here" (Zechariah 3:7). We have been let out of jail to perform community service, but there is a difference. Community service is not punishment, nor is it even a part of our rehabilitation. Having access to God, we are free to serve Him and others out of gratitude. "For we are His workmanship, created in Christ Jesus for good works, which God prepared beforehand so that we would walk in them" (Ephesians 2:10).

RECOGNIZING A CRITICAL DIFFERENCE

There is a major difference between the devil's accusations and the Holy Spirit's conviction, as Paul explained in 2 Corinthians 7:9-10:

> I now rejoice, not that you were made sorrowful, but that you were made sorrowful to the point of repentance; for you were made sorrowful according to the will of God, so that you might not suffer loss in anything through us. For the sorrow that is according to the will of God produces a repentance without regret, leading to salvation, but the sorrow of the world produces death.

The sorrow of this world and the Holy Spirit's conviction both produce the same sorrowful feeling. However, the sorrow resulting from Satan's accusation leads to death, while the sorrow of conviction leads to repentance and life without regret. Paul wasn't rejoicing that the Corinthians felt sorrowful; he was rejoicing that their sorrow would lead to repentance, eternal life, and freedom. The moment we choose to walk according to the flesh, the Holy Spirit brings conviction because what we have just chosen to do is not compatible with who we really are. The "hound of heaven" will track us down because He loves us.

If you have been honest with God and confessed every known sin, and you are still being pummeled with accusing thoughts, rest assured that those thoughts are not from God. But if you are sorrowful because your behavior doesn't reflect who you are in Christ, that's the sorrow according to the will of God prompting you to repent. "If we say that we have no sin, we are deceiving ourselves and the truth is not in us. If we confess our sins, He is faithful and righteous to forgive us our sins and to cleanse us from all unrighteousness" (1 John 1:8-9).

Satan "entered into Judas," and Judas plotted to betray Jesus for 30 pieces of silver (Luke 22:3-5). Afterward, Judas came under the sorrow of the world and hung himself. Satan also found a weakness in Peter when the disciples argued as to who was the greatest among them

(Luke 22:24-30). Jesus told Peter, "Simon, Simon, behold, Satan has demanded permission to sift you like wheat" (verse 31). Jesus allowed Satan to put Peter through the mill because Peter had given the enemy a foothold in his life. Jesus looked at Peter and said, "I have prayed for you, that your faith may not fail; and you, when once you have turned again, strengthen your brothers" (verse 32).

Peter vowed to go to jail or die for Jesus, but Jesus told Peter that he would deny his Lord three times (verses 33-34), which he did. The remorse Peter felt was every bit as painful as that which Judas experienced, but Peter's sorrow was conviction from the Holy Spirit, which led to repentance (John 21:15-17). When feelings of remorse pound you into the ground and drive you from God, you are being accused by Satan. When your sorrow results in confession, you are being convicted by the Holy Spirit. The good news is that Christ's continuing work is to intercede for us as He did for Peter. We have a persistent adversary, but we have an even more persistent and eternal advocate who defends us before the Father day and night.

THE QUICKSAND OF ACCUSATION

When we feel like worthless nobodies, we act like worthless nobodies, and our lives and ministries suffer. That was true about Janelle. Her pastor asked if he could bring her to me because he suspected that she was more than a psychological case. Janelle professed to be a Christian, but she was constantly berating herself and questioning her salvation. Janelle's fiancé, Curt, came with them. After introducing me to Janelle and Curt, the pastor started to leave. "Please stay," I said. "I'd prefer that you be here with us so you can provide responsible follow-up."

"I've got a weak heart," the pastor replied. He may have had heart trouble, but I'm guessing what he really feared was the enemy.

"I don't think anything will happen here today that will affect your heart," I assured him. "Besides, you're her pastor, and I would appreciate your prayer support." The pastor reluctantly agreed to stay.

Janelle had long been a victim of different kinds of abuse, beginning in her early childhood. One of her former boyfriends had been involved in the occult. She believed that she was the cause of her troubles, and that she was of no value to God or anybody else. There was little question in my mind that she was in spiritual bondage. I assured her that she was a child of God and that she could overcome her victimization by God's authority. As soon as I spoke those words, Janelle went catatonic. She sat as still as a stone, with her eyes staring into space.

"Have you ever seen this before?" I asked her pastor and fiancé.

"No," they answered fearfully. The oppression in the room was palpable. "There's nothing here to fear. I've seen it before," I said. "We're going to take authority over it, but it's important that you are in submission to God and wearing His armor."

I encouraged the pastor to confess any known sin, which I said he could do privately. When I turned to Curt, he started to shake.

"Curt, is there something you need to confess?" I asked. "I encourage you take this opportunity to do it right now."

Under the circumstances, Curt didn't need much prompting! He began confessing many sins, including the revelation that he and Janelle had been sleeping together. Curt committed himself to stop having sex and renounced every sexual use of his body as an instrument of unrighteousness. All the while, Janelle sat motionless.

I gave Curt the last step in The Steps to Freedom in Christ. As soon as he began, Janelle let out a menacing growl. Then she lashed out, slapping the paper out of Curt's hands. The suddenness of her action startled us, but it was just a scare tactic. We exercised God's authority and agreed in prayer that the evil one be bound in the name of the Lord Jesus Christ.

I wish I could have videotaped my encounter with Janelle that day so I could show skeptics what happens when Satan is confronted by God's authority. It was as if Wonder Woman had lassoed Janelle and tied her to the chair. She just sat there squirming, bound to the chair by the ropes of God's authority. Her eyes blazed at Curt with hatred, which was further evidence of the demonic power that was controlling her. Janelle didn't hate Curt; she loved him. They were going to be married. Satan hated the fact that his strongholds in Curt and Janelle were being torn down, and his hatred was mirrored in Janelle's countenance.

Curt finished the renunciations and read the prayer while Janelle continued to squirm in her chair. Then I prayed, "Lord, we declare our dependence upon You, for apart from Christ we can do nothing. Now, in the name and authority of the Lord Jesus Christ, we command Satan and all his forces to release Janelle and to remain bound so she will be free to obey her heavenly Father."

Janelle immediately slumped in her chair and snapped out of her catatonic state.

"Do you remember anything we've been doing here?" I asked her.

"No…what happened?" she responded with a weary and puzzled expression.

"It's nothing we can't deal with," I told her. "Satan has gained a foothold in your life, and with your permission we can lead you through The Steps to Freedom in Christ." It was an exhausting afternoon, but Janelle left free in Christ, and the pastor had the experience of his life.

What right did Satan have to control Janelle as he did? Only the right that she gave him by yielding to his lies and by living in sin. The accuser had convinced her that she was of little value, and that what she did was of little consequence. She had opened the door to immorality and the occult, so why not throw the door wide open as long as she was already guilty? It's similar to failing on a diet—once you have crossed a certain threshold, you reason, *I've already gone this far. Why not pig out?* For the person who feels remorseful over losing their virginity, it's easy to think, *Why not just give up and have more sex?* But that only leads to greater bondage.

Don't believe anything Satan says about you; he is a liar. Believe everything God says about you; it's the truth that will set you free.

I was staying in Canada with one of our staff. While setting up for a conference, he told me to go ask one of the helpers about her list. She pulled out the list I shared earlier in this book about who we are in Christ. She kept the list with her in a clear binder, and every time she thought things were in danger of getting out of hand, she pulled out the list, read it out loud, then wrote down the date. I looked at the sheet, and every available space on it was covered with dates. She was a ritual abuse victim that worldly counselors had given up on. She credits the truth of her identity in Christ to being the major reason for her freedom.

I was conducting a conference in Holland, which concluded with The Steps to Freedom in Christ. Afterward, a woman asked why the Steps didn't work for her. She was a ritual abuse victim, and such people can't resolve all that in one setting. I had no time to help her, so I gave her as much encouragement and advice as I could at the time. Five years later, her husband invited me to do a conference for pastors in Holland, and she attended. Afterward, she came to see me again and said, "You make it sound so easy." Once again I had no time to give her, but I called her husband over and asked if he would help her do something on a daily basis. There is a daily prayer in the Steps, along with what we call "Statements of Truth," and there's the list of scriptures that confirm who we are in Christ. I asked if she would be willing to read all three out loud every day for a month in the presence of her husband. Twenty-eight days later, I received an email from her husband, who said that she was finally free. This is just one example of why I can't overstate the value of knowing our true identity in Christ.

THE UNPARDONABLE SIN

Despite all the biblical assurances to the contrary, many believers struggle with the fear that they have committed the unpardonable sin. This is a critical matter to resolve because one of the pieces of the armor of God is the helmet of salvation (Ephesians 6:17). Those who are tormented by the possibility they've done the unpardonable sin usually suffer in silence. Many pastors would be amazed to know how many people in their church believe that they have committed an unforgivable sin. Our ministry conducted a conference in a federal prison, and every one of the prisoners believed that they had committed the unpardonable sin. They whooped and hollered when they learned otherwise. Jesus explains the unpardonable sin in Mark 3:22-30:

> The scribes who came down from Jerusalem were saying, "He is possessed by Beelzebul," and "He casts out the demons by the ruler of the demons." And He called them to Himself and began speaking to them in parables, "How can Satan cast out Satan? If a kingdom is divided against itself, that kingdom cannot stand. If a house is divided against itself, that house will not be able to stand. If Satan has risen up against himself and is divided, he cannot stand, but he is finished! But no one can enter the strong man's house and plunder his property unless he first binds the strong man, and then he will plunder his house. Truly I say to you, all sins shall be forgiven the sons of men, and whatever blasphemies they utter; but whoever blasphemes against the Holy Spirit never has forgiveness, but is guilty of an eternal sin"—because they were saying, "He has an unclean spirit."

Have you noticed that people frequently use the name of Jesus when they curse, but seldom, if ever, do they mention the Holy Spirit? Why can we utter blasphemies against others, including Jesus, and be forgiven, but not against the Holy Spirit? God the Father, and God the Son, and God the Holy Spirit are one God. The distinction is made because the three members of the Trinity have unique roles. For example, the work of Jesus was to be our kinsman redeemer. He came to shed His blood on the cross for the forgiveness of sins, and to be resurrected so that we may have new life "in Him." Those who come to Christ are forgiven of all their sins—past, present, and future. When Christ "died to sin once for all" (Romans 6:10), how many of your sins were future?

It is the unique work of the Holy Spirit to draw all people to Christ and to bear witness of His work. If you reject that witness, then you can never come to Christ to experience salvation. The only unpardonable sin, then, is the sin of unbelief. The scribes were attributing the work of the Holy Spirit to Satan. They rejected the witness and refused to believe. By contrast, those who do come to Christ are the sons of God, and their sins and blasphemies are forgiven, because they are in Christ.

That is why no Christian can commit the unpardonable sin. Standing in front of the scribes and Pharisees was Jesus the Messiah, the Son of God, and yet they attributed His ministry of delivering people from demonic bondage to the devil. They even accused Jesus of being possessed by Satan! They totally rejected the witness of the Spirit.

These were the same men who so hated Jesus that they maliciously plotted for Him to be betrayed, arrested, tried in a mock court, scourged, beaten, and crucified. They detested Jesus and cursed Him, spat upon Him, and sneered at Him while He hung on the cross. If you have come under the conviction of the Holy Spirit and have trusted in Christ, you have done the *opposite* of committing the unpardonable sin.

Many believers question their salvation and are under heavy conviction. The very fact that they are feeling convicted for their sins is the best evidence they are Christians, or about to become one. If the Holy Spirit were not at work in them, willful sin wouldn't be bothering them. Those who willfully sin and sense no conviction are not a part of God's family.

The devil is an accuser. He is like a prosecuting attorney who deceptively seeks to discredit and discourage a witness on the stand. He points his slimy finger and says, "Aha—you've done it now! There's no hope for you. You've blasphemed the Holy Spirit!" Perhaps you have questioned some spiritual gift, an anointed preacher, or apparent supernatural manifestation. Is that blaspheming the Holy Spirit? Of course not. In fact, it could be you are exercising necessary discernment. "Beloved, do not believe every spirit, but test the spirits to see whether they are from God, because many false prophets have gone out into the world" (1 John 4:1). A Christian can grieve the Holy Spirit (Ephesians 4:30) and even quench the Holy Spirit (1 Thessalonians 5:19)—but neither of these is unpardonable.

CHAPTER ELEVEN

THE DANGER OF DECEPTION

Because the devil was the first to be locked into sin, everyone who now sins acts according to his bidding. For the devil rules in the sinner by a mass of evil thoughts, as in the case of Judas. Some might say that the devil is present in sinners even before they sin, because they have made room for him. The answer to this is that committing sin and making room for the devil amount to one and the same thing—sin.

JOHN CHRYSOSTOM (AD 347–407)

n the beginning God created the heavens and the earth" (Genesis 1:1). Thus begins the story of creation and the history of humanity in the Old Testament. Two chapters later, Satan has deceived Eve, and Adam has sinned. The New Testament begins with the genealogy of Jesus. Three chapters later, Satan is tempting Jesus in yet another attempt to stop the plan of God. Once again, he failed. You can't deceive Jesus, who is the Truth, and there was nothing in Him to tempt.

How was it that Satan was able to tempt Eve? Paul explains how in 2 Corinthians 11:3, then follows that with a statement of concern for the believers in Corinth: "I am afraid that, as the serpent deceived Eve by his craftiness, your minds will be led astray from the simplicity and purity of devotion to Christ."

I'm concerned too, because "the serpent of old who is called the devil and Satan, who deceives the whole world" (Revelations 12:9) is why "the whole world lies in the power of the evil one" (1 John 5:19). Deception is more devious than temptation and accusation, because when you are tempted, you know it. When you are accused, you know it. But when you are deceived, you don't know it. If you did know it, you wouldn't be deceived. If we don't know the truth and don't know who our enemy is, we will be like blindfolded children striking out at ourselves and each other, unaware that we are being deceived.

Every movement by God is countered by Satan. Jesus said, "The kingdom of heaven may be compared to a man who sowed good seed in his field. But while his men were sleeping, his enemy came and sowed tares among the wheat, and went away" (Matthew 13:24-25). The wheat represents sons of God, and "the tares are the sons of the evil one" (verse 38). Tares and wheat both look like a blade of grass, and they are hard to tell apart until the harvest. Late in the season, the difference becomes more obvious. Wheat sprouts a head of grain, but the tares bear no fruit. They propagate underground while the church is sleeping.

The only defense against deception is to know the truth and to be spiritually discerning. That is why Jesus prayed to the Father, "I do not ask You to take them out of the world, but to keep them from the evil one...Sanctify them in the truth; Your word is truth" (John 17:15-17). "Having girded [our] loins with truth" (Ephesians 6:14) is the first piece of the armor of God. Paul used very specific language when he warned us about the end times: "The Spirit clearly says that in later times some will abandon the faith and follow deceiving spirits and things taught by demons" (1 Timothy 4:1 NIV). We are living in an age where "evil men and impostors will proceed from bad to worse, deceiving and being deceived" (2 Timothy 3:13). The manipulation of information both written and visual has become so commonplace that what you see, hear, and read in the mainstream media can't be trusted.

BEWARE OF SELF-DECEPTION

There is no class of people harder to help than those who are self-deceived. Usually they don't ask for help because they perceive there is nothing wrong with them and that they have done nothing wrong. For example, alcoholics believe they don't have a problem and that they can quit anytime. That is why recovery ministries stage interventions, hoping the alcoholic will acknowledge his or her problem and seek treatment.

However, self-deception may be accompanied by another culprit. Notice in the following passages how hardening our hearts and choosing not to believe make room for the devil: "Even if our gospel is veiled, it is veiled to those who are perishing, in whose case the god of this world [Satan] has blinded the minds [Greek, *noema*] of the unbelieving so that they might not see the light of the gospel of the glory of Christ, who is the image of God" (2 Corinthians 4:3-4). Which came first—the blinding, or the unbelieving? There is a veil over the hearts of those who have hardened their hearts (3:14). "But whenever a person turns to the Lord, the veil is taken away" (verse 16). The word of the Lord came to Ezekiel, saying, "Son of man, you live in the midst of the rebellious house, who have eyes to see but do not see, ears to hear but do not hear; for they are a rebellious house" (12:1-2). Which came first, the blinding or the rebellion?

Several passages of Scripture warn us not to deceive ourselves. First, we are deceiving ourselves if we hear or read God's Word but don't do what it says. "Prove yourselves doers of the word, and not merely hearers who delude themselves. For if anyone is a hearer of the word and not a doer, he is like a man who looks at his natural face in a mirror; for once he has looked at himself and gone away, he has immediately forgotten what kind of person he was" (James 1:22-24). The 90-pound anorexic looks in a mirror and says, "I'm fat!" The legalist reads Matthew 23, where Jesus denounced the scribes and Pharisees, but can't see that he himself is no different than the scribes and the Pharisees. Jesus said, "If you know these things, you are blessed if you do them" (John 13:17).

Second, John wrote that "if we say that we have no sin, we are deceiving ourselves and the truth is not in us" (1 John 1:8). We are not sinless saints; we are saints who sin. The moment we become aware of our sin, we should confess it. True confessors don't just say, "I'm sorry." They say, "I did it." To confess means to agree with God. It is the same as walking in the light—that is, consciously living in moral agreement with God. "Therefore, laying aside falsehood, speak truth each one of you with his neighbor, for we are members of one another. Be angry, and yet do not sin; do not let the sun go down on your anger, and do not give the devil an opportunity" (Ephesians 4:25-27). The Greek word translated "opportunity" is more commonly translated as "place" or "room." So don't give the devil a place in your life.

Third, we are deceiving ourselves if we believe that we are someone other than who we really are. "If anyone thinks he is something when he is nothing, he deceives himself" (Galatians 6:3). "For through the grace given to me I say to everyone among you not to think more highly of himself than he ought to think; but to think so as to have sound judgment, as God has allotted to each a measure of faith" (Romans 12:3). You have sound judgment if you say, "I know who I am. I'm a child of God, seated with Christ in the heavenlies, and I can do all things through Him who strengthens me." By contrast, a phony deceives himself and lacks sound judgment.

Fourth, we are deceived if we possess worldly wisdom yet lack an eternal perspective. "Let no man deceive himself. If any man among you thinks that he is wise in this age, he must become foolish, so that he may become wise. For the wisdom of this world is foolishness before God" (1 Corinthians 3:18-19). Knowledgeable people may seem wise from a temporal perspective, but true wisdom is seeing life from God's eternal perspective. "For even though they knew God, they did not honor Him as God or give thanks, but they became futile in their speculations, and their foolish heart was hardened. Professing to be wise, they became fools" (Romans 1:21-22).

Fifth, we have deceived ourselves if we think that we are mature but can't control what we say. "If anyone thinks himself to be religious, and yet does not bridle his tongue but deceives his own heart, this man's religion is worthless" (James 1:26). "Let no unwholesome word proceed from your mouth, but only such a word as is good for edification according to the need of the moment, so that it will give grace to those who hear. Do not grieve the Holy Spirit of God" (Ephesians 4:29-30). Many of the problems in our homes and churches would disappear if every believer obeyed that passage.

Sixth, we are deceived if we think we will face no consequences for our behavior. "Do not be deceived, God is not mocked; for whatever a man sows, this he will also reap" (Galatians 6:7). We are forgiven, but we still have to live with the consequences of our thoughts, words, and actions, whether good or bad.

Seventh, we are deceived if we believe that the unrighteous will inherit the kingdom of God. "Do not be deceived; neither fornicators, nor idolaters, nor adulterers, nor effeminate, nor homosexuals, nor thieves, nor the covetous, nor drunkards, nor revilers, nor swindlers, will inherit the kingdom of God" (1 Corinthians 6:9-10). The liberal "church" is deceived when they appoint a practicing homosexual to be a bishop or perform same-sex marriages. A revivalist in Florida was casting out demons and healing in Jesus's name, but afterward he abruptly left the revival to live with a woman who was not his wife. The Lord warned us of such people: "Many will say to Me on that day, 'Lord, Lord, did we not prophesy in Your name, and in Your name cast out demons, and in Your name perform many miracles?' And then I will declare to them, 'I never knew you; depart from Me, you who practice lawlessness'" (Matthew 7:22-23).

Eighth, we are deceived if we think we are incorruptible when we associate with the wrong crowd. Paul wrote, "Do not be deceived: 'Bad company corrupts good morals'" (1 Corinthians 15:33). Alexander Pope wrote the following, and I believe he said it well:

> Vice is a monster of so frightful mien,
> As, to be hated, needs but not to be seen;
> Yet seen too oft, familiar with her face;
> We first endure, then pity, then embrace.[17]

BEWARE OF FALSE
PROPHETS AND TEACHERS

For several years, Alvin believed he had a special gift from God. He was invited by several churches to share his prophetic message. Then his personal life began to fall apart. Alvin reached the point where he could no longer function in society, so he completely withdrew from people. By the time he came to see me he was unemployed, heavily medicated, and was being cared for by his father.

After a lengthy discussion about false prophets and teachers, Alvin said, "I think my problems began when I failed to test the 'gifts' of tongues and prophecy conferred on me by what I now know to be false teachers. Not only was I deceived, but I have deceived others."

"Would you be willing to test your gift of tongues?" I asked. I explained that we were going to test the spirit, not him. He agreed, so I instructed him to begin praying in tongues. As Alvin began, I said, "In the name of Christ and in obedience to God's Word, I ask this spirit to identify itself."

Alvin's demeanor changed, and he said, "I am he."

That could intimidate a novice, but it was not bearing witness with my spirit, so I said, "Are you the Christ who was crucified under Pontius Pilate, buried, raised on the third day, and who now sits at the right hand of the Father?"

He responded emphatically, "No! Not He!"

Obviously the wrong spirit!

Before you come to the wrong conclusion about what was happening here, remember Paul's instruction: "Desire earnestly to prophesy, and do not forbid to speak in tongues" (1 Corinthians 14:39). If you are zealous for spiritual gifts, you must be equally willing to submit spiritual manifestations to God. One young man said, "The voice in my head says it wants to go to heaven with me." I said, "Ask God to reveal to your mind the true nature of that voice." He said, "Lord, please show me...ugh!" I had no idea what he heard or saw, but there was little doubt about the true nature of that voice in his head. Yes, we are to acknowledge the reality of the supernatural, but we are also to be certain of the origin. "Do not quench the Spirit; do not despise prophetic utterances. But examine everything carefully; hold fast to that which is good; abstain from every form of evil" (1 Thessalonians 5:19-22). False prophets and teachers flourish simply because Christians accept their ministry without exercising spiritual discernment.

Comparing the Counterfeit with the Real

Every true prophet of God in the Old Testament was essentially an evangelist. A prophet draws people back to God and His Word. A prophetic voice speaks before people and time, but the major emphasis is on speaking before people. Because Daniel didn't preach, the Jewish order of Scripture doesn't include Daniel with the prophets, even though Daniel includes significant end-of-time prophecies. The call to righteousness was the standard that separated the genuine prophet from the false. Jeremiah wrote: "Thus says the LORD of hosts, 'Do not listen to the words of the prophets who are prophesying to you...I did not send these prophets, but they ran. I did not speak to them, but they prophesied. But if they had stood in My council, then they would have announced My words to My people, and would have turned them back from their evil way and from the evil of their deeds'" (23:16,21-22).

Jeremiah continued, "I have heard what the prophets have said who prophesy falsely in My name, saying, 'I had a dream, I had a dream!'... The prophet who has a dream may relate his dream, but let him who has My word speak My word in truth. What does straw have in common with grain?" (verses 25,28). God did communicate through dreams, but in comparison to the nutritious grain of His Word, dreams are mere straw. If the only food you give to cattle is straw, they'll die. They will sleep on it, but they won't eat it because it has no nutrients. Share your dreams, but don't equate them with God's Word, and don't make them the basis for your faith.

Next we read, "'Is not My word like fire?' declares the LORD, 'and like a hammer which shatters a rock?'" (verse 29). I wouldn't expect prophecies like "I love you, My children" or "I'm coming soon" if members of a congregation are living in sin (although such statements are true, and those who know Scripture should already know that). The Spirit of God is not going to lull His people into an unrighteous complacency. Remember, judgment begins in the household of God (1 Peter 4:17).

A prophetic message should motivate people to righteousness, not placate them in their sin. According to Paul, the gift of prophecy will disclose the secrets of a person's heart, causing him to fall on his face and worship God (1 Corinthians 14:24-25). God is more concerned about church purity than about church growth because church purity is an essential prerequisite for church growth. Comfort comes to those who are suffering and persecuted for righteousness's sake. Comfortable churches lead to colorless conformity to the zeitgeist (spirit of the age).

Jeremiah continued his exposure of false prophets: " 'Behold, I am against the prophets,' declares the LORD, 'who steal My words from each other' " (23:30). That's plagiarism—taking what God gave someone else and using it as if it were your own. " 'I am against the prophets,' declares the LORD, 'who use their tongues and declare, "*The Lord declares*" ' " (verse 31).

Declaring that your words are directly from the Lord when they aren't is deceiving, and an offense to God. Manipulating people by claiming a word from the Lord is spiritual abuse. Through the years, I have heard from a number of wives who were told by their husbands-to-be, "God revealed to me that we are supposed to get married." Any man who asked for my daughter's hand in marriage had to come with a humble request, not a mandate.

A lady said to me at a conference, "The Lord told me you are supposed to do such and such." As kindly as I could, I said, "No, I don't think He did." If God had wanted me to do something specific, why hadn't His Holy Spirit guided me as promised? Also, Scripture tells us "there is one God, and one mediator also between God and men, the man Christ Jesus" (1 Timothy 2:5). No Christian is ever called to function as a medium. A prophetic message would call me to get right with God so He could guide me.

Signs and Wonders: Who's Being Tested?

When a true prophet proclaims what will happen in the future, it always comes to pass. A false prophet is exposed when his prophecies don't come true. Moses instructed us not to believe the prophet whose prophecies fail (Deuteronomy 18:22). Deuteronomy 13:1-3 sounds another warning: "If a prophet or a dreamer of dreams arises among you and gives you a sign or a wonder, and the sign or the wonder comes true, concerning which he spoke to you, saying, 'Let us go after other gods (whom you have not known) and let us serve them,' you shall not listen to the words of that prophet or that dreamer of dreams; for the LORD your God is testing you to find out if you love the LORD your God with all your heart and with all your soul" (see also Matthew 24:4-11,23-25; Revelation 13:11-14).

Not every miraculous manifestation is from God. God can use signs and wonders to confirm the Word, but the Bible also warns that "false Christs and false prophets will arise, and will show signs and wonders, in order to lead astray, if possible, the elect" (Mark 13:22). Satan can also perform signs and wonders, and he does so to direct our worship away from God to himself. Deuteronomy 13:5-11 reveals the seriousness of attributing to God the activity of Satan. Persons who misled in this way were to be executed, even if they were relatives. Every use of the word "sign" or "wonder"—either together or separate in the context of Christ's second coming—is associated with a false prophet, false teacher, or false Messiah. God may perform signs and wonders today, but so does Satan.

Counterfeits in the Church

The apostle Peter devoted an entire chapter in one of his letters to warning about false prophets and teachers who operate *within* the church: "False prophets also arose among the people, just as there will be false teachers among you, who will secretly introduce destructive heresies, even denying the Master who bought them, bringing swift destruction upon themselves" (2 Peter 2:1). Notice how false teachers lure you into their deceptive teaching: "Many will follow their sensuality, and because of them the way of the truth will be maligned" (verse

2). The deceived "follow their sensuality" when they elevate appearance, performance, charm, and personality above the truth: *He's such a nice guy. She's a very charismatic person. He's a real dynamic speaker. She's so sweet and sounds so sincere.* But being physically attractive and having a charismatic personality are not the biblical criteria for validating a ministry or a teacher. The standards are *truth* and *righteousness*, and false teachers malign both.

Peter revealed two ways by which we can identify false prophets and teachers who operate within the church. First, they indulge "the flesh in its corrupt desires" (verse 10). Their immorality may not be easy to spot at first, but eventually it will surface (2 Corinthians 11:13-15). Their preaching will be lawless, overly emphasizing God's love and grace while ignoring the call to be holy "like the Holy One" (1 Peter 1:15).

Second, false prophets and teachers "despise authority" and are "daring, self-willed" (2 Peter 2:10). They have an independent spirit—they do their own thing and refuse to be accountable to anyone.

There are three Old Testament leadership roles that have functional equivalents in the church: prophet (preaching and teaching), priest (pastoring and shepherding), and king (administration). Only Jesus, in His perfection, is capable of fulfilling all three roles simultaneously. I believe we need the checks and balances of a plurality of elders in the church so that the three critical roles can be delegated to more than one person. As we all know, absolute authority corrupts absolutely. Committed Christians in leadership roles need to submit themselves and their ideas to other mature believers who will hold them accountable. If your pastor is not accountable to others or he doesn't display the heart of a shepherd and a servant, you need to go to another church.

BEWARE OF DECEIVING SPIRITS

John cautioned us to test the spirits so that we can unmask the many antichrists at work in this world (1 John 2:18) and distinguish the spirit of truth from the spirit of error (4:1-6). Satan's demonic forces are at work attempting to pollute our mind with lies in order to keep us from walking in the truth.

A lady attended one of my conferences because she was severely depressed. She had gone to see her pastor because she was plagued by thoughts that she was a lesbian, which was confusing to her because she was attracted to men. Rather than help her, the pastor said, "Oh, that is unfortunate." From the conference she learned that she was being deceived. She is no longer depressed and is one of our ministry associates.

I received an email from a man who wrote, "I love my girlfriend, but why am I having thoughts that I am gay?" We can find the answer in these words from Hannah Whitall Smith:

> There are the voices of evil and deceiving spirits, who lie in wait to entrap every traveler entering these higher regions of spiritual life. In the same epistle that tells us that we are seated in the heavenly places in Christ, we are also told that we shall have to fight with spiritual enemies. These spiritual enemies, whoever or whatever they may be, must necessarily communicate with us by means of our spiritual faculties, and their voices, as the voice of God, are an inward impression made upon our spirit. Therefore, just as the Holy Spirit may tell us by impressions what the will of God is concerning us, so also will these spiritual enemies tell us by impression what is their will concerning us, though not, of course, giving it their name.[18]

If you have any questions about the origin of certain mental impressions, the validity of spiritual gifts, or the credibility of those who speak for God, I encourage you to petition God as follows:

Prayer

Dear heavenly Father, I commit myself unreservedly to You. I desire to know and do Your will. I ask You to show me the true nature of this spirit, gift, or of this person claiming to be hearing from You. If I have been deceived in any way, I pray that

You will open my eyes to the deception. Lord, if these impressions or gifts are from You, or if this person is sent by You, I gladly receive the message that I may grow and be edified by it. In Jesus's name I pray. Amen.

Declaration

Now in the name of the Lord Jesus Christ and by His authority, I command all deceiving spirits to depart from me, and I renounce and reject all counterfeit gifts and all other spiritual manifestations that are not from God.

SPIRITUAL DISCERNMENT

Spiritual discernment is our God-given early warning system that lets us know something is wrong in the spiritual realm even though nothing appears wrong in the natural realm. The Holy Spirit indwells every believer, and He isn't passive when we encounter wrong spirits.

Motive plays a role in developing a discerning spirit. In 1 Kings 3, Israel's young King Solomon cried out to God for help. God came to Solomon in a dream and asked him what he wanted. Solomon responded, "Give Your servant an understanding heart to judge Your people to discern between good and evil" (verse 9). God answered, "Because you have asked this thing and have not asked for yourself long life, nor have asked riches for yourself, nor have you asked for the life of your enemies, but have asked for yourself discernment to understand justice, behold, I have done according to your words. Behold, I have given you a wise and discerning heart" (verses 11-12).

The motive for true discernment is never self-promotion, personal gain, or to secure an advantage over another person—even an enemy. The Greek word translated discernment—*diakrino*—means "to make a judgment or a distinction." Discernment has one function: to distinguish right from wrong. Paul mentioned various effects of the Holy Spirit, and one manifestation is the "distinguishing of spirits"

(1 Corinthians 12:10), which is the divinely enabled ability to distinguish a good spirit from a bad one.

The ability to discern increases as we grow in character and in the knowledge of God's Word. "Everyone who partakes only of milk is not accustomed to the word of righteousness, for he is an infant. But solid food is for the mature, who because of practice have their senses trained to discern good and evil" (Hebrews 5:13-14).

Spiritual discernment is not a function of the mind; it's a function of the spirit. We rightly divide the Word of truth with our minds, but the Spirit enables us to discern that which cannot be objectively verified. There will be times when you can *discern* that something is wrong, but not *know* what is wrong. In such cases, just share that you are sensing that something is wrong, and don't guess what it is. If you guess wrong, it will discredit your discernment. That would be like a parent saying, "What's wrong, Tommy? Have you been doing such and such again?" The discernment was probably right, but the guess will probably be wrong, and Tommy will be mad if he is wrongly accused. I have been in many board and committee meetings during which I or someone else sensed something was wrong. When that happened, we would stop and pray, asking God for wisdom as to how we should proceed.

Two missionary ladies came to me with a young woman who was asking for help. After hearing her story, I asked if she would like to resolve her problems, and she agreed to go through The Steps to Freedom in Christ. In the process of forgiving a number of people, I sensed that one attempt to forgive was illegitimate, and I said, "That is not her." As soon as I said that, we heard from the mouth of the young lady, "She will never forgive that person." We bound the spirit and were able to complete the Steps. Later, the missionaries asked, "How did you know that wasn't her?" The honest answer is I didn't know—I only sensed it. That was discernment in action.

Another manifestation of the Spirit is "the word of knowledge" (1 Corinthians 12:8). I believe that God has, at times, given me or others words of knowledge. For instance, while listening to a man who was telling me his story, I sensed that the real problem at hand was homosexuality. Rather than confront him, I tested the spirit. I waited for an appropriate moment, then asked, "Have you ever struggled with homosexual thoughts or tendencies?" If he had said no, then I would have known where that thought had come from, or that he was choosing not to disclose that fact to me. In this case, the man did acknowledge that he was struggling with homosexual thoughts and tendencies, and we were able to discuss the real issue and not dance around it.

There is also counterfeit discernment, which leads some to think they have a God-given ability or gift to see the sins in others. Lana, an undergraduate student, could point out the sins of other students. The best I could tell, she was right—but oddly, her own life was spiraling downward. She had been seeing a professional counselor for years before coming to see me. I asked her what that was like. She admitted to playing mental games with her counselor by telling him what he was going to do or say next. In response, I said, "You like having that power over people, don't you, Lana?" As soon as I said that, an evil spirit manifested itself in my office. When Lana found her freedom in Christ, she no longer had the ability to point out the sins of others. Her mind became so quiet that she had to learn to live without the noise from her "companions" who had cluttered her mind for years.

If we don't have an accurate diagnosis, we can't prescribe the right remedy. Deceived people don't understand what is going on in their minds, so how can they accurately explain it to others? Even if they could, attempts to help them would garner varying results depending on the encouragers' experience and education. To illustrate, the following testimony depicts one person's inner struggle. As you read her story, ask yourself these questions: Does she have a split personality? Is she psychotic? Does she have multiple personalities or an inner child from her past? Is she experiencing normal self-talk? Any one of those diagnoses could be made by secular counselors depending on their education or experience. She called her testimony—

Silence

When I sit and think, I think of many things—my life, what I want to do, what I think about various issues and people. I have conversations with myself inside my head. I talk to myself and answer myself...I am my own best friend. We get along great! Sometimes I talk to myself so much during the day that I am very tired by the end of the day. But I keep myself occupied, and the conversations help me to think things through.

Sometimes I think of myself as two people...The one who has a low self-esteem and is afraid to be herself in front of everyone. And then there's the one inside me...the confident me whom I wish would come out but for some reason won't. I call that part of me "her." She is a "she," and I refer to her as such. She is very bold, and everybody loves her—at least that's what I think would happen if I would just let her out. If I could just be myself, life would be so much easier and happier.

But until then, I talk to her inside of me. We talk about what we will do today, where we will go to eat, what we will wear, who we will talk to. Sometimes she comes up with very good ideas, and I am impressed with myself that I am so smart and clever. *If only people knew the real me,* I think, *they would really love me.* And sometimes I hear her say things to me that don't make sense. *I shouldn't do that,* I think. *That's not very nice. That would hurt someone. That is a stupid thing to do.* I don't listen to her those times. But I don't mind. I like talking to her, so I continue talking.

One day, things changed between us. My life was going okay, but I wanted a closer walk with God. I wanted to be free from the past and to be healed in my heart from the pain that I have been carrying. Someone told me I should go through something called The Steps to Freedom in Christ, and I made an appointment with a counselor. I

wasn't thinking about my friend inside me; I was thinking about myself.

In the counseling session, I was asked to read some prayers
and scriptures out loud. While I was doing this, my mind
became fuzzy and I couldn't concentrate. Most of all, when
I tried to speak to her in my mind, I became confused. I
couldn't hear her clearly. I became scared, my heart raced,
and I became enraged inside. I shook. Where was my
friend inside me? Why was she so mad all of a sudden?
What was going on? What was wrong with me?

Then I found out. She wasn't my friend. She wasn't really
me. She didn't want me to get right with God. It didn't
make sense, because these were things that I wanted to do.
I thought she was on my side. But I was wrong. I had to tell
her to leave…out loud. Out loud? It seemed weird when
I was told that she couldn't read my thoughts, but it made
sense…She wasn't God, and she wasn't omniscient. So I
told her, out loud, to leave…and she was gone.

Then there was silence. There were no more conversations
going on in my mind anymore. And I missed her. I knew
I shouldn't, but I did. I knew that she wasn't good for me
and that God wanted me to talk to Him and not her. I
struggled with the thought of not talking to her. I couldn't
stand the silence…I felt alone. She tried to come back, and
when she did, it scared me. She was angry and hostile. I felt
betrayed. But after a time, I got used to the silence. I used
it to remind me to talk to God, and I did. He didn't answer
like she did. I couldn't hear His voice like I could hers. But
I began to love talking to Him, singing to Him. I really felt
close to Him…like He cared. And after a while, I forgot
about the silence.

After some time, I found myself lonely again. I forgot about
the silence and found myself in conversation without even
realizing it. My life was in confusion, and I couldn't figure

out why, until one day I had to pray. My friend who had been discipling me wanted to help me, and I wanted help. She talked to me about my rebellion and how I needed to stop living independent of God. It was then that I heard a loud voice inside of me say, "I AM INDEPENDENT OF GOD." It scared me. Was that me? Did I really feel that way? No, I didn't…she was back. Then I got angry because I had let her back. I wanted her gone, but I couldn't move, and I couldn't say anything. My friend prayed with me, and I bowed my head. She told me to picture heaven with a light, the lampstands, and the throne of God. I started to "see" these and to feel calm again. But then the voice started yelling, "No! No! No!" So I opened my eyes and gave up. My heart became hard, and I didn't want to give everything to God. I still wanted control. There were some things that I did not want to give up.

But inside, I longed for the silence again. *How ironic,* I thought. *Something that I didn't like at first had become my freedom.* How I fought inside trying to struggle with praying to God or running away from Him! It is so easy to run, so easy to put off what I can do right now. But I didn't FEEL repentant. I didn't FEEL like letting go, even though I knew I needed to. I wondered if I would ever feel like it again.

And that is when I saw the words from The Steps to Freedom in Christ jump out at me from the page. They read, "Faith is something you decide to do, not something you feel like doing." So I did it.

And now I live in wonderful silence.

PART THREE

WALK FREE!

CHAPTER TWELVE

HELPING OTHERS

The shepherd of sheep has the flock following him wherever he leads; or if some turn aside from the direct path and leave the good pasture to graze in barren and precipitous places, it is enough for him to call more loudly, lead them back again and restore to the flock those that were separated. But if a man wanders away from the right path, the shepherd needs a lot of concentration, perseverance, and patience. He cannot drag by force or constrain by fear but must by persuasion lead him back to the true beginning from which he has fallen away. He needs, therefore, a heroic spirit, not to grow despondent or neglect the salvation of wanderers but to keep on thinking and saying, "God perhaps may give them the knowledge of the truth and they may be freed from the snare of the devil."

CHRYSOSTOM (AD 347–407)

God has provided all the spiritual protection we need, but when it comes to spiritual attacks, we have to assume our responsibility or suffer the consequences. We are told to put on the armor of God, stand firm, and resist. What will happen if we don't? We are told to "put on the Lord Jesus Christ, and make no provision for the flesh in regard to its lusts" (Romans 13:14). What if we do make provision for the flesh? We are told to "[take] every thought captive to the obedience of Christ" (2 Corinthians 10:5). What if we don't? It is our responsibility to not allow sin to reign in our mortal bodies by using our bodies as instruments of unrighteousness (Romans 6:12-13). What if we do? We are told to submit to God and resist the devil (James 4:7). What if we don't?

Can we assume a spiritually neutral position without any negative consequences? To believe that Satan won't take advantage of our indecision or indiscretion is scripturally wrong, and it creates a false hope for us. "For by what a man is overcome, by this he is enslaved" (2 Peter 2:19). To illustrate how enslaved one can become, read the following testimony I received after a Resolving Personal and Spiritual Conflicts conference:

> Dear Neil,
>
> I have been set free—praise the Lord! Yesterday, for the first time in years, the voices stopped. I could hear the silence. When we sang, I could hear myself sing.
>
> For the first 14 years of my life I lived with an oppressive, abusive mother who never said, "I love you" or put her arms around me when I cried. I received no affection, no kind words, no affirmation, no sense of who I was—only physical and emotional abuse. At 15, I was subjected to three weeks of Erhard Seminar Training (EST), which really screwed up my mind. The year that followed was pure hell. My mother threw me out, so I went to live with another family. Eventually they also threw me out.
>
> Three years later, I found Christ. My decision to trust Christ was largely based on my fear of Satan and the power of evil I had experienced in my life. Even though I knew Satan had lost his ownership of me, I was unaware of how vulnerable I still was to his deception and control. For the first two years of my Christian life I was in bondage to a sin. I didn't even know it was a sin. Once I realized my sin, confessed it to God, and received forgiveness, I thought I was finally free of Satan's attempts to control me. I didn't realize that the battle had only begun.

I suffered from unexplainable rashes, hives, and welts all over my body. I lost my joy and closeness to the Lord. I could no longer sing or quote Scripture. I turned to food as my comfort and security. The demons attacked my sense of right and wrong, and I became involved in immorality in my search for identity and love.

But that all ended yesterday when I renounced Satan's control in my life. I have found the freedom and protection that comes from knowing I am loved. I'm not on a high; I'm writing with a clear mind, a clean spirit, and a calm hand. Even my previous bondage to food suddenly seems foreign to me.

I never realized that a Christian could be so vulnerable to Satan's control. I was deceived, but now I am free. Thank You, thank You, Jesus!

Her testimony is a sobering example of a dimension of spiritual vulnerability that most Christians don't like to talk about: losing control. Yet every recovery ministry works with people who have lost control of their lives to food, sex, drugs, alcohol, and gambling. When we lose control, life becomes unmanageable. Christians generally agree that we are vulnerable to the enemy, but they hesitate to consider what would happen if we were to willfully surrender to demonic influences.

KINGDOMS IN CONFLICT

If a believer believes the devil's accusations, gives in to his temptations, and believes his lies, does that mean he or she is demon-possessed? No, but that person is likely defeated, stagnant in terms of spiritual growth, and enslaved to sin. The term "demon-possessed" in Matthew 4:24 (NIV); 9:32; 15:22; and Mark 5:15 is translated from one Greek word—*daimonizomai* (verb) or *daimonizomenos* (participle). It would have been more helpful if translators had transliterated the word as "demonized," meaning to be under the influence of one or more demons. The term never occurs in the epistles, so we have no way of knowing precisely how it would apply in the church age. The problem word is "possession," which doesn't occur in the original Greek text. Possession often implies ownership. In that sense, Christians are Holy Spirit–possessed. We have been bought and purchased by the blood of the Lamb. We belong to God. We are temples of God, indwelt by the Holy Spirit, who will never leave us nor forsake us. The translators were probably thinking of another aspect of possession, such as, "Whatever possessed you to do that?" In other words, "What has overcome or influenced you to do that?"

A related Greek phrase that appears in the Gospels is *echein daimonion*, which means "to have a demon." The Jewish religious leaders used this phrase when they accused both John the Baptist and Jesus of having a demon (Luke 7:33; John 7:20). They wrongly assumed that a demon was giving them supernatural knowledge and power, which enabled them to know what the religious leaders were thinking and to work miracles.

Given the fact that, as believers, our bodies are temples belonging to God, can an evil spirit coexist with the Holy Spirit in us? Satan is the God of this world, and the Holy Spirit is omnipresent. The kingdom of darkness and the kingdom of God's beloved Son are coexisting and in conflict all around us. Spatial arguments don't apply to the spiritual realm. There are no natural barriers or physical boundaries for spirits, including our skin. The sole purpose of armor is to stop penetration. If a person is paying attention to a deceiving spirit, the influence is not limited to the external part of his life. Every testimony in this book was written by professing Christians who were struggling to win the battle for their minds. You are serving the enemy when you give fellow believers a false hope of immunity. Give them real hope by telling them that when they repent and believe the truth, they will be alive and free in Christ.

A struggling Christian is like a house filled to overflowing with garbage that hasn't been taken out in months. That is going to attract a lot of flies. The knee-jerk response is to get rid of those pesky little creatures, but the right answer is to get rid of the garbage. Repentance and faith in God has been and always will be the right answer throughout this church age.

I am aware that some deliverance ministries study the flight patterns of the flies, call up the demons, ask them their names and ranks, then cast them out. That was what I heard from others, so that was what I tried to do at first. But it doesn't make sense to gather information from demons. We should never believe deceiving spirits. The moment we dialogue with them, the person we are trying to help is being totally bypassed. The person won't recall anything that happened during the session, and no human agent can take another person's garbage out. If I managed to expel a demon, it would likely go find seven others and tell them where the garbage is.

There are no instructions in the epistles for that methodology, and I believe Paul taught a different approach. The deliverer is Christ, and He has already come. We should be getting our information from the Holy Spirit, who will guide us into all truth, and that is the truth that will set us free. That perspective is taught in 2 Timothy 2:24-26:

> The Lord's bond-servant must not be quarrelsome, but be kind to all, able to teach, patient when wronged, with gentleness correcting those who are in opposition, if perhaps God may grant them repentance leading to the knowledge of the truth, and they may come to their senses and escape from the snare of the devil, having been held captive by him to do his will.

The first prerequisite is to be the Lord's bond-servant. We need to be totally dependent upon God because He is the only One who can set a captive free and heal the wounds of the brokenhearted. What sets Christian ministry apart from secular work is the presence of God. And as is evident in the passage we just read, we have to understand what God's role is, and what our role is. I believe there is a precise line between God's sovereignty and human responsibility. The line will appear a little blurred to us, and the Calvinists and the Arminians will adjust the line to the left or the right. However, both theological perspectives acknowledge that Scripture teaches God's sovereignty and human responsibility. On the left side of the line is what God, and only God, can do. We can be creative, but we can't speak and bring something into existence out of nothing. We can't even save ourselves or others. God created the universe, and He accomplishes His purposes by working through His created order. The providence of God refers to His direction and care over all creation. God "upholds all things by the word of His power" (Hebrews 1:3). He is the ultimate reality, and if He disappeared, so would all creation. We fulfill our purpose when we live in harmony with Him. We do that by knowing Him and His ways and living accordingly by faith.

God's Sovereignty | Human Responsibility

Everything on the right side of the line depicts human responsibility. We are either ignorant or irresponsible when we ask God to do for us what He told us to do. If you have a Bible quiz tomorrow, you can't ask God to study for it on your behalf. You have to do that yourself in order to present yourself approved to God as a workman who does not need to be ashamed (2 Timothy 2:15). Don't ask God to think for you, because He told you "to think so as to have sound judgment" (Romans 12:3). We have to assume responsibility for our own attitudes and actions. Suppose there is a problem person in your church and some well-meaning Christians ask God to remove him from your fellowship, and nothing happens. *Why not, God? Don't You love Your church?* Of course He loves His church, but He told us to go to such a person in private for the purpose of restoration. And if he doesn't repent, then we are to bring two more witnesses to confront the person (Matthew 18:15-20). The person should be removed from fellowship if there is no repentance. Will God bail us out if we don't carry out our responsibility? I have not seen that happen.

Suppose a person is frightened by some spiritual manifestation in their room and cries out, "God, do something," and nothing happens. So the person hides under the covers and wonders, *Why not, God? You are all-powerful. Why won't You help me? Don't You love me? Maybe I'm not a Christian, and that is why God hasn't answered.* That is the mental and emotional state of most people I have worked with. They question God's presence, question His love for them, and question their salvation. *Why didn't God do something?* He did. He disarmed the devil, forgave our sins, made us new creations in Christ, and positioned us with Christ in the heavenlies at the Father's right hand. Whose responsibility is it to submit to God and resist the devil? Whose responsibility is it to put on the armor of God, take every thought captive to the obedience of Christ, stand firm in the faith, and make no provision for the flesh in regard to its lusts? Can we assume that there will be no negative consequences if we don't carry out our responsibility? Will God bail us out if we don't? I have not seen that happen.

WHO IS RESPONSIBLE FOR WHAT?

When I am asked to help another individual, I do so with the awareness that God is always present and there is a role that God and only God can play in the other person's life. On the right side of the line in the above diagram there is another role relationship that exists, and that is between the encourager and the inquirer, or the discipler and the disciple. Imagine a triangle with God at the top, as follows:

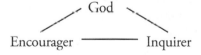

Each side of the triangle represents a relationship. The most important one is my own relationship with God. I need to make sure that the barriers to an intimate relationship with God have been removed through my own repentance from sin and belief in Him. It is also very important how I relate to the inquirer. Secular counselors focus all their attention on that relationship because their own relationship with God and their client's relationship with God are never even considered. Most counselors are taught not to be a rescuer, an enabler, or a codependent. They are also taught how to show empathy and be genuine, but they have left God out of the picture.

The third side of the triangle is the relationship that the inquirer has or doesn't have with God. Our goal is to help the inquirer have an intimate personal relationship with their heavenly Father through genuine repentance and faith in Him. God has given us "the ministry of reconciliation" (2 Corinthians 5:18). The whole world is in the kingdom of darkness because of the fall, and God's plans are as follows: to "destroy the works of the devil" (1 John 3:8), and to present every believer "complete in Christ" (Colossians 1:28).

With the triangle in mind, ask yourself, "Who is responsible for what?" A lot of problems in our homes, marriages, and ministries would disappear if we had a balanced answer to that question. Have you ever tried to play the role of the Holy Spirit in the life of your spouse? Your staff? An inquirer? How did that work for you? There is a sovereign role that God and only God can play in the life of another, and we will foul up the process if we usurp His role. Have you ever tried to assume other people's responsibilities? They won't think or make decisions for themselves, so you do their thinking and deciding for them. Doing that makes them dependent upon you instead of God.

Jesus said, "The time is fulfilled, and the kingdom of God is at hand; repent and believe in the gospel" (Mark 1:15). The big question is this: Do we really believe that repentance and faith in God are the means by which we resolve personal and spiritual conflicts? The answer is *no* if we usurp each other's roles and fail to include God in the process. The answer is *yes* if we acknowledge God's role and assume responsibility for ours.

When I have the opportunity to help another, I do so with the realization that there are three parties present: God, myself, and the inquirer. The first thing I do is make sure that I am in a right relationship with God. Then I pray, "Lord, I come before Your presence with thanksgiving. I declare my dependence upon You because I believe that apart from Christ, I can accomplish nothing. Please fill me with Your Holy Spirit, and guide me into all truth." In addition, I strive to make sure I am always kind, gentle, and patient.

To help inquirers assume their responsibility and to ensure lasting results, I ask them to read either this book or *Victory Over the Darkness.* There won't be much success if they are not willing to assume some responsibility for their own freedom and growth. That responsibility also enables them to maintain their freedom afterward. However, some people are in such serious bondage that they can't read the book or the Bible. In such cases, I lead them through the Steps and set aside enough time to instruct them about who they are in Christ, the nature of the battle for their mind, and how they can continue on in their growth in Christ.

After hearing an inquirer's story, I always ask if he or she would like to resolve their issues. No one has ever said no. Then I say,

> With your permission, I will lead you through The Steps to Freedom in Christ. What is going to happen here today is not based on what I do, but what you do. I need one major cooperation from you. If you have any thoughts contrary to what we are trying to do, share them with me. These thoughts could be condemning, threatening, intimidating, vulgar, or blasphemous. They are just thoughts, and they have no control over you unless you believe them. The best way to maintain control is to expose them to the light. You may not sense any spiritual opposition, but I want you to be prepared in case we experience some interference with what we are doing.

It is important to pay close attention to the inquirer. If you see her eyes starting to cloud over or look around the room, get her attention immediately. Even in the most difficult cases you don't have to lose control.

Some people have been conditioned to have a thought and then carry it out. It may seem to them that they have no control, but in reality, they do. Some have told me that they never even considered the possibility that they didn't have to obey the thought. I tell them, "If a thought comes to your mind telling you to do something, don't do it. Just share it." The power is broken the moment the thought is brought into the light. Whatever they share, I say, "Thank you for sharing that." Then I continue onward with the Steps. In extreme cases, some inquirers could go catatonic. If that happens, say out loud, "Satan, you have no authority here. You can open your eyes now," and the inquirer will. Some are so uncertain about their ability to exert their will that I have taken them for a walk just to show them that they have a will and can exercise it. Others will feel nauseous, and when they share that, I say, "Thank you for sharing that. The nauseous feeling will be gone when we are done." That has been true in every case I've handled.

In Romania, I was asked by a missionary to help a man addicted to pornography. I was working through an interpreter, which always makes the process more difficult. When we started going through the Steps, the man's eyes rolled upward and he started making a strange noise with his lips. The oppression in the room was heavy. I let the man go on for half a minute or so, then said, "You don't have to do that, but you can if you want to." He stopped.

A pastor asked if I would help him with a lady who had been using drugs for 20 years. I listened as she shared her story, and it appeared that her legs were cramping because she kept massaging them. One could easily be fooled into thinking that was a symptom of withdrawing from drugs. As soon as we started, she said, "I have to get out of here," and she left. The pastor asked, "Now what?" I said, "She is probably right outside the door. Go ask her if she wants to come back." She did, and I reminded her that she was supposed to share with us any thoughts that arose in her mind.

When we finished the Steps, the voices were gone and the cramping stopped. Now, it is very important to understand that going through the Steps is just a beginning, and not the end. This woman was 40 years old but had the maturity of a teenager. When people turn to medications to ease their pain, stress, anxiety, and fears, their emotional development is often stymied.

If you want to help others experience their freedom in Christ, you can learn how through my book *Discipleship Counseling* (Bethany House Publishers). I am often asked if people still need counseling after they go through The Steps to Freedom in Christ. That question probably wouldn't have been asked 50 years ago. Back then, "Do they need to be discipled?" would have been the more logical question. But over the last few decades, the massive growth of professional counseling has almost replaced the ministry of discipleship. Many Christians today—and Christian educational institutions—view discipleship and counseling as two different entities. But I believe they are the same ministry. A good Christian discipler is a good counselor, and vice versa.

I also have written two books that help marriage partners and ministries resolve personal and spiritual conflicts through genuine repentance and faith in God. If your church is full of people in bondage to sin or there are many bad marriages, you have a "church bondage" situation. The whole can't be greater than the sum of its parts. Trying to help a marriage work when both parties have unresolved conflicts is like trying to help two people on crutches learn how to dance. Even if both spouses have resolved their own problems, they will still have couple-related issues they need to work through, and I explain how to do that in *Setting Your Marriage Free* (Bethany House Publishers).

I have had the privilege of leading the top faculty and administrators in a seminary, the executives of two well-known global ministries, and many churches through The Steps to Setting Your Ministry Free. Every Christian organization has corporate conflicts that can be resolved through repentance, which I explain in *Setting Your Church Free* (Bethany House Publishers). In all cases, I am not the Wonderful Counselor or the church consultant—Jesus is. All seven letters to the churches in Revelation chapters 2 and 3 end with the same statement: "He who has an ear, let him hear what the Spirit says to the churches." The question is, are we listening?

I close with this encouraging letter from an interim pastor:

I purchased a set of Neil's CDs on Resolving Personal and Spiritual Conflicts. After listening to them, I began applying his principles to my problems. I realized that some of my problems could be spiritual attacks, and I learned how to take a stand and won victories over some of my problems in my life.

But that was only a tip of the iceberg. I'm a deacon and preacher in a Baptist church. My pastor was suffering from depression and other problems that I was not aware of, and he committed suicide. This literally brought our church to its knees. I knew of some of the problems of the previous pastors and felt the issues were spiritual in nature, but I didn't know how to relay that to the people, because supposedly the devil or a demon cannot affect a Christian, right?

The church elected me as their interim pastor. While in a local bookstore, I saw your book *Setting Your Church Free.* I purchased and read it. I felt that with all the spiritual suppression taking place in our church, this was the answer. There was only one problem: How to get others in the church to see this as well. After a few weeks of preaching on spiritual issues, I knew we had to follow the instructions in your book *Setting Your Church Free.* The previous pastor, who had killed himself, would not have believed your material; he would never have read or listened to your message.

Slowly, very slowly, the people listened to my messages and I was able to contact one of your staff. He flew to Houston and led the leaders of our church through The Steps to Setting Your Church Free. The leaders loved it. I felt step one was now behind us. Next, I wanted to take all the people through The Steps to Freedom in Christ. Six weeks later, I was able to do so. I don't understand exactly what all happened, but we were set free from the spiritual bondage of multiple problems. I can't put it all in a letter, or I would write a book.

During all of this, one of our middle-aged members, who was an evangelist, was set free. He learned who he was in Christ and is now back in ministry—praise the Lord! I saw the daughters of the deceased pastor set free and able to forgive their father, and they were able to move on with their lives. At one point, one of the daughters was contemplating suicide.

This is a new church; God is free to work here! In September, we founded our pulpit committee. Our church voted 100 percent for our new pastor. This has never happened in our church before, and this is an independent and fundamental Baptist church. Well, when you do things God's way, you get God's results.

I also work one night a week in our county jail, which is the second largest in the country. I work with the homosexual men, and I have seen many set free.

THE STEPS TO FREEDOM IN CHRIST

God created Adam and Eve in His image and in His likeness. They were physically and spiritually alive, and the latter means that their souls were in union with God. Living in a dependent relationship with their heavenly Father, they were to rule over the birds of the sky, the beasts of the field, and the fish of the sea. They were accepted, secure, and significant. Acting independently of God, they chose to disobey Him, and their choice to sin separated them from God. They immediately felt fearful, anxious, depressed, and insecure. Because Eve was deceived by Satan and because Adam sinned, all their descendants are born physically alive but spiritually dead (Ephesians 2:1). Since all have sinned (Romans 3:23), those who remain separated from God will struggle with personal and spiritual conflicts. Satan became the rebel holder of authority and the god of this world. Jesus referred to him as the ruler of this world, and the apostle John wrote that the whole world lies in the power of the evil one (1 John 5:19).

Jesus came to undo the works of Satan (1 John 3:8) and take upon Himself the sins of the world. By dying for our sins, Jesus removed the barrier that existed between God and those He created in His image. The resurrection of Christ brought new life to those who put their trust in Him. Every born-again believer's soul is again in union with God, and that is most often communicated in the New Testament by the phrases "in Christ" and "in Him." The apostle Paul explained that anyone who is in Christ is a new creation (2 Corinthians 5:17). The apostle John wrote, "As many as received Him, to them He gave the right to become children of God, even to those who believe in His name" (John 1:12). He also wrote, "See how great a love the Father has bestowed on us, that we would be called children of God; and such we are" (1 John 3:1). No amount of effort on your part can save you, and neither can any religious activity—no matter how well intentioned. We are saved by faith—that is, by what we choose to believe. All that remains for us to do is put our trust in the finished work of Christ. "By grace you have been saved through faith; and that not of yourselves, it is a gift of God; not as a result of works, so that no one may boast" (Ephesians 2:8-9). If you have never received Christ, you can do so right now. God knows the thoughts and intentions of your heart, so all you have to do is put your trust in Him alone. You can express your decision in prayer as follows:

Dear heavenly Father, thank You for sending Jesus to die on the cross for my sins. I acknowledge that I have sinned and that I cannot save myself. I believe that Jesus came to give me life, and by faith I now choose to receive You as my Lord and Savior. May the power of Your indwelling presence enable me to be the person You created me to be. I pray that You would grant me repentance leading to a knowledge of the truth so that I can experience my freedom in Christ and be transformed by the renewing of my mind. In Jesus's precious name I pray. Amen.

ASSURANCE OF SALVATION

Paul wrote, "If you confess with your mouth Jesus as Lord, and believe in your heart that God raised Him from the dead, you will be saved" (Romans 10:9). Do you believe that God the Father raised Jesus from the dead? Did you invite Jesus to be your Lord and Savior? Then you are a child of God, and nothing can separate you from the love of Christ (Romans 8:35-39). "The testimony is this, that God has given us eternal life, and this life is in His Son. He who has the Son has the life; he who does not have the Son of God does not have the life" (1 John 5:11-12).Your heavenly Father has sent His Holy Spirit to bear witness with your spirit that you are a child of God (Romans 8:16). "You were sealed *in Him* with the Holy Spirit of promise" (Ephesians 1:13). The Holy Spirit will guide you into all truth (John 16:13).

RESOLVING PERSONAL AND SPIRITUAL CONFLICTS

Because we are all born dead (spiritually) in our trespasses and sins (Ephesians 2:1), we had neither the presence of God in our lives nor the knowledge of His ways. Consequently, we all learned to live independently of God. When we became new creations in Christ, our minds were not instantly renewed. That is why Paul wrote, "Do not conform to the pattern of this world, but be transformed by the renewing of your mind. Then you will be able to test and approve what God's will is—his good, pleasing, and perfect will" (Romans 12:2 NIV). That is why new Christians struggle with many of the same old thoughts and habits. Their minds have long been programmed to live independently of God, and that is the chief characteristic of our flesh. As new creations in Christ, we now have the mind of Christ, and the Holy Spirit will lead us into all truth.

To experience your freedom in Christ and grow in the grace of God requires repentance, which literally means "a change of mind." God will enable that process as you submit to Him and resist the devil (James 4:7). The Steps to Freedom in Christ are designed to help you do that. Submitting to God is the critical issue. He is the Wonderful Counselor and the One who grants repentance leading to a knowledge of the truth (2 Timothy 2:24-26). The Steps cover seven critical issues that affect your relationship with God. You will not experience your freedom in Christ if you seek false guidance, believe lies, fail to forgive others as you have been forgiven, live in rebellion, respond in pride, fail to acknowledge your sin, and continue in the sins of your ancestors. "He who conceals his transgressions will not prosper, but he who confesses and forsakes [renounces] them will find compassion" (Proverbs 28:13). "Therefore, since we have this ministry, as we received mercy, we do not lose heart, but we have renounced the things hidden because of shame, not walking in craftiness or adulterating the word of God, but by the manifestation of truth" (2 Corinthians 4:1-2).

Even though Satan is defeated, he still rules this world through a hierarchy of demons who tempt, accuse, and deceive those who fail to put on the armor of God, stand firm in their faith, and take every thought captive to the obedience of Christ. Our sanctuary is our identity and position in Christ, and we have all the protection we need to live a victorious life. But if we fail to assume our responsibility and give ground to Satan, we will suffer the consequences of our sinful attitudes and actions. The good news is that we can repent and reclaim all that we have in Christ, and that is what the Steps will enable you to do.

PROCESSING THE STEPS

The best way to go through the Steps is to process them with a trained encourager. The book *Discipleship Counseling* explains the theology and process. However, you can also go through the Steps on your own. Every step is explained so you will have no trouble doing that. If you are part of a group study, the leader will introduce each step after the discussion questions and ask you to pray the beginning prayer out loud. The rest you will process on your own.

If you experience some mental interference, just ignore it and continue on. Thoughts such as *This isn't going to work*, or *I don't believe this*—or blasphemous, condemning, and accusing thoughts—have no power over you unless you believe them. They are just thoughts, and it doesn't make any difference whether they originate from yourself, an external source, or from Satan and his demons.

Such thoughts have no power over you unless you believe them. They will be resolved when you have fully repented. The mind is the control center of your life, and you will not lose control if you don't lose control of your mind. The best way to do that, if you are being mentally harassed, is to share it. Exposing the lies to the light breaks the power.

The apostle Paul wrote that "Satan disguises himself as an angel of light" (2 Corinthians 11:14). It is not uncommon for some people to have thoughts or hear voices that claim to be friendly, offer companionship, or say they are from God. They may even say that Jesus is Lord, but they cannot say that Jesus is their Lord. If there is any doubt about their origin, verbally ask God to show you the true nature of such spirit guides. You don't want any spirit other than the Holy Spirit to guide you.

Remember, you are a child of God and seated with Christ in the heavenlies (the spiritual realm). That means you have the authority and power to do His will. The Steps don't set you free. Jesus sets you free, and you will progressively experience that freedom as you respond to Him in faith and repentance. Don't worry about any demonic interference; most people do not experience any. It doesn't make any difference whether Satan has a little role or a bigger role; the critical issue is your relationship with God, and that is what you are to focus on. This is a ministry of reconciliation. Once any issues are resolved, Satan has no right to remain.

Successfully completing this repentance process is not an end; it is the beginning of growth. Unless any sin issues are resolved, however, the growth process will be stalled, and your Christian life will remain stagnant.

BREAKING MENTAL STRONGHOLDS

On a separate piece of paper, write down any false beliefs and lies that surface as you go through the Steps, especially those that are not true about yourself and God. When you are finished, verbally say the following for each exposed falsehood: "I renounce the lie that [what you have believed], and I announce the truth that [what you are now choosing to believe is true based on God's Word]." It may be best to have the encourager keep this list for you if you are being led by another through the Steps. It is strongly recommended that you repeat the process of renouncing lies and choosing truth for 40 days, because we are transformed by the ongoing renewal of our minds (Romans 12:2), and it is very easy to defer back to old flesh patterns when tempted.

PREPARATION

Processing these Steps will play a major role in your journey of becoming more and more like Jesus so that you can be a fruitful disciple. The purpose is to become firmly rooted in Christ. It doesn't take long to establish your identity and freedom in Christ, but there is no such thing as instant maturity. Renewing your mind and conforming to the image of God is a lifelong process. May God grace you with His presence as you seek to do His will. Once you have experienced your freedom in Christ, you can then help others experience the joy of their salvation. You are now ready to begin the Steps by saying the prayer and declaration below.

Prayer

Dear heavenly Father, You are present in this room and in my life. You alone are all-knowing, all-powerful, and everywhere present, and I worship You alone. I declare my dependency upon You, for apart from You I can do nothing. I choose to believe Your Word, which teaches that all authority in heaven and on earth belongs to the resurrected Christ, and being alive in Christ I have the authority to resist the devil as I submit to You. I ask that You fill me with Your Holy Spirit and guide me into all truth. I ask for Your complete protection and guidance as I seek to know You and do Your will. In the wonderful name of Jesus I pray. Amen.

Declaration

In the name and authority of the Lord Jesus Christ, I command Satan and all evil spirits to release their hold on me in order that I can be free to know and choose to do the will of God. As a child of God who is seated with Christ in the heavenly places, I declare that every enemy of the Lord Jesus Christ that is in my presence be bound. God has not given me a spirit of fear; therefore, I reject any and all condemning, accusing, blasphemous, and deceiving spirits of fear. Satan and his demons cannot inflict any pain or in any way prevent God's will from being done in my life today because I belong to the Lord Jesus Christ.

STEP ONE
Counterfeit Versus Real

The first step toward experiencing your freedom in Christ is to renounce (verbally reject) all involvement (past or present) with occultic, cultic, or false religious teachings or practices. Participation in any group that denies that Jesus Christ is Lord or elevates any teaching or book to the level of—or above—the Bible must be renounced. In addition, groups that require dark and secret initiations, ceremonies, vows, pacts, or covenants need to be renounced. God does not take false guidance lightly. "As for the person who turns to mediums and to spiritists...I will also set My face against that person and will cut him off from among his people" (Leviticus 20:6). Ask God to guide you as follows:

> *Dear heavenly Father, please bring to my mind anything and everything that I have done knowingly or unknowingly that involves occultic, cultic, or false religious teachings and practices. Grant me the wisdom and grace to renounce any and all spiritual counterfeits, false religious teachings and practices. In Jesus's name I pray. Amen.*

The Lord may bring events to your mind that you have forgotten, even experiences you participated in as a game or as part of a joke. The purpose is to renounce all the counterfeit spiritual experiences and beliefs that God brings to your mind. Begin this Step by processing the following ten questions:

1. Do you now have, or have you ever had, an imaginary friend, spirit guide, or "angel" offering you guidance or companionship? If it has a name, renounce it by name. **I renounce...**

2. Have you ever seen or been contacted by beings you thought were aliens from another world? Such deceptions should be identified and renounced. **I renounce...**

3. Have you ever heard voices in your head or had repeating, nagging thoughts such as *I'm dumb, I'm ugly, Nobody loves me, I can't do anything right*—as if there were a conversation going on inside your head? If so, renounce all deceiving spirits and the lies that you have believed. **I renounce…**

4. Have you ever been hypnotized, attended a New Age seminar, consulted a psychic, medium/channeler, or spiritist? Renounce all the specific false prophecies and guidance they offered. **I renounce…**

5. Have you ever made a secret covenant or vow to any organization or persons other than God, or made an inner vow contrary to Scripture, such as "I will never…"? Renounce all such vows. **I renounce…**

6. Have you ever been involved in a satanic ritual or attended a concert in which Satan was the focus? Renounce Satan and all his works and ways. **I renounce…**

7. Have you ever made any sacrifices to idols, false gods, or spirits? Renounce each one. **I renounce…**

8. Have you ever attended a counterfeit religious event or entered a non-Christian shrine that required you to participate in their religious observances, such as washing your hands or removing your shoes? Confess your participation and renounce your involvement in false worship. **I confess and renounce…**

9. Have you ever consulted a shaman or witch doctor for the purpose of manipulating the spiritual world to place curses, or seek psychic healing or guidance? All such activity needs to be renounced. **I renounce…**

10. Have you ever tried to contact the dead in order to send or receive messages? Renounce such practices. **I renounce…**

Continue this Step using the following Non-Christian Spiritual

Experience Inventory as a guide. Then pray the prayer following the checklist to renounce each activity or group the Lord brings to mind. He may reveal to you counterfeit spiritual experiences that are not on the list. Be especially aware of your need to renounce non-Christian religious practices that were part of your culture growing up. Prayerfully renounce them *out loud* if you are working through these Steps on your own.

Non-Christian Spiritual Experience Inventory

Check all those that you have participated in:

- ☐ Out-of-body experiences
- ☐ Ouija board
- ☐ Bloody Mary
- ☐ Charlie Charlie
- ☐ Occult games such as Light as a Feather
- ☐ Magic 8-Ball
- ☐ Table or body lifting
- ☐ Spells and curses
- ☐ Mental telepathy/ mind control
- ☐ Tarot cards
- ☐ Automatic writing
- ☐ Astrology/horoscopes
- ☐ Palm reading
- ☐ Fortune telling/ divination
- ☐ Blood pacts
- ☐ Sexual spirits
- ☐ Séances and circles

- ☐ Wicca
- ☐ Black and white magic/The Gathering
- ☐ Paganism
- ☐ Reiki
- ☐ Channeling/Chakras
- ☐ Reincarnation/previous life healing
- ☐ Mediums and channelers
- ☐ Mormonism
- ☐ Freemasonry
- ☐ Christian Science
- ☐ Church of Scientology
- ☐ Nature worship (Mother Earth)
- ☐ Unitarianism/ universalism
- ☐ Hinduism/ Transcendental Meditation
- ☐ Silva Mind Control
- ☐ Buddhism (including Zen)
- ☐ Islam

☐ Trances

☐ Spirit guides

☐ Clairvoyance

☐ Rod and pendulum
  (dowsing)

☐ Hypnosis

☐ Satanism

☐ Witchcraft/sorcery

☐ Bahaism

☐ Spiritism/animism/
  folk religions

☐ Ancestor worship

☐ Jehovah's Witnesses

Once you have finished reviewing the checklist, confess and renounce every false religious practice, belief, ceremony, vow, or pact that you were involved in by praying the following prayer out loud. Take your time and be thorough. Give God time to remind you of every specific incident, ritual, etc. as needed:

> *Dear heavenly Father, I confess that I have participated in [specifically name every belief and involvement with all that you have checked above], and I renounce them all as counterfeits. I pray that You will fill me with Your Holy Spirit so that I may be guided by You. Thank You that in Christ, I am forgiven. Amen.*

STEP TWO

Deception Versus Truth

The Christian life is lived by faith according to what God says is true. Jesus is the truth, the Holy Spirit is the Spirit of truth, God's Word is truth, and we are to speak the truth in love (see John 14:6; 16:13; 17:17; Ephesians 4:15). The biblical response to truth is faith regardless of whether we feel it is true or not. Christians are to forsake all lying, deceiving, stretching the truth, and anything else associated with false-hood. Believing lies will keep us in bondage. Choosing to believe the truth is what sets us free (John 8:32). David wrote, "How blessed [happy] is the man…in whose spirit there is no deceit!" (Psalm 32:2). The liberated Christian is free to walk in the light and speak the truth in love. We can be honest and transparent before God because we are already forgiven, and God already knows the thoughts and intentions of our hearts (Hebrews 4:12-13).

So why not be honest and confess our sins? Confession means to agree with God. People in bondage eventually get tired of living a lie. Because of God's great love and forgiveness, we can walk in the light and fellowship with God and others (see 1 John 1:7-9). Begin this commitment to truth by praying the following prayer out loud. Don't let any opposing thoughts, such as *This is a waste of time,* or *I wish I could believe this but I can't,* keep you from pressing forward. God will strengthen you as you rely on Him.

> *Dear heavenly Father, You are the truth, and I desire to live by faith according to Your truth. The truth will set me free, but in many ways I have been deceived by the father of lies, the philosophies of this fallen world, and even by myself. I choose to walk in the light, knowing that You love and accept me just as I am. As I consider areas of possible deception, I invite the Spirit of truth to guide me into all truth. Please protect me from all deception as You "search me, O God, and know my heart; try me and know my anxious thoughts; and see if there*

be any hurtful way in me, and lead me in the everlasting way"
(Psalm 139:23-24). In the name of Jesus I pray. Amen.

Prayerfully consider the lists in the three exercises over the next few pages, using the prayers at the end of each exercise in order to confess any ways you have given in to deception or wrongly defended yourself. It's not possible to instantly renew your mind, but the process of renewal will never get started unless you acknowledge your mental strongholds or defense mechanisms, also known as flesh patterns.

WAYS YOU CAN BE DECEIVED BY THE WORLD

☐ Believing that having an abundance of money and possessions will make me happy (Matthew 13:22; 1 Timothy 6:10)

☐ Believing that eating food, drinking alcohol, or using drugs can relieve my stress and make me happy (Proverbs 23:19,21)

☐ Believing that an attractive body, personality, or image will meet my needs for acceptance and significance (Proverbs 31:10; 1 Peter 3:3-4)

☐ Believing that gratifying sexual lust will bring lasting satisfaction without any negative consequences (Ephesians 4:22; 1 Peter 2:11)

☐ Believing that I can sin and suffer no negative consequences (Hebrews 3:12-13)

☐ Believing that I need more than Jesus to meet my needs of acceptance, security, and significance (2 Corinthians 11:2-4,13-15)

☐ Believing that I can do whatever I want regardless of others and still be free (Proverbs 16:18; Obadiah 3; 1 Peter 5:5)

☐ Believing that people who refuse to receive Jesus will go to heaven anyway (1 Corinthians 6:9-11)

☐ Believing that I can associate with bad company and not become corrupted (1 Corinthians 15:33-34)

☐ Believing that I can read, see, or listen to anything I want and not be corrupted (Proverbs 4:23-27; Matthew 5:28)

☐ Believing that there are no earthly consequences for my sin (Galatians 6:7-8)

☐ Believing that I must gain the approval of certain people in order to be happy (Galatians 1:10)

☐ Believing that I must measure up to certain religious standards in order for God to accept me (Galatians 3:2-3; 5:1)

☐ Believing that there are many paths to God, and Jesus is only one of the many ways (John 14:6)

☐ Believing that I must live up to worldly standards in order to feel good about myself (1 Peter 2:1-12)

Dear heavenly Father, I confess that I have been deceived by [confess the items you checked above]. I thank You for Your forgiveness, and I choose to believe Your Word and believe in Jesus, who is the Truth. In Jesus's name I pray. Amen.

WAYS TO DECEIVE YOURSELF

☐ Hearing God's Word but not doing what it says (James 1:22)

☐ Saying I have no sin (1 John 1:8)

☐ Thinking I am something or someone when I'm not (Galatians 6:3)

☐ Thinking I am wise in this worldly age (1 Corinthians 3:18-19)

☐ Thinking I can be truly religious yet not control what I say (James 1:26)

☐ Thinking that God is the source of my problems (Lamentations 3)

☐ Thinking I can live successfully without anyone else's help (1 Corinthians 12:14-20)

Dear heavenly Father, I confess that I have deceived myself by [confess the items checked above]. Thank You for Your forgiveness. I commit myself to believing only Your truth. In Jesus's name I pray. Amen.

WAYS TO WRONGLY DEFEND YOURSELF

☐ Denial of reality (conscious or unconscious)

☐ Fantasy (escaping reality through daydreaming, TV, movies, music, computer or video games, drugs, alcohol)

☐ Emotional insulation (withdrawing from people or keeping people at a distance to avoid rejection)

☐ Regression (reverting back to less-threatening times)

☐ Displaced anger (taking out frustrations on innocent people)

☐ Projection (attributing to another what you find unacceptable in yourself)

☐ Rationalization (making excuses for your poor behavior)

☐ Lying (protecting self through falsehoods)

☐ Hypocrisy (presenting a false image)

Dear heavenly Father, I confess that I have wrongly defended myself by [confess the items checked above]. Thank You for Your forgiveness. I trust You to defend and protect me. In Jesus's name I pray. Amen.

Frequently we'll respond to pain and rejection the wrong ways, and those ways, over time, become deeply ingrained in our lives. You may need additional discipling/counseling to learn how to allow Jesus to be your rock, fortress, deliverer, and refuge (see Psalm 18:1-2). The more you learn how loving, powerful, and protective God is, the more you'll be likely to trust Him. The more you realize how much God unconditionally loves and accepts you, the more you'll be released to be open, honest, and (in a healthy way) vulnerable before God and others.

The New Age movement has twisted the concept of faith by teaching that we make something true by believing it. That is false. We cannot create reality with our minds; only God can do that. Our responsibility is to face reality and choose to believe what God says is true. True biblical faith, then, is choosing to believe and act upon what is true because God has said it is true, and He is the Truth. Faith is something you decide to do, not something you feel like doing. Believing something doesn't make it true; it's already true—therefore, we choose to believe it! Truth is not conditioned by whether we choose to believe it or not.

Everybody lives by faith. The only difference between Christian faith and non-Christian faith is the object of our faith. If the object of our faith is not trustworthy or real, then no amount of believing will change that. That's why our faith must be grounded on the solid rock of God's perfect, unchanging character and the truth of His Word. For 2,000 years Christians have known the importance of verbally and publicly declaring truth. Read aloud the following Statements of Truth, and carefully consider what you are professing. You may find it helpful to read these statements out loud every day for at least six weeks, which will increasingly allow your mind to be renewed by the truth.

STATEMENTS OF TRUTH

1. **I recognize** that there is only one true and living God who exists as the Father, Son, and Holy Spirit. He is worthy of all honor, praise, and glory as the One who made all things and holds all things together. (See Exodus 20:2-3; Colossians 1:16-17.)

2. **I recognize** that Jesus Christ is the Messiah, the Word who became flesh and dwelt among us. I believe that He came to destroy the works of the devil, and that He disarmed the rulers and authorities and made a public display of them, having triumphed over them. (See John 1:1,14; Colossians 2:15; 1 John 3:8.)

3. **I believe** that God demonstrated His own love for me in

that while I was still a sinner, Christ died for me. I believe that He has delivered me from the domain of darkness and transferred me to His kingdom, and in Him I have redemption, the forgiveness of sins. (See Romans 5:8; Colossians 1:13-14.)

4. **I believe** that I am now a child of God and that I am seated with Christ in the heavenly realms. I believe that I was saved by the grace of God through faith, and that it was a gift and not a result of any works on my part. (See Ephesians 2:6,8-9; 1 John 3:1-3.)

5. **I choose** to be strong in the Lord and in the strength of His might. I put no confidence in the flesh, for the weapons of warfare are not of the flesh but are divinely powerful for the destruction of strongholds. I put on the full armor of God. I resolve to stand firm in my faith and resist the evil one. (See 2 Corinthians 10:4; Ephesians 6:10-20; Philippians 3:3.)

6. **I believe** that apart from Christ I can do nothing, so I declare my complete dependence on Him. I choose to abide in Christ in order to bear much fruit and glorify my Father. I announce to Satan that Jesus is my Lord. I reject any and all counterfeit gifts or works of Satan in my life. (See John 15:5,8; 1 Corinthians 12:3.)

7. **I believe** that the truth will set me free and that Jesus is the truth. If He sets me free, I will be free indeed. I recognize that walking in the light is the only path of true fellowship with God and man. Therefore, I stand against all of Satan's deceptions by taking every thought captive in obedience to Christ. I declare that the Bible is the only authoritative standard for truth and life. (See John 8:32,36; 14:6; 2 Corinthians 10:5; 2 Timothy 3:15-17; 1 John 1:3-7.)

8. **I choose** to present my body to God as a living and holy

sacrifice and the members of my body as instruments of righteousness. I choose to renew my mind by the living Word of God in order that I may prove that the will of God is good, acceptable, and perfect. I put off the old self with its evil practices and put on the new self. I declare myself to be a new creation in Christ. (See Romans 6:13; 12:1-2; 2 Corinthians 5:17; Colossians 3:9-10.)

9. **By faith** I choose to be filled with the Spirit so that I can be guided into all truth. I choose to walk by the Spirit so that I will not carry out the desires of the flesh. (See John 16:13; Galatians 5:16; Ephesians 5:18.)

10. **I renounce** all selfish goals and choose the ultimate goal of love. I choose to obey the two greatest commandments: to love the Lord my God with all my heart, soul, mind, and strength, and to love my neighbor as myself. (See Matthew 22:37-39; 1 Timothy 1:5.)

11. **I believe** that the Lord Jesus has all authority in heaven and on earth, and He is the head over all rule and authority. I am complete in Him. I believe that Satan and his demons are subject to me in Christ because I am a member of Christ's body. Therefore, I obey the command to submit to God and resist the devil, and I command Satan, in the name of Jesus Christ, to leave my presence. (See Matthew 28:18; Ephesians 1:19-23; Colossians 2:10; James 4:7.)

STEP THREE

Bitterness Versus Forgiveness

We are called to be merciful just as our heavenly Father is merciful (Luke 6:36) and to forgive others as we have been forgiven (Ephesians 4:31-32). Doing so sets us free from our past and prohibits Satan from taking advantage of us (2 Corinthians 2:10-11). Ask God to bring to your mind the people you need to forgive by praying the following prayer out loud:

> *Dear heavenly Father, I thank You for the riches of Your kindness, forbearance, and patience toward me, knowing that Your kindness has led me to repentance. I confess that I have not shown that same kindness and patience towards those who have hurt or offended me (Romans 2:4). Instead, I have held on to my anger, bitterness, and resentment toward them. Please bring to my mind all the people I need to forgive in order that I may now do so. In Jesus's name I pray. Amen.*

On a separate sheet of paper, list the names of people who come to your mind. At this point, don't question whether you need to forgive a specific person or not. Often we hold things against ourselves as well, punishing ourselves for wrong choices we've made in the past. Write "myself" at the bottom of your list if you need to forgive yourself. Forgiving yourself is accepting the truth that God has already forgiven you in Christ. If God has forgiven you, you can forgive yourself!

Also write "thoughts against God" at the bottom of your list. Obviously, God has never done anything wrong so He doesn't need our forgiveness, but we need to let go of any disappointments we may have with our heavenly Father. People often harbor angry thoughts against Him because He did not do what they wanted Him to do. Those feelings of anger or resentment toward God need to be released. Before you begin working through the process of forgiving those on your list, review what forgiveness is and what it isn't. Each subhead below is part of the definition of true, biblical forgiveness.

Forgiveness is not forgetting. People who want to forget all that was done to them will find they cannot do it. When God says He will remember our sins no more, He is saying that He will not use the past against us. Forgetting is a long-term by-product of forgiveness, but it is never a means toward it. Don't put off forgiving those who have hurt you, hoping the pain will go away. Once you choose to forgive someone, then Christ will begin to heal your wounds. We don't heal in order to forgive; we forgive in order to heal.

Forgiveness is a choice, a decision of the will. Because God requires you to forgive, it is possible for you to extend it. Some people hold on to their anger as a means of protecting themselves against further abuse, but all they are doing is hurting themselves. Others want revenge. The Bible teaches, " 'Vengeance is mine, I will repay,' says the Lord" (Romans 12:19). Let God deal with the person. Let him or her off your hook because as long as you refuse to forgive someone, you are still hooked to that person. You are still chained to your past, bound up in your bitterness. By forgiving, you let the other person off your hook, but he or she is not off God's hook. You must trust that God will deal with the person justly and fairly, something you simply cannot do.

You might say, "But you don't know how much this person hurt me!" No human truly knows another person's pain, but Jesus does, and instructs us to forgive others for our own sake. Until you let go of your bitterness and hate, the person is still hurting you. No one can fix your past, but you can be free from it. What you gain by forgiving is freedom from your past and from those who have abused you. To forgive is to set a captive free, then realize you were the captive.

Forgiveness is agreeing to live with the consequences of another person's sin. We are all living with the consequences of someone else's sin. It's up to us whether we do so in the bondage of bitterness or in the freedom of forgiveness. But what about seeking justice? The cross makes forgiveness legally and morally right. There, Jesus died for all our sins. We are to forgive as Christ has forgiven us. He did that by taking upon Himself the consequences of our sins. God "made Him who knew no sin to be sin on our behalf, so that we might become the righteousness of God in Him" (2 Corinthians 5:21). Do not wait for the other person to ask for your forgiveness. Remember, Jesus did not wait for those who were crucifying Him to apologize before He forgave them. Even while they mocked and jeered at Him, He prayed, "Father, forgive them; for they do not know what they are doing" (Luke 23:34).

Forgive from your heart. Allow God to bring to the surface any painful memories you have, and acknowledge how you feel toward those who have hurt you. If your forgiveness doesn't touch the emotional core of your life, it will be incomplete. Too often we're afraid of the pain, so we bury our emotions deep down inside us. Let God bring them to the surface so He can begin to heal those damaged emotions.

Forgiveness is choosing not to hold someone's sin against him or her anymore. It is common for bitter people to bring up past offenses to those who have hurt them. They want the instigator to feel as bad as they do! But we must let go of the past and choose to reject any thought of revenge. This doesn't mean you continue to put up with the abuse. God does not tolerate sin, and neither should you. You will need to set up scriptural boundaries that put a stop to further abuse. Take a stand against sin while continuing to exercise grace and forgiveness toward those who have hurt you. If you need help setting scriptural boundaries to protect yourself from further abuse, talk to a trusted friend, counselor, or discipler.

Don't wait until you feel like forgiving. You will never get there. Make the hard choice to forgive even if you don't feel like doing so. Once you choose to forgive, Satan will lose his hold on you, and God will begin to heal your damaged emotions. Start with the first person on your list, and make the choice to forgive him or her for every painful memory that comes to your mind. Stay with that individual until you are sure you have dealt with all the remembered pain. Then work your way down the list and do the same with the other names.

As you begin forgiving people, God may bring to your mind painful memories you've totally forgotten. Let Him do this even if it hurts. God is surfacing those painful memories so you can face them once and for all, then let them go. Don't excuse the offender's behavior, even if it is someone you are close to. Don't say, "Lord, please help me to forgive." He is already helping you, and He will be with you all the way through the process. Don't say, "Lord, I *want* to forgive" because that bypasses the hard choice you have to make. Say, "Lord, I *choose* to forgive these people and what they did to me." For every painful memory that God reveals in connection with each person on your list, pray,

> *Dear heavenly Father, I choose to forgive [name the person] for [what they did or failed to do], because it made me feel [share the painful feelings—i.e., rejected, dirty, worthless, inferior, etc.].*

After you have forgiven every person for every painful memory, then pray as follows:

> *Lord Jesus, I choose not to hold on to my resentment. I relinquish my right to seek revenge and ask You to heal my damaged emotions. Thank You for setting me free from the bondage of my bitterness. I now ask You to bless those who have hurt me. In Jesus's name I pray. Amen.*

Note: During this Step, God may have brought to your mind people whom you have knowingly or unknowingly wounded. With that in mind, let's look at how to seek the forgiveness of others.

SEEKING THE FORGIVENESS OF OTHERS

If someone has hurt you, then go to God. You don't need to go to the offender to extend forgiveness, and in many cases, that would be unadvisable. Your need to forgive another person is primarily an issue between you and God. On the other hand, Jesus said, "If you are presenting your offering at the altar and there remember that your brother has something against you, leave your gift there before the altar and go; first be reconciled to your brother, and then come and present your offering. Make friends quickly with your opponent" (Matthew

5:23-25). However, if you have offended others, you need to go to those people and ask for their forgiveness and make amends when appropriate. The following are guidelines for asking others to forgive you for offending them:

1. Be certain about what you did that was wrong and why it was wrong.

2. Make sure you have forgiven the person for whatever he or she has done to you.

3. Think through exactly how you will ask that person to forgive you.

4. Be sure to state that what you did was wrong.

5. Be specific and admit that you did it.

6. Don't offer any excuses or try to defend yourself.

7. Do not place blame on others.

8. Don't expect that the person will ask you for your forgiveness, and don't let that be the reason for what you are doing.

9. Your confession should lead to this direct question: "Will you forgive me?"

10. Seek the right place and the right time, but the sooner the better.

11. If it's safe to do so, ask for forgiveness in person whenever possible.

12. Unless there is no other option, do not write a letter. It can be misunderstood, and others who are not involved in the situation may see it. Also, it could be used against you in a court case or some other legal proceeding.

"If possible, so far as it depends on you, be at peace with all men" (Romans 12:18), but it doesn't always depend on you. If the other person doesn't want to be reconciled, it won't happen. Reconciliation between two people requires repentance and forgiveness by both parties. Rarely is there one who is completely innocent. However, if you have forgiven the other person and genuinely asked for his or her forgiveness, then you have done all God requires of you. Be at peace with God.

PRAYER FOR THE RESTORATION OF BROKEN RELATIONSHIPS

Dear heavenly Father, I confess and repent of my sins against my neighbor [spouse, parents, children, relatives, friend, neighbors, brothers and sisters in Christ]. Thank You for Your forgiveness, and I forgive them for what they have done to me, and I choose not to hold it against them in the future. I ask that You bless them and enable them to live with the consequences of my sin against them. I pray that You would heal the wounds from the sins I have inflicted on them. I ask the same for myself—that I may be set free from the consequences of their sin, or that You would give me the grace to live with the consequences without bitterness. I pray that You would heal my wounds and set me free so that I can live in peaceful coexistence with my neighbors and with You. In Jesus's name I pray. Amen.

STEP FOUR
Rebellion Versus Submission

We live in rebellious times. Many people sit in judgment of those in authority over them, and they submit only when it is convenient, or they do so out of fear and not because they want to. The Bible instructs us to pray for those in authority over us (1 Timothy 2:1-2) and submit to governing authorities (Romans 13:1-7). Rebelling against God and His established authority leaves us spiritually vulnerable. The only time God permits us to disobey earthly leaders is when they require us to do something morally wrong, or they attempt to rule outside the realm of their authority. To have a submissive spirit and servant's heart, pray the following prayer:

> *Dear heavenly Father, You have said that rebellion is like the sin of witchcraft and arrogance like the evil of idolatry [see 1 Samuel 15:23]. I know that I have not always been submissive, but instead have rebelled both in attitude and action against You and against those You have placed in authority over me. Please show me all the ways I have been rebellious. I choose now to adopt a submissive spirit and a servant's heart. In Jesus's name I pray. Amen.*

It is an act of faith to trust God to work in our lives through less-than-perfect leaders, but that is what God is asking us to do. Should those in positions of leadership or power abuse their authority and break the laws designed to protect innocent people, you need to seek help from a higher authority. Many governments require certain types of abuse to be reported to a governmental agency. If that is your situation, we urge you to get the help you need immediately.

Don't, however, assume that someone in authority is violating God's Word just because he or she is telling you to do something you don't like. God has set up specific lines of authority to protect us and give order to society. It is the position of authority that we respect. Without governing authorities, every society would be in chaos. From the list below, allow God to show you any specific ways you have been rebellious, and use the prayer that follows to confess those sins He brings to mind.

- Civil government (including traffic laws, tax laws, attitude toward government officials) (Romans 13:1-7; 1 Timothy 2:1-4; 1 Peter 2:13-17)
- Parents, stepparents, or legal guardians (Ephesians 6:1-3)
- Teachers, coaches, school officials (Romans 13:1-4)
- Employers (past and present) (1 Peter 2:18-23)
- Husband (1 Peter 3:1-4) or wife (Ephesians 5:21; 1 Peter 3:7) (*Note to Husbands:* Ask the Lord if a lack of love for your wife could be fostering a rebellious spirit within her. If so, confess that as a violation of Ephesians 5:22-33.)
- Church leaders (Hebrews 13:7)
- God (Daniel 9:5,9)

For each way that you have been rebellious, use the following prayer to specifically confess that sin:

> *Heavenly Father, I confess that I have been rebellious toward [name or position] by [specifically confess what you did or did not do]. Thank You for Your forgiveness. I choose to be submissive and obedient to Your Word. In Jesus's name I pray. Amen.*

STEP FIVE

Pride Versus Humility

Pride comes before a fall, but God gives grace to the humble (James 4:6; 1 Peter 5:1-10). Humility is confidence properly placed in God, and we are instructed to "put no confidence in the flesh" (Philippians 3:3). We are to be "strong in the Lord and in the strength of His might" (Ephesians 6:10). Proverbs 3:5-7 urges us to trust in the Lord with all our hearts and to not lean on our own understanding. Use the following prayer to ask for God's guidance:

> *Dear heavenly Father, You have said that pride goes before destruction and an arrogant spirit before stumbling. I confess that I have focused on my own needs and desires and not those of others. I have not always denied myself, picked up my cross daily, and followed You. I have relied on my own strength and resources instead of resting in Yours. I have placed my will before Yours and centered my life around myself instead of You. I confess my pride and selfishness and pray that all ground gained in my life by the enemies of the Lord Jesus Christ would be canceled as I repent and overcome these sinful flesh patterns. I choose to rely upon the Holy Spirit's power and guidance so that I will do nothing from selfishness or empty conceit. With humility of mind, I choose to regard others as more important than myself. I acknowledge You as my Lord, and confess that apart from You I can do nothing of lasting significance. Please examine my heart and show me the specific ways I have lived my life in pride. In the gentle and humble name of Jesus I pray. Amen. (See Proverbs 16:18; Matthew 6:33; 16:24; Romans 12:10; Philippians 2:3.)*

Pray through the list below, then use the prayer that follows to confess any sins of pride the Lord brings to mind.

☐ Having a stronger desire to do my will than God's will

☐ Leaning too much on my own understanding and experience rather than seeking God's guidance through prayer and His Word

☐ Relying on my own strengths and resources instead of depending on the power of the Holy Spirit

☐ Being more concerned about controlling others than in developing self-control

☐ Being too busy doing "important" and selfish things rather than seeking and doing God's will

☐ Having a tendency to think that I have no needs

☐ Finding it hard to admit when I am wrong

☐ Being more concerned about pleasing people than pleasing God

☐ Being overly concerned about getting the credit I feel I deserve

☐ Thinking I am more humble, spiritual, religious, or devoted than others

☐ Being driven to obtain recognition by attaining degrees, titles, and positions

☐ Feeling that my needs are more important than another person's needs

☐ Considering myself better than others because of my academic, artistic, athletic, or other abilities and accomplishments

☐ Not waiting on God

☐ Other ways I have thought more highly of myself than I should

For each of the above areas that has been true in your life, pray,

> *Dear heavenly Father, I agree I have been proud by [name what you checked above]. Thank You for Your forgiveness. I choose to humble myself before You and others. I choose to place all my confidence in You and none in my flesh. In Jesus's name I pray. Amen.*

STEP SIX

Bondage Versus Freedom

Many times we feel trapped in a vicious cycle of "sin-confess, sin-confess" that never seems to end. But Scripture gives us these promises: "God is faithful, who will not allow you be tempted beyond what you are able, but with the temptation will provide the way of escape" (1 Corinthians 10:13), and "Submit therefore to God. Resist the devil and he will flee from you" (James 4:7). If you did not choose the way of escape and instead you yielded to sin, then you should confess that sin to God, ask Him to fill you with His Holy Spirit, and resist the devil by putting on the full armor of God (see Ephesians 6:10-20). Then he will flee from you.

Sin that has become a habit may require that you seek help from a trusted brother or sister in Christ. James 5:16 says, "Confess your sins to one another, and pray for one another so that you may be healed. The effective prayer of a righteous man can accomplish much." Sometimes the assurance of 1 John 1:9 is enough: "If we confess our sins, He is faithful and righteous to forgive us our sins and to cleanse us from all unrighteousness." Remember, confession is not saying, "I'm sorry." Rather, it is openly admitting, "I did it." Whether you need help from other people or simply the accountability of walking in the light before God, pray the following prayer:

Dear heavenly Father, You have told me to put on the Lord Jesus Christ and make no provision for the flesh in regard to its lusts. I confess that I have given in to fleshly lusts that wage war against my soul. I thank You that in Christ my sins are already forgiven, but I have broken Your holy law and I have allowed sin to wage war in my body. I come to You now to confess and renounce these sins of the flesh so that I might be cleansed and set free from the bondage of sin. Please reveal to my mind all the sins of the flesh I have committed and the ways I have grieved the Holy Spirit. In Jesus's holy name I pray. Amen. (See Romans 6:12-13; 13:14; 2 Corinthians 4:2; James 4:1; 1 Peter 2:11; 5:8.)

The following list contains many sins of the flesh, but a prayerful examination of Mark 7:20-23; Galatians 5:19-21; Ephesians 4:25-31 and other passages will help you to be even more thorough. Look over the list below and ask the Holy Spirit to bring to your mind the sins you need to confess. He may reveal others to you as well. For each sin the Lord shows you, lift up a prayer of confession from your heart. There is a sample prayer following the list.

Note: Sexual sins, marriage and divorce issues, gender identity, abortion, suicidal tendencies, perfectionism, eating disorders, substance abuse, gambling, and bigotry will be dealt with later in this step.

☐ Stealing   ☐ Quarreling/fighting
☐ Jealousy/envy   ☐ Gossip/slander
☐ Complaining/criticism   ☐ Sarcasm
☐ Swearing   ☐ Apathy/laziness
☐ Lying   ☐ Drunkenness
☐ Hatred   ☐ Anger
☐ Cheating   ☐ Avoiding responsibility
☐ Greed/materialism   ☐ Others: _____

Dear heavenly Father, I confess that I have sinned against You by [name the sins]. Thank You for Your forgiveness and cleansing. I now turn away from these expressions of sin and turn to You, Lord. Fill me with Your Holy Spirit so that I will not carry out the desires of the flesh. In Jesus's name I pray. Amen.

RESOLVING SEXUAL SIN

It is our responsibility not to allow sin to rule in our physical bodies. To avoid that, we must not use our bodies or another person's body as an instrument of unrighteousness (see Romans 6:12-13). Sexual immorality is not only a sin against God, it is also a sin against your body, the temple of the Holy Spirit (1 Corinthians 6:18-19). Sex was intended by God to be the means for procreation and for the pleasure of a husband and wife. When the marriage relationship is consummated, they become one flesh. If we sexually join our bodies to another person outside of the context of marriage, we become "one flesh" with that person (1 Corinthians 6:16). This creates a spiritual bond that leads to spiritual bondage, whether it is heterosexual or homosexual. Sexual relations between people of the same sex are explicitly forbidden by God, and so is sex with someone of the opposite sex who is not your spouse. To find freedom from sexual bondage, pray the following prayer:

> *Dear heavenly Father, I have allowed sin to reign in my mortal body. I ask You to bring to my mind every sexual use of my body as an instrument of unrighteousness so that I can renounce these sexual sins and break those sinful bondages. In Jesus's name I pray. Amen.*

As the Lord brings to your mind every sexually immoral use of your body, whether it was done to you (rape, incest, sexual molestation) or you initiated it (pornography, masturbation, sexual immorality), renounce these using the prayer that follows:

> *Dear heavenly Father, I renounce [name the sexual experience] with [name]. I ask You to break that sinful bond with [name] spiritually, physically, and emotionally. In Jesus's name I pray. Amen.*

If you have used pornography, say the following prayer:

> *Dear heavenly Father, I confess that I have looked at sexually suggestive and pornographic material for the purpose of*

stimulating myself sexually. I have attempted to satisfy my lustful desires and polluted my body, soul, and spirit. Thank You for cleansing me and for Your forgiveness. I renounce any satanic bonds I have allowed in my life through the unrighteous use of my body and mind. Lord, I commit myself to destroying any objects in my possession that I have used for sexual stimulation, and to turn away from all media that are associated with my sexual sin. I commit myself to the renewing of my mind and to thinking pure thoughts. Fill me with your Holy Spirit that I may not carry out the desires of the flesh. In Jesus's name I pray. Amen.

After you have finished, commit your body to God by praying:

Dear heavenly Father, I renounce all the uses of my body as an instrument of unrighteousness, and I admit to any willful participation. I choose to present my physical body to You as an instrument of righteousness, a living and holy sacrifice acceptable to You. I choose to reserve the sexual use of my body for marriage only. I reject the devil's lie that my body is not clean or that it is dirty or in any way unacceptable to You as a result of my past sexual experiences. Lord, thank You that You have cleansed and forgiven me and that You love and accept me just the way I am. Therefore, I choose now to accept myself and my body as clean in Your eyes. In Jesus's name I pray. Amen.

SPECIAL PRAYERS AND DECISIONS FOR SPECIFIC SITUATIONS

The following prayers will enhance your growth process and help you to make wise choices when you are faced with critical decisions. On their own they are unlikely to bring complete resolution or recovery, but they serve as excellent starting points. You will then need to work on renewing your mind. Please don't hesitate to seek godly counsel for additional help when needed.

Marriage

Dear heavenly Father, I choose to believe that You created us male and female, and that marriage is a spiritual bond between one man and one woman who become one in Christ. I believe that bond can be broken only by death, adultery, or desertion by an unbelieving spouse. I choose to stay committed to my vows and to remain faithful to my spouse until physical death separates us. Give me the grace to be the spouse You created me to be, and enable me to love and respect my partner in marriage. I will seek to change only myself and accept my spouse as You have accepted me. Teach me how to speak the truth in love, to be merciful as You have been merciful to me, and to forgive as You have forgiven me. In Jesus's name I pray. Amen.

Divorce

Dear heavenly Father, I have not been the spouse You created me to be, and I deeply regret that my marriage has failed. I choose to believe that You still love and accept me. I choose to believe that I am still Your child, and that Your desire for me is that I continue serving You and others in Your kingdom. Give me the grace to overcome the disappointment and the emotional scars that I carry, and I ask the same for my ex-spouse. I choose to forgive him/her and to forgive myself for all the ways I contributed to the divorce. Enable me to learn from my mistakes and guide me so that I don't repeat the same old flesh patterns. I choose to believe the truth that I am still accepted, secure, and significant in Christ. Please guide me to healthy relationships in Your church, and keep me from seeking a marriage on the rebound. I trust You to supply all my needs in the future, and I commit myself to following You. In Jesus's name I pray. Amen.

Gender Identity

Dear heavenly Father, I choose to believe that You have created all humanity to be either male or female (Genesis 1:27) and commanded us to maintain a distinction between the two genders (Deuteronomy 22:5; Romans 1:24-29). I confess that I have been influenced by the social pressures of this fallen world and the lies of Satan to question my biological gender identity and that of others. I renounce all the accusations and lies of Satan that would seek to convince me that I am somebody other than who You created me to be. I choose to believe and accept my biological gender identity, and pray that You would heal my damaged emotions and enable me to be transformed by the renewing of my mind. I take up the full armor of God (Ephesians 6:13-17) and the shield of faith to extinguish all the temptations and accusations of the evil one (Ephesians 6:16). I renounce any identities and labels that derive from my old nature, and I choose to believe that I am a new creation in Christ. In the wonderful name of Jesus I pray. Amen.

Abortion

Dear heavenly Father, I confess that I was not a proper guardian and keeper of the life You entrusted to me, and I confess that I have sinned. Thank You that because of Your forgiveness, I can forgive myself. I commit the child to You for all eternity, and believe that he or she is in Your caring hands. In Jesus's name I pray. Amen.

Suicidal Tendencies

Dear heavenly Father, I renounce all suicidal thoughts and any attempts I've made to take my own life or in any way injure myself. I renounce the lie that life is hopeless and that I can find peace and freedom by taking my own life. Satan is a thief and comes to steal, kill, and destroy. I choose to remain alive in Christ, who said He came to give me life and give it abundantly. Thank You for Your forgiveness that allows me to forgive myself. I choose to believe that there is always hope in Christ and that my heavenly Father loves me. In Jesus's name I pray. Amen.

Drivenness and Perfectionism

Dear heavenly Father, I renounce the lie that my sense of worth is dependent upon my ability to perform. I announce the truth that my identity and sense of worth are found in who I am as Your child. I renounce seeking the approval and acceptance of other people for my affirmation, and I choose to believe the truth that I am already approved and accepted in Christ because of His death and resurrection for me. I choose to believe the truth that I have been saved not by deeds done in righteousness, but according to Your mercy. I choose to believe that I am no longer under the curse of the law because Christ became a curse for me. I receive the free gift of life in Christ and choose to abide in Him. I renounce striving for perfection by living under the law. By Your grace, heavenly Father, I choose from this day forward to walk by faith in the power of Your Holy Spirit according to what You have said is true. In Jesus's name I pray. Amen.

Eating Disorders or Self-Mutilation

Dear heavenly Father, I renounce the lie that my value as a person is dependent upon my appearance or performance. I renounce cutting or abusing myself, vomiting, using laxatives or starving myself as a means of being in control, altering my appearance, or trying to cleanse myself of evil. I announce that only the blood of the Lord Jesus Christ cleanses me from sin. I realize that I have been bought with a price and that my body, which is the temple of the Holy Spirit, belongs to God. Therefore, I choose to glorify God in my body. I renounce the lie that I am evil or that any part of my body is evil. Thank You that You accept me just the way I am in Christ. In Jesus's name I pray. Amen.

Substance Abuse

Dear heavenly Father, I confess that I have misused substances (alcohol, tobacco, food, prescription or street drugs) for the purpose of pleasure, to escape reality, or to cope with difficult problems. I confess that I have abused my body and programmed my mind in harmful ways. I have quenched the Holy Spirit as well. Thank You for Your forgiveness. I renounce any satanic connection or influence in my life through my misuse of food or chemicals. I cast my anxieties onto Christ, who loves me. I commit myself to yielding no longer to substance abuse, but instead I choose to allow the Holy Spirit to direct and empower me. In Jesus's name I pray. Amen.

Gambling

Dear heavenly Father, I confess that I have been a poor steward of the financial resources that have been in my possession. I have gambled away my future chasing a false god. I have not been content with food and clothing, and the love of money has driven me to behave irrationally and sinfully. I renounce making provision for my flesh with regard to this lust. I commit myself to staying away from all gambling casinos, gambling websites, bookmakers, and lottery sales. I choose to believe that I am alive in Christ and dead to sin. Fill me with Your Holy Spirit so that I don't carry out the desires of the flesh. Show me the way of escape when I am tempted to return to my addictive behaviors. I stand against all of Satan's accusations, temptations, and deceptions by putting on the armor of God and standing firm in my faith. I choose to believe that You will meet all my needs according Your riches in glory. In Jesus's name I pray. Amen.

Bigotry

Dear heavenly Father, You have created all humanity in Your image. I confess that I have judged others by the color of their skin, their national origin, their social or economic status, their cultural differences, and their sexual orientation. I renounce racism, elitism, and sexism. I choose to believe "there is neither Jew nor Greek, there is neither slave nor free man, there is neither male nor female; for you are all one in Christ" (Galatians 3:28). Please show me the roots of my bigotry that I may confess them and be cleansed from such defilement. I pledge myself "to walk in a manner worthy of the calling with which [I] have been called, with all humility and gentleness, with patience, showing tolerance for one another in love, being diligent to preserve the unity of the Spirit in the bond of peace" (Ephesians 4:1-3). In Jesus's name I pray. Amen.

STEP SEVEN

Curses Versus Blessings

The Bible declares that the iniquities of one generation can be visited on to the third and fourth generations of those who hate God, but God's blessings will be poured out on thousands of generations of those who love and obey Him (Exodus 20:4-6). The iniquities of one generation can adversely affect future ones unless those sins are renounced and your new spiritual heritage in Christ is claimed. This cycle of abuse and all negative influences can be stopped through genuine repentance. You are not guilty of your ancestors' sins, but because of their sins you have been affected by their influence. Jesus said that after we have been fully trained we will be like our teachers (Luke 6:40), and Peter wrote that you were redeemed "from your futile way of life inherited from your forefathers" (1 Peter 1:18). Ask the Lord to reveal your ancestral sins, then renounce them as follows:

> *Dear heavenly Father, please reveal to my mind all the sins of my ancestors that have been passed down through family lines. As a new creation in Christ, I want to experience my freedom from those influences and to walk in my new identity as a child of God. In Jesus's name I pray. Amen.*

Listen carefully to what the Holy Spirit may reveal, and list anything that comes to your mind. God may reveal cultic and occultic religious practices of your ancestors—practices that you were not aware of. Also, every family has instances of mental illness, sickness, divorce, sexual sins, anger, depression, fear, violence, abuse, etc. When nothing else comes to mind, conclude with this:

> *Lord, I renounce [name all the family sins that God brings to your mind].*

We cannot passively take our place in Christ. Rather, we must actively and intentionally choose to submit to God, resist the devil, and then he will flee from us. Verbally complete this final step with the following declaration and prayer:

Declaration

I here and now reject and disown all the sins of my ancestors. As one who has been delivered from the domain of darkness and transferred into the kingdom of God's Son, I declare myself to be free from those harmful influences. I am no longer "in Adam." I am now alive "in Christ." Therefore, I am the recipient of the blessings of God upon my life as I choose to love and obey Him. As one who has been crucified and raised with Christ and who sits with Him in heavenly places, I renounce any and all satanic attacks and assignments directed against me and my ministry. Every curse placed on me was broken when Christ became a curse for me by dying on the cross (Galatians 3:13). I reject any and every way in which Satan may claim ownership of me. I belong to the Lord Jesus Christ, who purchased me with His own precious blood. I declare myself to be fully and eternally signed over and committed to the Lord Jesus Christ. Therefore, having submitted to God, I now by His authority resist the devil, and I command every spiritual enemy of the Lord Jesus Christ to leave my presence. In putting on the armor of God, I stand against Satan's temptations, accusations, and deceptions. From this day forward, I will seek to do only the will of my heavenly Father.

Prayer

Dear heavenly Father, I come to You as Your child, bought out of slavery to sin by the blood of the Lord Jesus Christ. You are the Lord of the universe and the Lord of my life. I submit my body to You as a living and holy sacrifice. May You be glorified through my life and body. I now ask You to fill me with Your Holy Spirit. I commit myself to the renewing of my mind in order that I may prove that Your will is good, acceptable, and perfect for me. I desire nothing more than to be like You. I pray, believe, and do all this in the wonderful name of Jesus, my Lord and Savior. Amen.

INCOMPLETE RESOLUTION?

After you have completed the Steps, close your eyes and sit silently for a minute or two. Is your mind quiet? By this point, most believers who go through the Steps sense the peace of God within them and a clear mind. A small percentage don't, and usually they know that there is still some unfinished business to take care of with God. If you believe that you have been totally honest with God, and you have processed all the Steps to the best of your ability, then pray in this way to God:

Dear heavenly Father, I earnestly desire Your presence, and I am asking You to reveal to my mind what is keeping me from experiencing that. I ask that You take me back to times of trauma in my life and show me the lies that I have believed. I pray that You will grant me the repentance that leads to a knowledge of the truth that will set me free. I humbly ask that You would heal my damaged emotions. In Jesus's name I pray. Amen.

Don't spend your time trying to figure out what is wrong with you if nothing new surfaces. You are only responsible to deal with what you know. Instead, commit yourself to finding out what is right about you—that is, who you are in Christ. Some believers can sense a newfound freedom, and then days or weeks later, begin to struggle again. Chances are that God is revealing some more of your past that needs to be dealt with. Sometimes God works one layer at a time through the issues faced by those who have experienced severe trauma. Trying to deal with every abuse in one setting may be too overwhelming for some. If we show ourselves faithful in little things, God will put us in charge of bigger things. Claim your place in Christ with the following:

I renounce the lie that I am rejected, unloved, or shameful. In Christ I am accepted.

God says:

- I am His child (John 1:12).

- I am Christ's friend (John 15:15).

- I have been justified (Romans 5:1).

- I am united with the Lord and I am one spirit with Him (1 Corinthians 6:17).

- I have been bought with a price; I belong to God (1 Corinthians 6:19-20).

- I am a member of Christ's body (1 Corinthians 12:27).

- I am a saint, a holy one (Ephesians 1:1).

- I have been adopted as God's child (Ephesians 1:5).

- I have direct access to God through the Holy Spirit (Ephesians 2:18).

- I have been redeemed and forgiven of all my sins (Colossians 1:14).

- I am complete in Christ (Colossians 2:10).

I renounce the lie that I am guilty, unprotected, alone, or abandoned. In Christ I am secure.

God says:

- I am free from condemnation (Romans 8:1-2).

- I am assured that all things work together for good (Romans 8:28).

- I am free from any condemning charges against me (Romans 8:31-34).

- I cannot be separated from the love of God (Romans 8:35-39).

- I have been established, anointed, and sealed by God (2 Corinthians 1:21-22).

- I am confident that the good work God has begun in me will be perfected (Philippians 1:6).

- I am a citizen of heaven (Philippians 3:20).
- I am hidden with Christ in God (Colossians 3:3).
- I have not been given a spirit of fear, but of power, love, and self-control (2 Timothy 1:7).
- I can find grace and mercy to help in time of need (Hebrews 4:16).
- I am born of God, and the evil one cannot touch me (1 John 5:18).

I renounce the lie that I am worthless, inadequate, helpless, or hopeless. In Christ I am significant.
God says:

- I am the salt of the earth and the light of the world (Matthew 5:13-14).
- I am a branch of the true vine, Jesus, a channel of His life (John 15:1,5).
- I have been chosen and appointed by God to bear fruit (John 15:16).
- I am a personal, Spirit-empowered witness of Christ (Acts 1:8).
- I am a temple of God (1 Corinthians 3:16).
- I am a minister of reconciliation for God (2 Corinthians 5:17-21).
- I am a fellow worker with God (2 Corinthians 6:1).
- I am seated with Christ in the heavenly realms (Ephesians 2:6).
- I am God's workmanship, created for good works (Ephesians 2:10).

- I may approach God with freedom and confidence (Ephesians 3:12).

- I can do all things through Christ, who strengthens me (Philippians 4:13).

- I am not the great "I Am," but by the grace of God I am what I am (see Exodus 3:14; John 8:24,28,58; 1 Corinthians 15:10).

MAINTAINING YOUR FREEDOM

It is exciting to experience your freedom in Christ, but what you have gained must be maintained. You have won an important battle, but the war goes on. To maintain your freedom in Christ and grow as a disciple of Jesus in the grace of God, you must continue renewing your mind with the truths found in God's Word. If you become aware of lies that you have believed, renounce them and choose the truth. If more painful memories surface, then forgive those who hurt you and renounce any sinful part you played.

Many people choose to go through The Steps to Freedom in Christ again on their own to make sure they have dealt with all their issues. Often new issues will surface. The process can assist you in a regular "housecleaning." It is not uncommon, after going through the Steps, for people to have thoughts like *Nothing has really changed. You're the same person you always were. It didn't work.* In most cases, you should ignore such thoughts. You are not called to dispel the darkness; you are called to turn on the light. You don't get rid of negative thoughts by rebuking every one of them; you get rid of them by repenting and choosing the truth.

In the introduction, you were encouraged to write down any false beliefs and lies that surfaced as you went through the Steps. For the next 40 days, verbally work through that list, saying, "I renounce [the lies you have believed], and I announce the truth that [what you have chosen to believe is true based on God's Word]."

We encourage you to read *Victory Over the Darkness* if you haven't already done so, or to go through *The Freedom in Christ Course.* The 21-day devotional *Walking in Freedom* was written for those who have gone through the Steps. So that you may continue to grow in the grace of God, we suggest the following:

1. Get rid of or destroy any cult or occult objects in your home (see Acts 19:18-20).

2. Be part of a church where God's truth is taught with kindness and grace, and get involved in a small group where you can be honest and real.

3. Read and meditate on the truths of God's Word each day.

4. Don't let your mind be passive, especially concerning what you watch and listen to (Internet, music, TV, etc.). Actively take every thought captive to the obedience of Christ.

5. Be a good steward of your health and develop a godly lifestyle of rest, exercise, and proper diet.

6. Say the following daily prayer for the next 40 days, and the other prayers as needed.

Daily Prayer and Declaration

Dear heavenly Father, I praise You and honor You as my Lord and Savior. You are in control of all things. I thank You that You are always with me and will never leave me nor forsake me. You are the only all-powerful and all-wise God. You are kind and loving in all Your ways. I love You and thank You that I am united with Jesus and spiritually alive in Him.

I choose not to love the world or the things in the world, and I crucify the flesh and all its passions. Thank You for the life I now have in Christ. I ask You to fill me with the Holy Spirit so I can be guided by You and not carry out the desires of the flesh. I declare my total dependence upon You and I take my stand against Satan and all his lying ways. I choose to believe the truths in Your Word despite what my feelings may say.

I refuse to be discouraged; You are the God of all hope. Nothing is too difficult for You. I am confident that You will supply all my needs as I seek to live according to Your Word. I thank You that I can be content and live a responsible life through Christ, who strengthens me.

I now take my stand against Satan and command him and all his evil spirits to depart from me. I choose to put on the full armor of God so I may be able to stand firm against all the devil's schemes. I submit my body as a living and holy sacrifice to You, and I choose to renew my mind by Your living Word. By so doing I will be able to prove that Your will is good, acceptable, and perfect for me. In the name of my Lord and Savior Jesus Christ I pray. Amen.

Bedtime Prayer

Thank You, Lord, that You have brought me into Your family and have blessed me with every spiritual blessing in the heavenly places in Christ Jesus. Thank You for this time of renewal and refreshment through sleep. I accept it as one of Your blessings for Your children, and I trust You to guard my mind and my body during my sleep. As I have thought about You and Your truth during the day, I choose to let those good thoughts continue in my mind while I am asleep. I commit myself to You for Your protection against every attempt of Satan and his demons to attack me as I sleep. Guard my mind from nightmares. I renounce all fear and cast every anxiety upon You. I commit myself to You as my rock, my fortress, and my strong tower. May Your peace be upon this place of rest. In the strong name of the Lord Jesus Christ I pray. Amen.

Prayer for Spiritual Cleansing
of Home/Apartment/Room

After removing and destroying all objects of false worship, pray this prayer out loud in every room:

Dear heavenly Father, I acknowledge that You are the Lord of heaven and earth. In Your sovereign power and love, You have entrusted many things to me. Thank You for this place where I live. I claim my home as a place of spiritual safety for me and my family, and I ask for Your protection from all the attacks of the enemy. As a child of God raised up and seated with Christ in the heavenly places, I command every evil spirit claiming ground in this place—based on the activities of past or present occupants, including me and my family—to leave and never return. I renounce all demonic assignments directed against this place. I ask You, heavenly Father, to post Your holy angels around this place to guard it from any and all attempts of the enemy to enter and disturb Your purposes for me and my family. I thank You, Father, for doing this in the name of the Lord Jesus Christ. Amen.

Prayer for Living in
a Non-Christian Environment

After removing and destroying all the objects of false worship in your home, pray this out loud in the place where you live:

Thank You, heavenly Father, for a place to live and to be renewed by sleep. I ask You to set aside my room [or portion of this room] as a place of spiritual safety for me. I renounce any allegiance given to false gods or spirits by other occupants. I renounce any claim to this room [space] by Satan based on the activities of past or present occupants, including me. On the basis of my position as a child of God and joint heir with Christ, who has all authority in heaven and on earth, I command all evil spirits to leave this place and never return. I ask You, heavenly Father, to station Your holy angels around me to protect me while I live here. In Jesus's mighty name I pray. Amen.

ENDNOTES

1. Conversation with Dr. Paul Hiebert, who formerly taught at Trinity Evangelical Divinity School in Deerfield, Illinois.

2. F.F. Bruce, *Commentary on the Book of Acts* (Grand Rapids, MI: Eerdmans, 1954), 114.

3. Ernst Haenchen, *The Acts of the Apostles* (Philadelphia: Westminster Press, 1971), 237.

4. Formerly Campus Crusade for Christ.

5. Neil T. Anderson, *Living Free in Christ* (Ventura, CA: Regal Books, 1993).

6. Luther, *Table Talk*, IV, 5097, cited by Father Louis Coulange (pseud. Joseph Turmell), *The Life of the Devil* (London: Alfred A. Knopf, 1929), 147-48.

7. Coulange [Turmell], 150ff.

8. David Powlison, *Power Encounters: Reclaiming Spiritual Warfare* (Grand Rapids, MI: Baker, 1995), 135.

9. Thomas Brooks, *Precious Remedies Against Satan's Devices* (Carlisle, PA: Banner of Truth, 1984).

10. Neil T. Anderson, *Becoming a Disciple Making Church* (Minneapolis, MN: Bethany House, 2016), 52-53.

11. Jessie Penn-Lewis, *War on the Saints*, 9th ed. (New York: Thomas E. Lowe, Ltd., 1973).

12. Theodore H. Epp, *Praying with Authority* (Lincoln, NE: Back to the Bible Broadcast, 1965), 98.

13. C. Fred Dickason, *Demon Possession and the Christian* (Chicago, IL: Moody Press, 1987), 255.

14. C.S. Lewis, *The Screwtape Letters* (Old Tappan, NJ: Fleming H. Revell, 1978).

15. As cited by Michael Scanlan and Randall J. Cirner, *Deliverance from Evil Spirits* (Ann Arbor, MI: Servant Books, 1980), 16.

16. Neil T. Anderson and Steve Russo, *The Seduction of Our Children* (Eugene, OR: Harvest House, 1991), 34, 39.

17. Alexander Pope, *Essay on Man, Epistle II*.

18. As cited by Martin Wells Knapp, *Impressions* (Wheaton, IL: Tyndale House, 1984), 14-15.

FREEDOM IN CHRIST MINISTRIES BOOKS AND RESOURCES

Victory Over the Darkness offers a study guide, audiobook, and DVD (Bethany House Publishers, 2000). With more than 1,400,000 copies in print, this core book explains who you are in Christ, how to walk by faith in the power of the Holy Spirit, how to be transformed by the renewing of your mind, how to experience emotional freedom, and how to relate to one another in Christ.

The Bondage Breaker offers a study guide and audiobook (Harvest House Publishers, 2018). With more than 1,400,000 copies in print, this book explains spiritual warfare, what our protection is, ways that we are vulnerable, and how we can live a liberated life in Christ.

Discipleship Counseling (Bethany House Publishers, 2003) combines the concepts of discipleship and counseling and teaches the practical integration of theology and psychology for helping Christians resolve their personal and spiritual conflicts through repentance and faith in God.

The Steps to Freedom in Christ and accompanying interactive video (Bethany House Publishers, 2017) is a discipleship counseling tool that helps Christians resolve their personal and spiritual conflicts through genuine repentance and faith in God.

Restored (E3 Resources) is an expansion of The Steps to Freedom in Christ with additional explanations and instructions.

Walking in Freedom (Bethany House Publishers, 2008) is a 21-day devotional used for follow-up after leading someone through The Steps to Freedom.

Freedom in Christ (Bethany House Publishers, 2017) is a discipleship course for Sunday school classes and small groups. The course comes with a teacher's guide, a student guide, and a DVD covering 12 lessons and The Steps to Freedom in Christ. This course is designed to enable believers to resolve personal and spiritual conflicts and be established alive and free in Christ.

The Bondage Breaker DVD Experience (Harvest House Publishers, 2011) is also a discipleship course for Sunday school classes and small groups. It is similar to the one above, but the lessons are 15 minutes long instead of 30 minutes. It offers a student guide, but no teacher's guide.

"Victory Series" (Bethany House Publishers, 2014, 2015) is a comprehensive curriculum, including eight books that follow the growth sequence of being rooted in Christ, growing in Christ, living in Christ, and overcoming in Christ: *God's Story for You; Your New Identity; Your Foundation in Christ; Renewing Your Mind; Growing in Christ; Your Life in Christ; Your Authority in Christ; Your Ultimate Victory.*

SPECIALIZED BOOKS

The Bondage Breaker, The Next Step (Harvest House Publishers, 2011) has several testimonies of people who found their freedom from all kinds of problems, along with commentary by Dr. Anderson. It is an important learning tool for encouragers and gives hope to those who are entangled in sin.

Overcoming Addictive Behavior with Mike Quarles (Bethany House Publishers, 2003) explores the path to addiction and how a Christian can overcome addictive behaviors.

Overcoming Depression with Joanne Anderson (Bethany House Publishers, 2004) explores the nature of depression, which is a body, soul, and spirit problem. This resource presents a wholistic answer for overcoming this "common cold" of mental illnesses.

Daily in Christ with Joanne Anderson (Harvest House Publishers, 2000) is a popular daily devotional read by thousands of Internet subscribers every day.

Who I Am in Christ (Bethany House Publishers, 2001) has 36 short chapters describing who believers are in Christ and how their deepest needs are met in Him.

Freedom from Addiction with Mike and Julia Quarles (Bethany House Publishers, 1997) begins with Mike and Julia's journey into addiction and codependency, and explains the nature of chemical addictions and how to overcome them in Christ.

One Day at a Time with Mike Quarles (Bethany House Publishers, 2000) is a 365-day devotional that helps those who struggle with addictive behaviors and explains how to discover the grace of God on a daily basis.

Letting Go of Fear with Rich Miller (Harvest House Publishers, 2017) explains the nature of fear, anxiety, and panic attacks, and how to overcome them.

Setting Your Church Free with Charles Mylander (Bethany House Publishers, 2006, 2014) explains servant leadership and how the leaders of a church can resolve corporate conflicts through corporate repentance.

Setting Your Marriage Free with Charles Mylander (Bethany House Publishers, 2006, 2014) explains God's divine plan for marriage and the steps that couples can take to resolve their difficulties.

Christ-Centered Therapy with Dr. Terry and Julie Zuehlke (Zondervan Publishing House, 2000) explains the practical integration of theology and psychology for professional counselors and provides them with biblical tools for therapy.

Managing Anger with Rich Miller (Harvest House Publishers, 2018) explains the nature of anger and how to put away all anger, wrath, and malice.

Grace That Breaks the Chains with Rich Miller and Paul Travis (Harvest House Publishers, 2003, 2014) explains the bondage of legalism and how to overcome it by the grace of God.

Winning the Battle Within (Harvest House Publishers, 2008) shares God's standards for sexual conduct, examines the path to sexual addiction, and presents how to overcome sexual strongholds.

Restoring Broken Relationships (Bethany House Publishers, 2008) explains the primary ministry of the church, and how we can be reconciled to God and each other.

Rough Road to Freedom (Monarch Books) is Dr. Anderson's memoir.

The Power of Presence (Monarch Books) is about experiencing the presence of God during difficult times and what our presence means to each other. This book is written in the context of Dr. Anderson caring for his wife, who recently died from agitated dementia.

About Freedom in Christ Ministries

Freedom in Christ Ministries (FICM), established in 1988, now has staff and certified volunteers (Ministry Associates) in many locations around the United States. We also have offices and representatives in Canada, Europe, Asia and the Pacific region, and Africa.

FICM's vision is to see churches and Christian ministries vibrantly alive *in Christ;* walking in love, truth, and grace-filled, Spirit-empowered freedom; and becoming healthy, healing places having a powerful impact on their communities.

Our mission is to come alongside selected churches and ministries in long-term relationships to encourage their leaders to walk in freedom and equip those leaders to prayerfully guide their organizations into spiritual transformation in Christ.

Imagine the life-transforming truths of The Bondage Breaker and other FICM resources touching...

...your church or ministry leaders!
...the people in your church or organization—young and old, seeker and veteran believer!
...many churches in your community!

Could we perhaps begin to see the revival come to this nation and the world that we have dreamed of and prayed about for decades?

That is our heart passion and heart cry at Freedom in Christ Ministries! Is it yours?

For more information about our ministry and resources, or if you would like to know more about becoming a FICM Ministry Associate, please contact us at:

Freedom in Christ Ministries
9051 Executive Park Dr., Suite 503
Knoxville, TN 37923
Phone: 865.342.4000
Fax: 865.342.4001
Web site: www.ficm.org
E-mail: info@ficm.org

We are also looking for those whom God has called to pray for the ministry and ministers of FICM. If the Lord is calling you to pray for us, please contact us at:

prayer@ficm.org

Thank you!

To learn more about Harvest House books and
to read sample chapters, visit our website:

www.harvesthousepublishers.com

HARVEST HOUSE PUBLISHERS
EUGENE, OREGON